Praise for **Awaken Your Thir**

"Susan's books are a rich resou   .ching, and
with *Awaken Your Third Eye*, she thoroughly explains the key to inner
vision and spiritual brilliance—the 'God eye' that helps us see the world
through a lens of light."

—Cyndi Dale,
author of *The Subtle Body, The Intuition Guidebook,*
Energetic Boundaries, and *Kundalini*

"This book is a treasure trove of information, bridging science,
philosophy and actual practice. I can't imagine a more well-rounded
and thorough resource on the subject of opening the sixth chakra and
discovering the gateway to transcendent awakening. A jam-packed
gem full of spiritual insight."

—Anodea Judith, PhD,
author of *Wheels of Life* and *Eastern Body-Western Mind*

"Some books entertain while a few others awaken. It's rare to find one
that does both. Susan Shumsky's *Awaken Your Third Eye* illuminates.
The field-proven methods it reveals can help you open your third
eye—the source of power, intuition and wisdom—which can
transform you from a spiritual caterpillar to an enlightened butterfly."

—Dr. Joe Vitale,
author of *Zero Limits* and *The Attractor Factor*

"I doubt that anyone has written so extensively and done as
much research as Susan Shumsky regarding the third eye. In her
book *Awaken Your Third Eye* she has packed numerous historical
references, extensive scientific research, and a number of spiritual
exercises that can inspire you about the benefit (and ease) of opening
your third eye chakra and your inner knowing. Susan's background of
having served on Maharishi Mahesh Yogi's staff for seven years serves
as a backdrop to the information shared in this book."

—Denise Linn,
author of *Sacred Space, Soul Coaching,*
and *Unlock the Secret Messages of Your Body*

"With this book Susan Shumsky opens our eyes to all that can be revealed when we open our third eye. A whole new world opens up. As a comprehensive blueprint of the human energy field and a practical guide to spiritual awakening, well-supported with convincing scientific evidence, *Awaken Your Third Eye* will show you how to open your Third Eye and experience your own spiritual awakening. What could be better than that?"

—Colin Tipping,
author of *Radical Forgiveness*

"Susan Shumsky has combined ancient practices with her own 47 years of spiritual experience in meditation, prayer, yoga, and intuition to design powerful methods to help you awaken your third eye."

—Mas Sajady,
spiritual healer

AWAKEN YOUR THIRD EYE

How Accessing Your Sixth Sense Can Help You Find Knowledge, Illumination, and Intuition

SUSAN SHUMSKY, DD

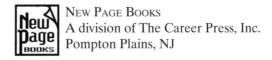

NEW PAGE BOOKS
A division of The Career Press, Inc.
Pompton Plains, NJ

AWAKEN YOUR THIRD EYE
TYPESET BY EILEEN MUNSON
Cover design by Howard Grossman/12E Design
Printed in the U.S.A.

To order this title, please call toll-free 1-800-CAREER-1 (NJ and Canada: 201-848-0310) to order using VISA or MasterCard, or for further information on books from Career Press.

The Career Press, Inc.
220 West Parkway, Unit 12
Pompton Plains, NJ 07444
www.careerpress.com
www.newpagebooks.com

Library of Congress Cataloging-in-Publication Data

Shumsky, Susan G.
  Awaken your third eye : how accessing your sixth sense can help you find knowledge, illumination, and intuition / by Susan Shumsky, DD.
      pages cm
  Includes bibliographical references and index.
  ISBN 978-1-60163-363-7 (alk. paper) -- ISBN 978-1-60163-389-7 (ebook : alk. paper) 1. Extrasensory perception. 2. Parapsychology. I. Title.

BF1321.S566 2015
131--dc23

2015002794

Disclaimer

Awaken Your Third Eye can familiarize you with the complex fields of meditation, spiritual development, and yoga, but in no way claims to fully teach the techniques described. Therefore, personal instruction is recommended. *Awaken Your Third Eye* is not an independent guide for self-healing. Susan Shumsky is not a medical doctor and does not diagnose diseases or prescribe treatments. No medical claims are implied about any methods, exercises, or postures suggested in this book, even if specific "benefits" or "healing" of conditions are mentioned. The methods and suggestions in this book should be followed with permission from a medical doctor or psychiatrist. Susan Shumsky, her agents, assignees, licensees, and authorized representatives, as well as Divine Revelation, Teaching of Intuitional Metaphysics, and New Page Books, make no claim or obligation and take no legal responsibility for the effectiveness, results, or benefits of reading this book, of using the methods described, or of contacting anyone listed in this book or at *www.divinerevelation.org*; deny all liability for any injuries or damages that you may incur; and are to be held harmless against any claim, liability, loss, or damage caused by or arising from following any suggestions made in this book, or from contacting anyone mentioned in this book or at *www.divinerevelation.org*.

| Dedication |

This book is offered, with great love, to those precious souls who struggle and sacrifice to attain spiritual illumination, and to those teachers who show the way to that mountaintop. To all aspirants and teachers devoted to supreme truth, I share this gift of light in gratitude for every tear you shed on the pathway.

| Acknowledgments |

I wish to give appreciation to those who have helped bring this book to press. Foremost, I want to thank Jeff and Deborah Herman, who, in addition to being agents and advisors, have also been the most loyal of friends. I give gratitude to Michael Pye and Laurie Kelly-Pye, who requested that I write this book, who have stood by me for well over a decade, and for whom I have the greatest admiration and respect. Thank you to Adam Schwartz, Eileen Munson, Jeff Piasky, and everyone else at New Page Books, who have worked so diligently to bring this book to publication.

During the time of writing this book, I was under the care and watchful eye of several friends and supporters who helped me master some difficult challenges. I wish to acknowledge and thank Til Luchau, Amy Valenta, Marsha Clark, Hani Saeed, Pat Dorsey, Annette Gore, Helaine Hayutin, Gail Hayutin, Abbie Hayutin, and Sid Hayutin for their love and support.

I wish to give special thanks to those mentors who have assisted in my quest to open and explore my own third eye, including Maharishi Mahesh Yogi, Peter Victor Meyer, Raman Kumar Bachchan, and all my inner teachers and divine beings of light, such as the immortal Mahamuni Babaji and the Holy Spirit. Without these magnificent guiding stars, I would have no comprehension of subtle energies and no awakened third eye.

| Contents |

Part I: Discovering the Third Eye

Part II: Anatomy of the Third Eye

Part III: Treasures of the Third Eye

Part IV: Opening the Third Eye

Part V: Bliss of the Third Eye

Discovering

the

Third Eye

1

| What's a Third Eye, Anyway? |

The light of the body is the eye: therefore if thine eye be single, thy whole body shall be full of light.

—Jesus of Nazareth[1]

Recently a gentleman named Craig Loverich from New Zealand shared his third-eye experience with me:

"When I first began reading your book *Ascension,* that night I got into bed. Just moments after closing my eyes to go to sleep, I had a wonderful experience...like an explosion in my mind's eye. I had no idea what it was. It was as if brilliant white paint exploded all over/within my mind's eye. The experience only lasted for a moment. However it was awesome, and like nothing I ever had before. It left me with a sense of peace and being cleansed.

"At the time I had no idea what had taken place. However later in your book I read the information you provided about this. Since then, it has happened again."

Craig's description is typical of what might occur when your third eye opens. This fortunate experience is a sign of awakening to higher consciousness.

Seeing Through Your Third Eye

What is your third eye? And how can you open it?

Through the window of your eyes, you can view the ever-changing landscape of your beauteous, miraculous world. You can delight in beholding the glorious manifest creation around you—both the natural world and man-made objects. You perceive this magnificent world with your five senses: seeing, hearing, tasting, smelling, and feeling.

But there is a sixth sense. With this sixth, higher sense perception, you can open the gateway to subtler realms of existence. You can develop an inner eye and view an invisible world, consisting of multiple dimensions, alternate realities, subtle planes, spiritual worlds filled with light, and parallel universes of indescribable wonders. This eye of wisdom, knowledge, illumination, and intuition is aptly named "the third eye."

The mechanism of sight, according to science, is a marriage between the object of perception, your two eyes, and your brain. It is believed that the mechanism of inner sight (insight or intuition) uses an inner third eye, seated in the pineal gland. This gland, somewhat of a mystery to modern allopathic medicine, is well known to Ayurvedic medicine of India; to Chinese medicine; to Druidic, Judaic, Islamic, Taoist, Mayan, Tibetan, Aboriginal and other cultures; and to ancient Egypt, Sumeria, Assyria, Babylonia, Greece, Rome, and Mesoamerica.

In India this third eye is known as *ajna chakra,* a subtle energy plexus in the center of your brain, seated in the pineal gland. It is the portal of higher vision, where you can see what is not evident to your eyes. The ajna chakra is not in your physical body. If you were to dissect a cadaver, you would not find it anywhere. It is located in your subtle body.

Throughout the ancient and modern world, this third eye seated in the pineal gland has been named "divine eye," "all-seeing eye," "mind's eye," "eye of the soul," "inner eye," "eye of illumination," "eye of wisdom," "Eye of Horus," "third eye," "eye of providence," "eye of God," "sixth chakra," "ajna chakra," and "brow chakra."

In this book you will explore the third eye in depth. You will discover the workings of your subtle body and its relation to your physical body. Through using the methods in this book, you will learn how to awaken your third eye and develop super-sensory perception by various traditional and non-traditional methods, both ancient and modern.

Why Develop Your Third Eye?

There are untold benefits to exploring your third eye. This eye of wisdom and intuition is literally your inner teacher. In India, the planet Jupiter, associated with the third eye, is called *Guru,* which can be translated as "spiritual preceptor" or "teacher." Therefore, by awakening and developing your third eye, you are opening lines of communication between your ego self and your higher self.

What can this inner teacher do for you? In one word: miracles! When you open the eye of inner wisdom, you begin a flow of divine guidance. When you learn how to perceive that flow, allow it, trust it, learn how to test whether it is real, and then follow the true inner guidance you receive, then miracles will begin to happen everywhere, in every part of your life.

The third eye is the eye of illumination, which shines the light of wisdom upon your pathway. It is the wayshower, the beacon that guides you to your true destination—the home you have been longing for. It is the lighthouse of consciousness, which truth-seekers everywhere long to attain. Seated in that treasure trove is your inner wisdom, the very essence and source of your true Self. There you come home to the place of perfect peace, divine understanding, inner joy, fulfillment, and utter contentment.

The third eye is where truth lies, and where all that is untrue dies and disappears. Nothing false can live in the light of pure wisdom. The third eye is the seat of discernment and discrimination. There, you distinguish between what is real and what is unreal. The truth shines in that inner radiance, where you are enveloped in divine light, which shines upon all equally, the just and unjust, the rich and poor, the healthy and diseased, both male and female, in all religions, paths, social statures, and economic ranks.

Here is what you can expect from opening the miraculous inner eye of wisdom:

▷ Greater confidence as you discover your true purpose.

▷ Greater wisdom as you tap into the source of all wisdom.

▷ Access to inner counselors who will guide you on your path.

▷ The ability to make decisions effortlessly, with commitment, certainty, and assurance.

▷ Clarity of mind in all endeavors.

▷ Development of psychic and intuitive abilities.

▷ Spiritual development of higher consciousness.

▷ Direct communication with higher beings.

▷ Greater inner peace, fulfillment, contentment, and joy.

▷ The ability to see through illusions to perceive reality and truth.

▷ Spiritual gifts of subtle sensory perception, prophecy, and direct voice.

▷ Robust physical health, well-being, longevity, and youthfulness.

Take the Third Eye-Q Test

You might be completely unfamiliar with the concepts in this book—even the idea of the third eye. Or perhaps you have studied spiritual disciplines for decades. Even if you think you are an expert, this quiz just might stump you. Measure your Third Eye-Q here by circling the correct answers in this multiple-choice test:

1. **What is the third eye?**

A. The all-seeing eye in the forehead.

B. The Cyclopes.

C. Clairvoyant ability.

D. The seat of wisdom.

E. An endless peyote trip.

2. What is a chakra?

A. A wheel.

B. The center of the body.

C. A type of energy that should be balanced in the body.

D. A nerve in the body.

E. Chalk that smells rotten.

3. What is the ajna chakra?

A. The highest energy center.

B. The command center.

C. My chance for enlightenment.

D. A plexus in the nervous system.

E. Shock and awe.

4. What does the pineal gland do?

A. It produces male hormones.

B. It awakens the third eye.

C. It secretes pinoline in the dark.

D. It regulates sugar metabolism.

E. It produces pinecones for Santa.

5. Who dubbed the pineal gland "the principle seat of the soul"?

A. Plato.

B. Baruch de Spinoza.

C. René Descartes.

D. Ralph Waldo Emerson.

E. Dr. Scholl.

6. What is DMT?

A. A compound that triggers psychedelic experiences.

B. A compound that the third eye uses to see inner light.

C. A compound that awakens *prana* in the body.

D. A compound that produces melatonin.

E. Where I go to take my driver's test.

7. **What does the word *Guru* mean?**
   A. The ajna chakra.

   B. The planet Jupiter.

   C. The third eye.

   D. A teacher who knows better than me what is best for me.

   E. Who Gollum was in a past life.

8. **What does the word *prana* mean?**
   A. Moving or breathing forth.

   B. Subtle energy.

   C. The breath of life.

   D. A breathing exercise.

   E. A man-eating fish.

9. **What is a *nadi*?**
   A. A sound.

   B. A bull that Lord Shiva rides.

   C. A subtle energy conduit.

   D. A word that means "nothing."

   E. Where I look up prices of used cars.

10. **What is *kundalini*?**
    A. Energy in the third eye.

    B. Serpent power.

    C. A sign that I'm experiencing higher consciousness.

    D. A goddess from India.

    E. A type of pasta.

11. **What is *sushumna*?**
    A. A conduit of subtle energy.

    B. A conduit of energy that is always open.

    C. A conduit of energy in the brain.

    D. A conduit of energy through which kundalini flows.

    E. The name of the author of this book.

12. What are *ida* and *pingala?*

    A. Nerve plexuses in the body.

    B. Autonomic functions of resting, digesting, feeding, and breeding.

    C. Energy conduits associated with the autonomic nervous system.

    D. Male and female sides of the body.

    E. Conjoined twins from Siam.

13. What is a *granthi?*

    A. A distressed mind.

    B. A psychic knot.

    C. Attachment to material things.

    D. Stuck energy in all the chakras.

    E. What a fat guy does after eating too fast.

14. What is a *bandha?*

    A. A muscular lock.

    B. A yoga posture.

    C. A breathing exercise.

    D. The act of raising the diaphragm.

    E. A guy in a ski mask who robs me at gunpoint.

15. What is *soma?*

    A. The nectar of immortal life.

    B. The physical body.

    C. The subtle body.

    D. The life force energy in the body.

    E. Yo-Yo Ma's sister.

16. What is yoga?

    A. A physical exercise program.

    B. Breathing exercises.

    C. Eastern philosophy.

    D. A Sanskrit word that means "to yoke."

    E. Boo-Boo's pal.

17. What are the *Yoga Sutras?*

    A. A dialogue between Lord Shiva and Mother Divine.

    B. Aphorisms of ancient seers.

    C. Threads of divine union.

    D. Aphorisms of Hatha Yoga.

    E. What aliens used to sew the Space Needle.

18. What is a *siddhi?*

    A. A yoga sutra of Patanjali.

    B. The highest intention of the meditator.

    C. Withdrawal of the senses.

    D. Perfection.

    E. New York, New York.

19. What is an *asana?*

    A. A meditation practice.

    B. A seat.

    C. A chant.

    D. An exercise.

    E. J.Lo's backside.

20. What is *pranayama?*

    A. A yoga exercise for flexibility.

    B. A yogic meditation practice.

    C. The best way to develop clairvoyance.

    D. A way to increase life-force energy through breath.

    E. A pick-a-size paper towel.

21. What is *samadhi?*

A. Stillness of mind and body.

B. Meditation.

C. A philosophy from India.

D. Freedom from the karmic wheel.

E. Saturday in Paris.

22. What is ESP?

A. Seeing, hearing, and feeling things without the senses.

B. Getting higher knowledge.

C. Predicting the future.

D. Having subtle sensory experiences inwardly.

E. A cable TV sports network.

23. What is clairvoyance?

A. Clear seeing.

B. Clear sound.

C. Clear sensing.

D. Clear scent.

E. Clair de Lune's twin sister.

24. What is intuition?

A. Telepathy.

B. Something women have.

C. Insight.

D. Predicting the future.

E. What I have to pay to go to USC.

Scoring Your Test

Please mark one point for each correct answer. The answers are as follows:

___ **1: D.** Your third eye, located in the pineal gland, is known as the seat of wisdom, of spiritual illumination, of higher learning and intuition, and of senses of higher perception: clairvoyance, clairaudience, and clairsentience.

___ **2: A.** The Sanskrit word *chakra* means "wheel." These energy centers in your subtle body have a hub, where many conduits of energy converge, and they have spokes, or radiations of energy. When your chakras fully open, you are robust, healthy, and happy.

___ **3: B.** The *ajna chakra,* located in the pineal gland, is the seat of the third eye. All chakras are plexuses of energy, but this sixth major chakra is called *ajna,* which literally means "command center."

___ **4: C.** Pinoline is produced in the pineal gland during the metabolism of the hormone melatonin. Production of melatonin, stimulated by darkness, relates to circadian rhythms.

___ **5: C.** René Descartes dedicated himself to studying the pineal gland, and believed it to be the point of connection between the intellect and physical body. He was criticized by Baruch de Spinoza for this belief.

___ **6: A.** The chemical DMT, or dimethyltryptamine, is a powerful hallucinogenic drug that dramatically affects human consciousness. Some researchers believe it is produced by the pineal gland and, when ingested, awakens the third eye.

___ **7: B.** *Guru* is the Sanskrit word for Jupiter, known as the preceptor of the gods. The ajna chakra (third eye) is associated with Jupiter. The Sanskrit roots *gu* and *ru* mean "darkness" and "light," respectively. Therefore, a true *guru* (teacher) is one who dispels the darkness of ignorance and brings the light of knowledge.

___ **8: A.** The Sanskrit word *prana* means "moving or breathing forth." Prana is the life force energy within everything in the universe. It is also called *chi* or *ki*. The *pranamaya kosha* (energy sheath of the subtle body) is the seat of all chakras, including the third eye.

___ **9: C.** *Nadi* is a Sanskrit word for conduits of subtle energy, through which *prana* (life-force energy) flows in the subtle body. The Sanskrit word *nada* means "sound," and *Nandi* is Lord Shiva's bull. The Spanish word *nada* means "nothing."

___ **10: B.** The Sanskrit word *kundalini* literally means "curled-up." It is a powerful, vital life energy at the base of your spine that when awakened, brings unusual experiences, bodily sensations, supernormal powers, and higher awareness. *Kundalini* is often called "Mystic Coil" or "Serpent Power," because it is coiled at the base chakra, and then uncurls like a cobra with its hood over your head.

___ **11: D.** *Sushumna* is a specific energy conduit (*nadi*) through which kundalini flows. It begins at the base of the spine and runs all the way up through your spine and head until it reaches the crown chakra, above your head. Sushumna is closed in ordinary individuals, but as kundalini awakens, it forces sushumna to open and flow through it.

___ **12: C.** *Ida* and *pingala* are subtle energy tubes that regulate the autonomic nervous system. Ida is associated with the parasympathetic system, and pingala is associated with the sympathetic system.

___ **13: B.** Psychic knots, or *granthis*, are blockages that disallow the free flow of prana throughout the subtle energy body. The three main granthis are found in the root chakra at the base of the spine (bondage of physical gratification), the navel chakra at the abdomen (bondage of action and material life), and the third eye chakra at the pineal gland (bondage of ideas and psychic powers).

__ **14: A.** *Bandhas* are muscular locks—traditional yogic exercises that nudge kundalini, normally seated in the base chakra, to rise upward through sushumna nadi all the way above the top of the head to the crown chakra.

__ **15: A.** *Soma,* the nectar of immortal life, is a mysterious substance mentioned in the ancient scriptures of India. Yogis believe it to be manufactured in the pineal gland, the seat of the third eye. It is said to be stimulated by the yogic practice of *khechari mudra.*

__ **16: D:** The Sanskrit word *yoga* comes from the root *yuj,* which means "to yoke." The goal of yoga, therefore, is to yoke or unify individual spirit (the self) with universal Spirit (the divine). Yoga philosophy is one of the six main philosophical systems of India. Hatha yoga, which teaches physical culture, including postures and breathing exercises, is one of the eight major paths of yoga.

__ **17: C.** The Sanskrit scripture by the sage Patanjali called *Yoga Sutras,* written approximately 400 AD, literally means "threads of divine union." This is a book of aphorisms that teach *ashtanga yoga* (eight limbs of yoga), which forms the basis of the path known as Raja Yoga.

__ **18: D:** The Sanskrit word *siddhi* means "perfection." The *Yoga Sutras* of Patanjali is the ancient scripture of India that explains how to attain perfection through yogic practices that help you develop singularity (*kaivalya*)—a state of awakened consciousness.

__ **19: B:** The term *asana* is a Sanskrit word meaning "seat." Therefore yoga asanas, or yoga postures, are not exercises, nor are they meditative states. They are body positions that are held for various lengths of time.

__ **20: D.** *Pranayama* are breathing exercises that increase prana throughout your subtle energy system. They bring greater health, wellbeing, happiness, charisma, attractiveness, success, and inner peace.

__ **21: A.** The Sanskrit word *samadhi* comes from the roots *sama* (equanimity) and *dhi* (intellect). Therefore it connotes evenness of mind and stillness of body in deep meditation, where bodily functions slow down and breathing becomes imperceptible. When you attain a state of perpetual samadhi, your awareness is no longer disturbed by deleterious effects of karmic law (cause and effect, action and reaction).

__ **22: D.** ESP or "extrasensory perception" is actually a misnomer, because you cannot have any experience without using the senses. Subtle sensory experiences of other dimensions can occur through expanded awareness, either in or out of meditation.

__ **23: A.** *Clairvoyance* is from a French expression meaning "clear seeing." It means receiving ESP impressions through images— seeing messages in your mind's eye. The word is often used to describe receiving psychic impressions of any type—seeing, hearing, or feeling.

__ **24: C.** Intuition is your higher self or "in-house counselor" giving you insight—a "still, small voice" of inner wisdom, healing, love, and inspiration. Intuitive capacities are not gender-specific. Everyone can receive intuitive impressions through visions, words, and feelings.

__ TOTAL

Evaluating Your Test

Please add up your scores. Here are the results:

▷ If you got all 24 right, your Third Eye-Q is 200. You do not need to read any spiritual books. You should write your own.

▷ If you got 19–23 right, you are a DOCTOR OF THIRD EYE. You have tremendous understanding of the third eye and your Third Eye-Q is 175.

▷ If you got 12–18 right, you are a MASTER OF THIRD EYE. You know a lot, but you have a few things to learn. Your Third Eye-Q is 150.

▷ If you got 7–11 right, you are a BACHELOR OF THIRD EYE. You still know a lot, but you have more to learn. Your Third Eye-Q is 125.

▷ If you got 1–6 right, congratulations—the odds are with you. You have successfully proven that random selection works. Your Third Eye-Q is 100.

▷ If you got them all wrong, it is no surprise. Your Third Eye-Q is 75.

▷ If you chose any of the E's, congratulations—you can laugh at a joke.

Are you surprised at some of the answers in the quiz? That is because so many myths surround these words. Having some familiarity with esoteric terms is not the same as understanding them fully. In this book you will delve into the true meaning of spiritual development through the third eye. You will learn and practice methods to open that eye of wisdom in practical, powerful ways that are easy to learn and apply.

This book is the key to unlock a great adventure. Through opening a doorway to the subtle realms, you can begin to explore all the marvels of the multidimensional creation that are usually hidden from view. Through opening your third eye and developing your sixth sense, you can enrich your life, create greater success, and awaken higher consciousness.

Let us begin this journey to deep understanding and spiritual upliftment now.

2

| Lore of the Third Eye |

*In all men there is the eye of the soul, which can
be re-awakened by the correct means. It is far
more precious than ten thousand physical eyes.*

—Plato

Artifacts of the ancient world indicate that the third eye is more than just a graphic found on a 1960s psychedelic poster, or on the back of a U.S. one-dollar bill. Awakening this eye of wisdom and subtle perception has been sought as long as humans have walked the planet. This gateway to inner space and realms of higher awareness was well-known to the ancients.

The third eye is widely depicted by Buddhist, Hindu, Jain, and Taoist cultures, variously in temple sculptures, paintings, and wall murals appearing as a dot, spiral, jewel, or eye in the middle of the forehead, above and between the two human eyes. It is called *urna* or *urnakosa* in Sanskrit, *unna* in Pali, *byakugo* in Japan, and *trinetra* ("three-eyed"), a moniker of Lord Shiva.

In statues of Buddha and other deities, a jewel is placed between the eyebrows. Hindu deities are portrayed with a *tilaka* (dot of red *kumkum* powder) on the forehead. In fact, married women in India are traditionally required to wear the tilaka. Now it is fashionable for unmarried women also.

The third eye is symbolized by the "Eye of Providence" in a pyramid's capstone on the U.S. one-dollar bill. It is portrayed in myths and fables as Cyclops. Some UFO researchers believe it to be a vestigial organ of extraterrestrial human ancestors. It is represented in the Kabbalah as two of the 10 Sephiroth (lights) on the Tree of Life: *Binah* and *Hokhmah,* which embody wisdom and understanding.

The Pineal Body

Although the third eye is one of your chakras (*ajna* chakra), and therefore located in your subtle body, it is also associated with your physical body. Its home is your pineal gland (*conarium* or *epiphysis cerebri*), located at the center of your brain. Interestingly, the word "epiphany" is derived from the Greek and Latin *epiphania*. This is not a coincidence. The ancient Greeks believed the faculty of inspiration to be seated in the pineal gland.

The Hebrew word *peniel* translates as "face of God." This is appropriate, because mystics might see the face of God with their third eye. When the prophet Jacob wrestled with God face-to-face, he named the place "Peniel" where that vision occurred.[1]

Image 2a. *Angkor Wat*[2]

The pineal looks like a tiny pinecone, beehive, or corn stalk. According to the Greek physician Galen (circa 130 to 210 AD), its name (Greek: *kônarion*, Latin: *glandula pinealis*) derives from its resemblance to nuts found in pinecones of the stone pine (Greek: *kônos*, Latin: *pinus pinea*).

The symbol of the pinecone, representing the highest spiritual illumination, appears widely throughout ancient Indonesia, Babylonia, Sumeria, Egypt, Greece, and Rome. It is also prevalent in Freemasonry, Theosophy, Gnosticism, and Christianity. The beehive is a common Masonic symbol, and the corn stalk was widely portrayed by indigenous tribes of the Americas.

Image 2b. *Pinecone Fountain at Vatican*[3]

The largest religious monument in the world, Angkor Wat, is found in Cambodia. Its colossal domes are pinecone-shaped. Pinecones or beehives adorn the head of Buddha in statues throughout Asia. The world's largest pinecone statue, found in the Vatican's "Court of the Pine Cone," is flanked by two peacocks, representing resurrection and immortality. The pinecone appears in the staff of the Pope and in the coat of arms of the Holy See. Pigna (pinecone) is the name of rione IX (one of the 22 administrative districts) of Rome.

The thyrsus is a wand or staff of the ancient Greeks, wielded by the fertility god Dionysus (also known as the Roman god Bacchus), and his followers, the Satyrs and Maenads. Made of a stalk of giant fennel plant, twined with ivy and vine branches and decorated with a ribbon, it is topped with a pinecone.

Image 2c. *Thyrsus Staff*[4]

Third Eye in Greek Literature

In Homer's *Odyssey,* composed approximately eighth century BC, we find an allegory about the third eye. After the Trojan War, the hero Odysseus is traveling home to Ithaca. He lands on Sicily, island of the Cyclopes, where he encounters a cruel, savage giant Polyphemus (son of Poseidon) with a large eye in the middle of his forehead. Odysseus and his sailors are imprisoned in a cave by the giant, who makes meals of six of them. Odysseus tricks the giant into getting drunk. In his weakened and vulnerable state, Polyphemus falls asleep and Odysseus drives a firebrand into his eye, blinding him. Odysseus and his band barely escape the island with their lives.

In India, the word *chakra* literally means "wheel." The third eye chakra is found in the middle of the forehead, where the Cyclopes eye is located. Remarkably, in Greek the word *Cyclopes* means "wheel-eyed."

With that in mind, we might consider possible interpretations of the Polyphemus myth. One explanation is that piercing the eye of Polyphemus represents atrophy of the third eye and subsequent loss of divine wisdom. Another might be that if the spiritual gifts granted through opening the third eye are misused, one is vulnerable to destruction.

The ancient Greeks believed the pineal gland to be the entrance to the realms of thought. Plato (circa 428 BC–348 BC) and Hippocrates (circa 460 BC–377 BC) believed the third eye (*enkephalos*) to be the "eye of wisdom." Plato viewed the chakras as subtle organs through which the soul (*psyche*) communicates with the physical body. He thought the marrow or cerebrospinal fluid to be the essence of the soul, and that the chakras emanated spiritual energy by means of this spiritual sap, which he called "radical moisture." He saw the third eye as the controlling center for all the chakras. This concurs with wisdom of ancient India. In Sanskrit, the term *ajna chakra* literally means "command center."[5]

Plutarch, the first century AD Greek historian, biographer and essayist, stated that the Eye of Horus (Egyptian symbol of the third eye) represents not only keen vision, but also foreknowledge.[6] Plutarch further stated there is a spark of divinity in the highest capacity of the human soul.[7]

The All-Seeing Eye of God

On July 4, 1776, the Declaration of Independence was signed, and 13 colonies declared themselves as states of a new nation. That same day, the Continental Congress began to design the Great Seal—its national emblem. Benjamin Franklin, John Adams, and Thomas Jefferson directed the creative process, which spanned six years.

First, Pierre Eugene du Simitière designed a heraldic seal, crested by a single eye—already an established symbol for God in heraldic Renaissance art. Simitière described it as "the Eye of Providence in a radiant Triangle whose Glory extends over the Shield and beyond the Figures." His design influenced Jean-Jacques-François Le Barbier's design of the French Declaration of the Rights of Man, crowned by a similar eye.

Image 2d. *The Great Seal*[8]

A heraldry consultant who worked on the Great Seal committee in 1780, Francis Hopkinson had previously designed the $50 Continental Currency note, which featured a pyramid. Then in 1782, William Barton, who had studied heraldry in England, was hired to further the work. He suggested a pyramid of 13 steps (representing the 13 colonies) with a radiant eye above it, which he described: "In the Zenith, an Eye, surrounded with a Glory."

On June 13, 1782, Secretary of Congress Charles Thomson (1729–1824) was assigned to complete the design. The most highly respected member of Congress, he was an advocate for the cause of African slaves and native Indians. Using elements from the submitted drafts, Thomson created the two-sided design officially adopted on June 20, 1782. Ever since, the design has remained unchanged.[9]

Charles Thomson's description of the seal stated: "The pyramid signifies strength and duration. The eye over it and the motto *Annuit Coeptis* allude to the many signal interpositions of providence [signs of divine intervention] in favor of the American cause." *Annuit coeptis* translates as: "He [the All-Seeing Eye of God] sees and approves our undertaking (or enterprise)."[10]

Many American Revolutionaries felt Providence had often intervened to enable their independence from Britain. As George Washington stated on March 26, 1781, "The many remarkable interpositions of the divine government, in the hours of our deepest distress and darkness, have been too luminous to suffer me to doubt the happy issue of the present contest."[11]

The Latin motto under the pyramid, *Novus Ordo Seclorum,* signifies "the beginning of the new American Era," according to Thomson. Its literal translation is "A New Order of the Ages." Both mottos on the reverse of the Great Seal originated with the Roman poet, Virgil (70 BC to 19 BC).[12]

Image 2e.

Masonic All-Seeing Eye of God

Freemasons say the eye depicted on the Great Seal is not a Masonic symbol.[13] They believe the Eye of Providence represents God's active intervention in human affairs, but the Masonic All-Seeing Eye symbolizes God's passive watchfulness and ever-present care for the universe. The Masonic All-Seeing Eye is an official symbol for God—"the Great Architect of the Universe," also known as "G" in their symbology.

Freemasons claim the symbol was borrowed from nations of antiquity, such as Egypt, where an open eye was the hieroglyph for Osiris, the main deity of Egypt.[14] The All-Seeing Eye also appears in other secret societies, such as Shriners, Knights of Pythias, and Odd Fellows.

MASTERS CARPET

Image 2f. *Masonic Tracing Board*[15]

During secret meetings of Freemasonry, Tracing Boards, which depict emblems of the Craft, originated as chalk drawings created by the Tyler or Worshipful Master on a table or floor of the Lodge. After the meeting, the diagram was erased with a mop in order to preserve secrecy. Later these Tracing Boards evolved into floor-cloths and finally canvas paintings. The All-Seeing Eye of God would often crown and watch over the symbols appearing on the Tracing Board.

More than 20 times brighter than our Sun, Sirius, known as the "Dog Star," is the brightest star in the sky. In ancient civilizations, Sirius was of supreme importance to astronomy, mythology, and the occult. Deemed the "Sun behind the Sun" and true source of our Sun's potency, it was considered the light keeping the spiritual realm alive, the true light shining in the East, the spiritual light. It is associated with the pineal gland, the source of spiritual light in the body. Its true meaning is the eye of wisdom—the third eye, which every human can awaken.

Image 2g. *The Masonic Blazing Star*[16]

Sirius is considered the home of the spiritual hierarchy, the divine beings of light and ascended masters. The star is the central focus of Hermetic Orders and secret societies. It is the "Blazing Star" of Masonry, and described by author William Hutchinson as "the first and most exalted object that demands our attention in the Lodge." It is a symbol of the omniscient Creator.[17]

The Eye of Horus

The hieroglyphs of ancient Egypt depict the *Udjat* Eye, also known as *Wadjet* or "Eye of Horus." It is also known as *Uadjet, Utchat, Oudjat, Wedjoyet, Edjo,* or *Uto.* The Eye of Horus is a symbol for spiritual awakening, protection, the power of royalty, and good health.

Horus is the sky god. His right eye symbolizes the Sun god Ra, and the southern direction. It is called the "Eye of Ra." His left eye represents the moon, northern direction, and the god Djehuti, Tehuti, or Thoth. It is the "Eye of Thoth."

Seven hieroglyphs represent the eye in ancient Egypt. The meaning of these hieroglyphs is "to make" or "to do." Thus the eye represents activity rather than passive seeing. It denotes action, protection, or wrath. The Eye of Providence found on the back of the U.S. Treasury's dollar bill has a similar connotation.

The god Horus (known as "Heru"), son of Osiris, is represented in Egyptian art as the lanner falcon or peregrine falcon.[18] When Osiris (the creator god and ruler of the planet Saturn) died, his brother Seth and his son Horus fought over his throne. In the battle, Seth gouged out the left eye of Horus, and Seth lost his testicles. Seth either tossed the eye into the celestial ocean or tore it to pieces (subject to alternate versions).[19]

When Thoth, god of magic and wisdom, magically restored the eye to its full moon state, Horus then offered it to his father Osiris, in an attempt to resurrect him. When Osiris ate the eye, he was magically returned to life, and subsequently allowed to rule the underworld. Thus the word *udjat* means "intact, complete, healthy." It also symbolizes phases of the moon, because that eye in the sky is "torn out" every month.[20]

Horus is the hero of Egyptian mythology. He defeated powers of darkness, regulated the flow of the Nile, and established order, harmony, and productivity. Thus the eye of Horus allows us to see with greater awareness, shed light upon the darkness, and attain true enlightenment.

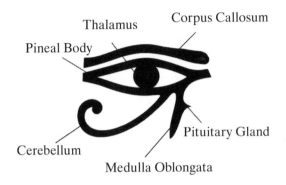

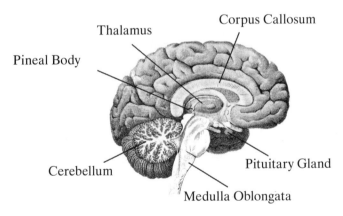

Image 2h. *Eye of Horus as a Map of the Brain*

A compelling theory is that the eye of Horus is a map of the brain. The eye represents the thalamus, the eyebrow is the corpus callosum, the tear duct and teardrop symbolize the pituitary and medulla oblongata, the long spiral arc is the cerebellum, and the small point on the end is the pineal body, or third eye.

In Ancient Egypt, the standard unit of measurement was known as a *hekat* (approximately 4.8 liters). Most fractions were written as the sum of two or more fractions with 1 as a numerator. For example, the fraction 3/4 was written 1/2 + 1/4. The Rhind Mathematical Papyrus was a table of "Horus Eye Fractions," written in 1650 BC by the Egyptian scribe Ahmes—the earliest identifiable contributor to mathematics.

The Wadjet is divided into six portions, representing its shattering into six pieces by Seth. These six pieces symbolize the six senses (hearing, sight, taste, touch, smell, and thought). According to Sir Alan Henderson Gardiner, in *Egyptian Grammar,* published in 1927, these fractions were written with hieroglyphs that resembled distinct pieces of the Wadjet as shown in the image of the Horus Eye fractions.[21]

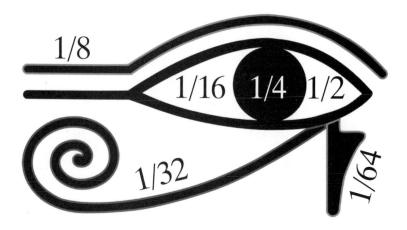

Image 2i. *Horus Eye Fractions*[22]

Parts of the Eye of Horus were used by ancient Egyptians to represent 1 divided by the first six powers of 2:

▷ The right side of the eye = 1/2, which represents the sense of smell.

▷ The iris = 1/4, which represents the sense of sight.

▷ The eyebrow = 1/8, which represents thought.

▷ The left side of the eye = 1/16, which represents the sense of hearing.

▷ The curved tail = 1/32, which represents the sense of taste.

▷ The teardrop = 1/64, which represents the sense of touch.

When these fractions are added together, they total 63/64, rather than 64/64 (or 1). Some researchers believe the remaining 1/64 might symbolize the magic used by Thoth to restore the eye to wholeness. Others think the missing portion might suggest that perfection is impossible.[23] But, because the Udjat represents perfection, that theory is illogical.

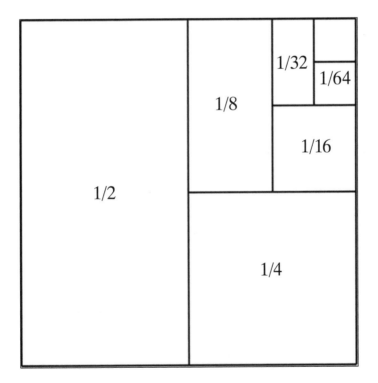

Image 2j. *Wadjet Proportions to Infinity*

A compelling idea is that the missing 1/64 was regarded by the Egyptian Mystery School as the secret name of God, and those in possession of this secret would attain higher consciousness.[24]

H. Peter Aleff, author of *Ancient Creation Stories Told by the Numbers,* offers an even more intriguing argument. He says the Eye of Horus hieroglyph is missing a pupil. However, a smaller circle than the one used for 1/4 hekat (which represents the iris in the Eye of Horus) did exist in Egyptian hieroglyphs. That small circle represented whole hekats from one to nine.

So the missing piece, in fact the most important piece, the piece that lets light in, the "window to the soul," does exist. It symbolizes wholeness (the numeral 1) and possibly infinity. The method of successively halving the fractions that led to 1/64 must eventually reach its ultimate conclusion—there is no end to the process. In order for one whole hekat to exist, infinity must be attained. And only the infinite has the power to resurrect the dead, as in the Osiris myth.[25]

It is believed the Eye of Horus was used as a medical measuring device. Its mathematical proportions allowed physicians to prepare medications by dispensing medical ingredients according to the Eye's proportions. The Ebers papyrus, circa 1550 BC (derivative of the books of Thoth, 3000 BC) listed 700 drugs and 800 compounds. The word "pharmacy" comes from the Egyptian *ph-ar-maki* ("bestower of security"). The God Thoth was patron of physicians.[26]

Image 2k. *Origin of R$_x$ Symbol*

In the second century AD, the Greek physician Claudius Galenus, popularly known as Galen, often used mystical symbols to impress his patients. He borrowed the Egyptian Udjat and the R_x symbol, commonly used to mean "prescription" in pharmacology today, from the hieroglyphs of ancient Egypt.

Amulets depicting the Udjat accompanied many Egyptians to the afterlife. Bracelets, pendants, and necklaces, fabricated with blue or green faience or semi-precious stones, protected the dead from harm and bad luck during their afterlife journey, and ensured their resurrection. The amulet was placed in the mummy wrappings over the incision where internal organs were removed by embalmers.

The Udjat was painted on the sides of rectangular coffins, carved on sarcophagi and stelae, and placed in or above a false door facing to the east. Through this doorway, the deceased could magically look toward the rising Sun. The Udjat sometimes decorated doors, and ancient texts mention a door-bolt of two eyes. Sailors of the Near East painted the symbol on their ship bows to ward off evil. The trireme, a warship used by the Phoenicians, Greeks, and Romans, is one example.[27]

Image 2l. *Trireme on a Carthage Mosaic*[28]

More Third Eye Symbols

The Hypocephalus of Tasheritkhons (305–330 BC) is an Egyptian disk made of linen, papyrus, gold, wood, or clay. Placed under the head of the deceased, it was believed to radiate heat and envelop the corpse's head with divine light. When used with a spell from the *Book of the Dead,* it supposedly brought new life to the dead.[29] This disk symbolizes the Eye of Horus. Its upper half represents the world of the living and daylight, and its lower half, the world of the dead and darkness of night.

Image 2m. *Hypocephalus of Tasheritkhons*[30]

Some researchers believe the disk is a map of the human brain, with the lower portion (upside-down in the image) representing the cerebellum (lower part of the brain) and the upper portion symbolizing the upper part of the brain. In the lower section, a serpent with a genital erection offers the Udjat to the Pharaoh. The erection symbolizes kundalini, the sacred energy that rises from the base of the spine up to the third eye.

Image 2n. *Uraeus: Symbol of Resurrection*[31]

As part of their headdress, priests, deities, and rulers of Egypt wore a *uraeus* ("the risen one" cobra, symbol of resurrection) on their forehead at the third eye point. Ancient Egyptians believed the center of the brain to be the Sun or "Eye of God," and the original name for Eye of Horus was Eye of Ra (Sun god). The uraeus cobra with its hood raised is the hieroglyph for Wadjet—one of the titles of goddess Sekhmet (daughter of Ra). The uraeus holds the Sun disk on Sekhmet's brow and on Pharaoh's crown. The name for the planet Uranus (known as the sky god, as is Horus) derives from *uraeus.*

Perhaps the oldest book in the world, the *Bopal Vuh* of the ancient Mayans, pictures the deity Quetzalcoatl wearing a multi-rayed Sun as a crown on his head along with a symbolic form of a snake.

In an ancient myth, Ra (the Sun god and also Pharaoh of Egypt) grew old and weak. His subjects no longer respected him nor obeyed his rule. He became the butt of their jokes. Infuriated, he yanked the uraeus (Wadjet—his own daughter) from his royal crown and dispatched her to earth as the lioness Sekhmet, to wreak vengeance on humanity.

But Sekhmet quickly became bloodthirsty. Even Ra could not call her back. He then tricked her into drinking 7,000 jugs of beer mixed with pomegranate juice, which resembled blood. Sekhmet gorged herself, fell asleep for three days, and woke with a hangover. Thus ended her campaign of devastation.[32]

Thus the Wadjet is not only a protecting, All-Seeing Eye. It is also a destructive, inescapable eye. Sekhmet ("she who is powerful"), also known as Wadjet, is the goddess of life-force power in the breath. Her temple is a mystery school for raising *sekhem*—the life energy known in India as kundalini.

In many cultures the eyes represent the universe. In the Taoist yin-yang symbol, the two eyes symbolize the masculine and feminine polarities of creation. The right eye is associated with masculine, solar energy, and left eye with feminine, lunar energy. In Egypt, the masculine energy is symbolized by the Sun god Ra, and the feminine energy, by the moon goddess Isis.

Image 2o. *Tai Chi Symbol*

In Egyptian art, Osiris, the creator god, is shown standing between Horus and Isis. He represents unity and wholeness. Horus, the masculine principle, stands to his right, symbolizing action and Isis, the feminine lunar goddess of emotion, stands to his left. So Horus is yang, Isis is yin, and Osiris is the unity between these two polar opposites.

Between the two hemispheres of the brain, in the very center of the brain, is the key to the connection between the inner male and inner female. That is the pineal gland, the third eye—the gateway between the material and spiritual worlds, the key to psychic development and higher vision.

The *ka* of Ancient Egypt represents the soul or subtle body, which was often symbolized by a phoenix, with the body of a man and wings of a bird, with arms turned upward and elbows bent. The phoenix is a symbol of death and rebirth. A tuft of feathers on its head represents the pineal gland and its function as the third eye.

Tefillin

The laying of *tefillin* in Orthodox Judaism might be a reminder of the third eye. Deuteronomy 6:8 states, *"And thou shalt bind them* [the sacred words of the holiest prayer of Judaism—the *Shema*] *for a sign upon thine hand, and they shall be as totafot between thine eyes,"* and Deuteronomy 11:18 says, *"Therefore shall ye lay up these my words in your heart and in your soul, and bind them for a sign upon your hand, that they may be as totafot between your eyes."*

Image 2p. *Laying Tefillin in Russia (circa 1898)*[33]

The totafot refer to cubed-shaped leather boxes, called tefillin (Greek: phylacteries), which contain four scriptural passages. According to Jewish scholars such as Chizkuni (Rabbi Hezekiah ben Rabbi Manoach, French rabbi of the 13th century), the root of *totafot* is from the Aramaic, meaning "to see."[34]

Jewish men attach them to the head and arm and wear them during morning prayers. They are meant to function as a reminder of God's laws. Could they also remind us that the true law of God is present in the area of the third eye, over which tefillin is worn? Could totafot show us that we see the truth through our third eye?

Trepanation

For more than 7,000 years, humans have been drilling holes in their skulls, for both medical and non-medical reasons. The earliest known trepanation, or trephination (from the Greek *trypanon*, "to bore") was discovered in 1685 in a Neolithic burial site at Ensisheim, France. In medical terminology, craniotomy surgery removes a piece of bone from the skull. This was practiced by ancient Egyptians, Arabs, Chinese, Indians, Romans, Greeks, Mesoamericans, and South Americans.

In the 19th century in Cusco, Peru, Ephraim George Squier acquired a frontal bone fragment (originating from an Incan cemetery) with a square, man-made hole measuring 15 by 17 millimeters. Paul Broca, illustrious anthropologist who founded the Societe d'Anthropologie de Paris in 1859, examined the bone and concluded that the trepanation was the result of advanced surgery performed by ancient Peruvians.

Hundreds of trepanned skulls have been found throughout the world. Many contain multiple holes. Why ancient civilizations performed trepanation for non-medical purposes is unknown. Anthropologists speculate that it was a tribal ritual or superstition.

The rite of trepanation for opening the third eye became widely known in 1956, when the book *The Third Eye* became a bestseller. Its author, Cyril Henry Hoskin, a British plumber, claimed his body was occupied by the spirit of a Tibetan monk named Tuesday Lobsang Rampa. The book included a hair-raising description of the trepanation that Rampa claimed to have undergone.

On Rampa's eighth birthday he ostensibly underwent the surgery. A muscular Lama braced the child's head between his knees and pressed a shining steel instrument against his forehead. The young Rampa felt as if thorns were pricking him, and time seemed to stand still. He felt a jolt and then a scrunch as the instrument penetrated his bone. A hard, clean sliver of wood, treated by fire and herbs, pierced the hole in his head. He felt a stinging, tickling sensation in the bridge of his nose and smelled unidentifiable subtle scents. Then he felt as though he had been pushed against a resilient veil.

Suddenly there was a blinding flash. An intense pain felt like a searing, white flame. He saw spirals of color and globules of incandescent smoke. The metal instrument was removed. But the sliver of wood remained in place for a few weeks, while the child was held in a small room in near-darkness.

This operation purportedly opened Rampa's clairvoyant sight, and from that moment, he could see auras. The child's mentor, Lama Mingyar Dondup, said to Rampa, "You are now one of us, Lobsang. For the rest of your life you will see people as they are and not as they pretend to be."[35]

Trepanning is still used today to treat traumatic brain injuries. Advocates of non-medical trepanation, such as Bart Hughes of the Netherlands, claim the procedure increases blood flow and expands brain size, just as a baby's skull with its *fontanelles* (soft spots) allows brain growth. They believe forehead trepanation opens the third eye. In 1965, Hughes performed trepanation on himself using an electric drill and a surgical knife, under local anesthetic. His followers have also performed self-trepanation or have practiced cranial surgery on their friends.

Please do not try this at home—or anywhere else!

Third Eye in Art and Architecture

Richard Cassaro, author of *Written in Stone,* explores the symbolism of the third eye in ancient architecture. He discovered that buildings of several cultures of antiquity, including Mexico, Indonesia, and Egypt (which scholars claim are completely unrelated), show a characteristic three-door pattern on their façades. Cassaro also shows this pattern in façades of buildings of secret societies: Shriners, Knights of Pythias, Freemasons, and Skull and Bones. Cassaro calls this pattern a "triptych," since it appears as a trinity.

Cassaro goes one step further, to show a third eye pattern over the middle doorway of the triptych in many buildings. The triptych can be equated with the three major energy conduits running through the midline of the human subtle body: *ida nadi* on the left, *pingala nadi* on the right, and *sushumna nadi* in the middle (see page 84 for information about the nadis), which meet at the third eye.

Image 2q. *Triptych and Third Eye: Reims Cathedral*[36]

These three energy tubes are also represented by the *caduceus*—the ancient symbol known as the staff of Hermes or Mercury in Greek or Roman mythology, respectively. It is also the Staff of Aesculapius, named for the Greek physician Asklepios, revered as the deity of medicine and healing by the ancient Romans. This symbol, first found on a libation vase of King Gudea of Lagash (circa 2000 BC), was later adopted by the medical profession as its emblem.

Image 2r. *Caduceus*

In India, the symbol for kundalini is a bamboo shoot with seven knots for the seven major chakras (energy centers). A barber pole, with its spiral of red and white bands and a knob on top, also symbolizes kundalini. This is known to represent the barber's former sideline of surgery. The pagan tree, later adapted as the Christmas tree, represents kundalini, and its lighted ornaments signify the chakra centers. The Jewish symbol for kundalini is the Kabbalistic tree of life.

In the next chapter, we will learn more about the pineal gland—seat of the third eye chakra.

3

| Seat of the Third Eye in the Brain |

And Jacob called the name of the place Peniel ["face of God"]: for I have seen God face to face, and my life is preserved. And as he passed over Penuel the sun rose upon him, and he halted upon his thigh.

—Genesis 32:30–31

Your third eye is centered in the pineal gland. Approximately the size of a raisin, its frequent calcifications ("brain sand") make it easily recognizable in brain X-rays. This endocrine gland rests in back of the eyes, behind the third cerebral ventricle in the midline (between the two cerebral hemispheres) of the brain. It is located in the geometric center of your cranium, near the entrance to the cerebral aqueduct, which connects the brain's third and fourth ventricles. As part of the epithalamus, between the two hemispheres, it rests in a groove where the two halves of the thalamus join.

The pineal is considered a "master" gland because it regulates bodily cycles, stimulates the production of many hormones, and controls other glands. Your endocrine system consists of glands that secrete hormones directly into porous capillaries of your blood. Your major endocrine glands are pineal, pituitary, pancreas, ovaries and testes, thyroid, para-thyroid, hypothalamus, and adrenals.

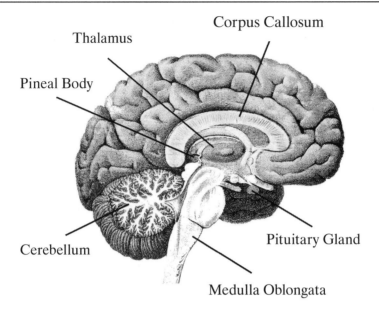

Image 3a. *Pineal Body in Brain*

The hormones manufactured by your endocrine glands are bio-chemical agents, transported via your blood to specific organs. These hormones regulate metabolism, digestion, respiration, reproductive cycle, immune system activation or inhibition, onset of puberty and menopause, sense perception, mood swings, wake-sleep cycle, circadian rhythms, hunger cravings, sexual arousal, flight-or-fight response, lactation, stress, stimulation or inhibition of growth, and movement.

The pineal gland, unlike the rest of the brain, is not isolated by the blood-brain barrier, which separates circulating blood from the brain's extracellular fluid found in cavities and channels of the brain and spinal cord. The pineal gland's blood flow is nearly the highest in the body, second only to that of the kidneys.

The Infamous "Worm"

Today it is known that light entering your eyes is sent to your hypothalamus and pineal gland. In response to cycles of light and darkness, your pineal body produces melatonin and other hormones that monitor and modulate sleep patterns in seasonal and circadian rhythms. It also controls sexual behavior, menstrual cycles, and sympathetic (fight-or-flight) nervous system responses.

Your pineal gland produces the hormone melatonin in varying amounts throughout the day and night. Derived from serotonin, melatonin induces drowsiness and lowers the core body temperature. Melatonin was not discovered until 1958. Nearly 2,000 years prior, physicians and philosophers of the West speculated about the functions of the pineal body.

In the second century AD, the Greek physician, surgeon, and philosopher Aelius Galenus (Galen) described the pineal gland in his anatomical book *On the Usefulness of the Parts of the Body*. He identified it as a gland and claimed its function (like that of all other glands) was to serve as a support for blood vessels. Galen never performed human autopsies, which were prohibited by law. Yet, astonishingly, his anatomical theories were considered gospel until the 16th century.

Both the Greek physician Hippocrates (460–370 BC) and Galen believed the ventricles in the brain were filled with *psychic pneuma,* a fine, volatile, airy, or vaporous substance and "the first instrument of the soul." Galen's theory was that the worm-shaped structure connecting the left and right sides of the cerebellum controls the flow of pneuma between the middle and rear ventricles. Today this connector is known as *cerebellar vermis* (Latin for "worm"). Galen vehemently rejected the prevailing view of his time that the pineal gland was that "worm."[1]

Medieval anatomists imagined that reason, memory, and imagination were seated in separate ventricles of the brain and that the "worm" separated them. These anatomists included Posidonius of Byzantium (end of the fourth century AD), Nemesius of Emesa (circa 400 AD), Avicenna (980–1037 AD), and Mondino dei Luzzi (1306).[2]

Qusta ibn Luqa (864–923), Byzantine Greek physician, speculated that the worm-like appendage controls the flow of "animal spirit" between the ventricles. He observed that people look upward when they are remembering, and downward when they are concentrating. He postulated that the eye movements raise or lower the wormlike appendage, which either retrieves memories from the posterior ventricle, or prevents memories residing in the posterior ventricle from disturbing the spirit.[3]

Authors of the late Middle Ages used the term *pinea* to denote the notorious wormlike valve. This is the very theory Galen had rejected. Adding to the mix-up, the medieval texts failed to distinguish between the pineal gland and the "worm-like appendage." Confusion only increased when the term "worm" ended up signifying three separate parts of the brain by various writers: the *vermis* of the cerebellum, the pineal gland, and the choroid plexus.[4]

Finally, Andreas Vesalius (1514–1564), a Belgian physician known as the founder of modern human anatomy, rejected all theories that mental functions were localized in specific ventricles. He also refuted the fabled "worm" regulating the flow of spirits in the brain's ventricles.[5]

"Principle Seat of the Soul"

René Descartes (1596–1650), French mathematician, writer, and father of modern philosophy, believed the human body functions as a machine, and the pineal gland produces sensation, imagination, memory, and bodily muscular movements. He viewed the pineal gland as the seat of perception, the universal sense faculty (*sensus communis*). He called it the "principal seat of the soul, and the place in which all our thoughts are formed." He also believed memories are stored there.

His logic was that because we see only one image with two eyes, and because we have two ears, yet hear only one sound, there must be an organ that unifies the two impressions before the soul can perceive them.[6] Because the pineal is the only body in the brain that does not appear in pairs, Descartes concluded the pineal "must necessarily be the seat of the common sense, i.e., of thought, and consequently of the soul." He also argued that the idea of the soul not being directly joined with the body is absurd.[7]

Descartes postulated that "animal spirits," swirling around in the ventricles, direct muscular responses by flowing through hollow tubes between the pineal and various muscles. These animal spirits, acting as intermediary between mind (seated in the pineal) and body, were seen as "a very fine wind, or rather a very lively and pure flame."

Descartes believed the brain tissue surrounding the pineal works as a sieve. Only the subtlest blood particles can pass through tiny openings that filter out the most subtle and active parts of matter (defined as animal spirits).[8]

He believed physical movements of the pineal gland drive the animal spirits "towards the pores of the brain" and then through the nerves to the limbs. Nerves are hollow tubes that contain fibers or threads connecting the sensory organs with tiny valves on the walls of the brain's ventricles.[9]

Although Descartes' ideas do not concur with those of modern anatomy, we might wonder whether he studied Ayurveda or Chinese medicine. Perhaps his "hollow tubes" or "pores" are the nadis, and his "animal spirits" are the five pranas that flow through our subtle body, granting life and movement. (Read my book *The Power of Chakras* for more information about the nadis and five pranas.)

Chronobiology

The field of chronobiology studies the relation between living organisms and solar-lunar cycles, mapped as a biological clock. The circadian rhythm (cycles that recur naturally in a 24-hour cycle) is chronobiology's most important cycle. Its biological processes enable brain activity to adapt to the time of day (light-dark cycles).

Organisms are fundamentally *diurnal*—most active during the day, *nocturnal*—active at night, or *crepuscular*—active during dawn and dusk. Humans tend to be early birds or night owls. Such classifications are called *chronotypes*.

Circadian cycles were first observed in plants during the 1700s by the French scientist Jean-Jacques d'Ortous de Mairan. In the same century, Carolus Linnaeus, a Swedish botanist and naturalist, created a "flower clock" that charted the opening of flowering plant blossoms during specific times of the day.[10]

In 1898, Dr. Otto Heubner, a German pediatrician, identified the pineal body as a gland. He discovered that pineal tumors were associated with both early and delayed puberty. From 1898 to 1958, it was thought this gland's sole function was to control puberty.

In 1918, a Swedish anatomist, Nils Holmgren, examined pineal glands of frogs and sharks. In the tip of the pineal gland, he discovered cells that resembled cone cells (color-sensitive photoreceptor cells). He concluded the pineal was not a gland, but a "third eye" in these animals.

The tuatara, a reptile of New Zealand that can grow to 31 inches, is a surviving species that flourished 200 million years ago. Its pronounced photoreceptive "third eye" (parietal eye) is believed to regulate seasonal cycles and circadian cycles. A similar third eye is found in extant lizards, iguanas, frogs, lampreys, brine shrimp, crustacean larvae, and fish, such as tuna and pelagic sharks. Arthropods such as spiders often have photoreceptive dorsal ocelli (extra eyes with separate visual pathways).

German biologist Erwin Bünning determined that plants and insects behave according to circadian rhythms, which are inherited. In 1935, he discovered the genetic origin of the "biological clock," a term he coined. His Bünning Hypothesis states that plants display endogenous phases of sensitivity to light and darkness—a *photophil* (light-loving) phase, and a *scotophil* (dark-loving) phase.[11]

In 1958, a breakthrough in pineal gland research occurred when Dr. Aaron B. Lerner, first chairman of the dermatology department at Yale University, isolated the hormone melatonin. He found the substance could be used to treat the human skin disorder vitiligo (loss of pigmentation on patches of skin). Later research showed that melatonin, produced by the pineal gland at night, regulates sleep-wake cycles and metabolic activity.[12]

Dr. Jürgen Walther Ludwig Aschoff studied how stimuli can alter circadian rhythms. In 1960 he conceived the term *zeitgeber*—an environmental cue that entrains, or synchronizes, biological rhythms. Through 20 years of experiments in an underground bunker, where subjects could turn lights on and off according to internal rhythms, Aschoff concluded that humans have endogenous (built-in, self-sustained) circadian (regular changes within each 24-hour period) oscillators (rhythms). He found that shifting the dark-light cycle can create harmful results, even mental illness.

Colin S. Pittendrigh, the British-born biologist who led the Society of Research in Biological Rhythms in the 1970s, is considered the father of the biological clock. He studied the circadian clock in various species, including fruit flies. He demonstrated that circadian rhythms, which synchronize to light-dark cycles, are intrinsic and independent of environmental cues.

Dr. Franz Halberg of the University of Minnesota, known as the father of American chronobiology, coined the word *circadian*. During a 50-year career, his challenge was convincing physicians that understanding bodily rhythms could prevent and treat disease. Halberg stated, "One of the big mistakes that's made is to believe that we can treat by clock hours...we have to treat by body times." He found that the white blood cell count of mice varied widely throughout the day in a regular rhythm. He was first to successfully treat cancer by timing radiation therapy with body rhythms. His research on blood pressure rhythms identified markers for potential disease. He found cycles of solar wind, sunspots, and geomagnetic storms had a greater physiological effect than seasonal changes.[13]

At Cold Spring Harbor Laboratory in New York, the field of chronobiology was launched at a famous 1960 symposium on biological clocks. That same year, Patricia DeCoursey invented the *phase response curve* (PRC), which is used to plot circadian rhythms.

In 1972, Robert Y. Moore and Victor B. Eichler of the University of Chicago, and Friedrich K. Stephan and Irving Zucker of the University of California in Berkeley, found that the suprachiasmatic nucleus (SCN) is a central timekeeper, tracking daily biological rhythms that manage cells, many of which have their own molecular clocks.[14, 15] Located in the mammalian hypothalamus, the SCN comprises two tiny, wing-shaped, paired bundles of 20,000 "clock cells." It coordinates the sleep cycle as well as fluctuations in heart rate, blood pressure, temperature, and some hormone secretion. Via nerve impulses, the SCN receives messages from the retina and sends them to the hypothalamus and pineal gland. [16, 17]

In 1989, Dr. Alfred J. Lewy and R.L. Sack, from Oregon Health Services University in Portland, found that the pineal gland naturally secretes melatonin starting two hours before bedtime, provided that lighting is dim. This is known as *dim-light melatonin onset* (DLMO). This helps prepare the body for sleep, and keeps the body on a regular sleep-wake schedule.[18]

Is the Pineal Gland a Third Eye?

The pineal gland is said to be a third eye, but it is not a third eye-ball. It has no iris, pupil, or lens. However, some of its cells resemble a retina. The primary cell found in the pineal is *pinealocyte,* commonly thought to have evolved from photoreceptor cells like those found in the retina.[19] Human pinealocytes were described by researcher Allan F. Wiechmann as "cone-like modified photoreceptor cells."[20]

Collaborative research in Bethesda, Maryland, conducted by Paul O'Brien of the National Eye Institute, and David Klein, PhD, of the National Institute of Child Health and Human Development, showed "the pineal gland was the evolutionary precursor to the modern eye," and found "surprising similarities between the two organs," including the presence of melatonin in both retina and pineal gland.[21]

Evidence of this link is a "pineal eye" in some animals. The Western fence lizard has a yellow-white spot in a 1-millimeter opening between the skull bones on top of its head. This eye-like extension of the pineal gland contains a retina, lens, and cornea. Other species, including lizards, frogs, and lampreys, have similarly elaborate pineal eyes.

Though this pineal eye resembles an actual eye, it does not react to light, nor does it focus. However, when illuminated, it does respond with electrical impulses. It senses ambient light, but not the detailed patterns perceived by the retina.

Though not possessing a pineal eye, many birds, fish, reptiles, and amphibians have a pineal gland that is sensitive to light, with photoreceptor rods and cones, though more rudimentary and randomly placed than in the retina.

Proteins formerly believed unique to the retina are also found in light-sensitive pineal glands of various vertebrates. In mammals, some pineal cells in the fetus resemble photoreceptor cells. In the human embryo, these cells have the potential (known as *differentiation potential*) to become lens, epithelial layer, or retina neuron cells. But instead they grow into a pineal gland.[22]

"It is now my view that the pineal gland—the so-called third eye—was the first eye," David Klein says. "The most primitive visual organ was a single 'eye' that had only to convert light into chemicals." Klein believes the pineal gland evolved to produce nerve signals and a hormonal response.[23]

This opinion is upheld by professor of developmental biology, Dr. Masasuke Araki of Nara Women's University, who, through 20 years of research, found the effects of the brain's very structure, as well as the peripheral nerves on the cells, cause a pineal gland to form, rather than an eye.[24]

A study in 1986 by Allen F. Wiechmann, Department of Cell Biology, University of Oklahoma College of Medicine, reported the pineal and retina have many similarities, including their common ability to synthesize the hormone melatonin. He said, "Many investigators suspect that the cyclic rhythm of retinal melatonin synthesis may be related to other cyclic events which normally occur in the retina."

The study further states that "the presence of proteins in the pineal gland which are morally involved in phototrasduction (light sensing) in the retina, raises the possibility that direct photic events may occur in the mammalian pineal gland."[25]

In 1995, in *USC Health & Medicine,* Cheryl C. Craft, PhD, chair of USC's department of Cell and Neurobiology, wrote, "The pineal gland is the 'mind's eye.' Dissected, the reptile's pineal looks much like an eye, with the same shape and tissue."[26]

In 2004, David C. Klein said the photoreceptor cells of the retina strongly resemble pineal gland cells, and the pineal cells of sub-mammals (such as fish, frogs, and birds) detect light.[27]

DMT Found in Pineal Gland

"The pineal gland has been an object of great interest regarding consciousness for thousands of years, and a pineal source of DMT would help support a role for this enigmatic gland in unusual states of consciousness." So says the website for the Cottonwood Research Foundation.

DMT (N-dimethyltryptamine) is an illegal substance that became popular in the 1960s as a recreational drug with a fast-acting, highly intense hallucinogenic effect. A psychedelic compound of the tryptamine family, DMT resembles a neurotransmitter and can cross the human blood-brain barrier. Ingesting the compound instantly evokes an altered state of consciousness, a sudden loss of connection with the physical world, complete immersion in hallucinatory experiences, communication with spiritual realms or otherworldly beings, and/or entry into strange environments likened to alien or parallel universes.

Recently, the jungle of the Amazon has become a popular tourist destination for those seeking DMT in the form of *ayahuasca,* a shamanic medicine sacred to indigenous South American cultures. It is used in potions for healing, and for opening awareness to subtle realms beyond the physical world.

Aguaruna Indians of the Amazon have used ayahuasca in ritual ceremonies since 500 BC. The concoction is made from leaves and stems of the psychedelic plants *Banisteriopsis caapi* (ayahuasca), *Psychotria viridis* (chacruna), and sometimes *Diplopterys cabrerana* (chagropanga, chaliponga, oco-yage). Known as *yagé, huasca, rambi, shuri, ayahuasca, nishi oni, natema, iona, mii, nixi, pae, ka-hee, mi-hi,* or *kuma-basere,* this sacred plant medicine is found throughout Amazonian Peru, Equador, Colombia, Bolivia, western Brazil, and in portions of the R'Orinoco basin.[28]

For those unwilling to travel to the Amazon, the church of Santo Daime, a Brazilian religion founded in the 1920s, has expanded to several countries. It blends Catholicism, native Amazonian rainforest rituals, and Afro-Caribbean animism. Its sacred church ritual involves drinking ayahuasca tea.

Since shamans of the Amazon claim that DMT awakens understanding of the self and communion with a higher power, scientists have sought to discover its connection with the pineal gland, which has been associated with the third eye and higher states of consciousness since antiquity.

In 1976, R.B. Gucchait's research indicated that the pineal contains an enzyme capable of synthesizing DMT.[29]

Dr. Rick Strassman, author of *DMT: The Spirit Molecule,* conducted extensive scientific research on DMT in the 1990s at the University of New Mexico. He speculated that the pineal gland is the most likely place where DMT is produced, because of the compound's chemical similarity to melatonin. He also conjectured that DMT is released by the pineal gland during REM sleep (dream state) and near death, resulting in the near-death experience (NDE).[30]

In 2011, Nicholas V. Cozzi, of the University of Wisconsin School of Medicine and Public Health, found *indolethylamine N-methyltransferase* (INMT), an enzyme associated with the biosynthesis of DMT and endogenous hallucinogens, is present in the pineal gland of the rhesus macaque monkey, in the retina's ganglion neurons, and spinal cord motor neurons.[31]

In 2013, Stephen A. Barker, Jimo Borjigin, Rick Strassman, and Izabela Lomnicka, of the Cottonwood Research Foundation, made a stunning discovery: Rodent pineal glands produce the psychedelic hallucinogen DMT: "We report here for the first time the presence of DMT in pineal gland dialysate obtained from the rat."[32]

Beach Barrett, researcher and associate of Dr. Rick Strassman, coined the term *metatonin* to designate the internally produced, endogenous DMT naturally occurring in the pineal gland, as differentiated from synthetically manufactured DMT. For you scientists reading this book, both melatonin and metatonin are derived from serotonin, which is in the tryptamine family. Melatonin is a methyltryptamine, and metatonin is a dimethyltryptamine. Melatonin derives from serotonin (serotonin plus one methyl molecule), metatonin derives from melatonin (melatonin plus one methyl molecule).

The most serotonin-rich tissue in the human body is in the pineal gland. However, serotonin produced by the pineal does not directly influence the brain. It is primarily used to create melatonin and metatonin. Metatonin is produced when the pineal internally secretes the enzyme *methyltransferase* (INMT).[33]

Some researchers believe the endogenous DMT produced by the pineal gland is responsible for out-of-body experiences (OBEs), near-death experiences (NDEs), spiritual experiences, inspiration, dreams, and even religious beliefs. DMT is found naturally in human blood, urine, and cerebrospinal fluid.

DMT floods the human body at birth, at death, and at the 13th week of gestation in the womb. Buddhists and Hindus believe that the soul of the newborn enters the fetus at about the 12th to 13th week of gestation. The pineal gland becomes visible in the human fetus 49 days after conception. Buddhists have long believed that the soul reincarnates within 49 days.

The implication of the discovery of DMT in mammals is enormous. Because DMT triggers the experience of altered states of consciousness, a connection between DMT and the pineal gland may indicate that the ancients of India were right all along—that the pineal gland is indeed the seat of the third eye.

In the next chapter, we will discover a lot more about the latest scientific research on the pineal gland and the third eye.

4

| The Third Eye Through the Eyes of Science |

*The Eye of the soul, which is blinded and
buried by other studies, is alone naturally
adapted to be resuscitated and excited by
the mathematical disciplines.*

—Plato

Melatonin, a hormone secreted by the pineal gland, was discovered in 1958 by Dr. Aaron B. Lerner and colleagues at Yale University School of Medicine. Derived from the amino acid tryptophan, melatonin is produced in the pineal gland of mammals, birds, reptiles, and amphibians, and it affects the daily wake-sleep cycle (circadian rhythms).[1]

The pineal gland converts serotonin into melatonin in a regular daily pattern. Melatonin and serotonin production are governed by cycles of light and darkness, detected by the eye's retina.[2] Melatonin output is higher at nighttime and lower during the day. Serotonin output is higher in daytime and lower at night. Also, melatonin is produced in greater quantities during the long nights of winter than the short days of summer.

Melatonin receptors are mainly found in the suprachiasmatic nucleus (SCN), where circadian rhythm is regulated. Generation of melatonin induces bodily changes that promote sleep, such as decreased temperature and respiratory rate. In the morning, melatonin production is inhibited. This stimulates wakefulness and maintains alertness throughout the day.[3]

In 2012, Peter McCormick and his team from the Faculty of Biology at the University of Barcelona discovered that dopamine in the pineal gland, when interacting with its receptors, inhibits the effects of norepinephrine and decreases melatonin production. Dopamine receptors only appear in the pineal at the end of the dark period. This stops melatonin production when the day begins.[4]

Benefits of Melatonin and Meditation

Melatonin is a free-radical scavenger in all cells and therefore a potent antioxidant with anti-aging and anti-cancer properties. It neutralizes harmful oxidative radicals and activates antioxidant enzymes. The decline of melatonin production with age contributes to age-related diseases. Melatonin protects embryonic fetuses and mediates many hormone functions.[5]

Professor Russell Reiter, a leading melatonin researcher, summarized melatonin's benefits as follows:

1. Vital for healthy sleep states, including lowering the body temperature.

2. Reduces cholesterol and risk of atherosclerosis and coronary heart disease.

3. Reduces blood pressure and the tendency for blood clots and strokes.

4. Reduces risk of heart attack, cancer, and viral replication.

5. Maintains and enhances immune system health.[6, 7]

Psychological health is greatly influenced by the pineal gland. If the pineal gland cannot find enough serotonin to produce adequate melatonin, sleep disorders arise and biological rhythms are disturbed. Fluctuating levels or low amounts of serotonin are found in the mentally ill.

The absence of natural sunlight decreases serotonin levels and consequently disrupts the biological clock. In climates with restricted sunlight, Seasonal Adjustment Disorder (SAD), develops. Residents of Norway and Finland suffer higher rates of irritability, fatigue, illness, insomnia, depression, alcoholism, and suicide. In contrast, sufficient sunshine promotes serotonin production, balances the circadian cycle, and increases melatonin production.

Mental illness is consistently correlated with the season of birth.[8] Incidences of schizophrenia and bipolar disorder are higher for those born in winter and spring. Research has shown a relationship between season, geomagnetic field fluctuation, melatonin production, and various physical and mental diseases.

Physician-astrologers of ancient Greece, the *iatromathematici,* as well as later European medical astrologers, believed that the heavenly bodies have a direct affect on human wellness. Greek physicians considered cosmic forces, planetary influences, climate, geography, and anatomy when treating patients.[9] Scientific research on circadian rhythms bears out this hypothesis.

In the second century, Aretaeus of Cappadocia, in *On Airs, Waters and Places* stated: "Human diseases change along with the seasons." The 18th-century English physician Richard Meade agreed. In *The Action of Sun and Moon in Animal Bodies* he emphasized seasonal factors in wellness and disease.[10]

The pineal gland is spiritually linked to consciousness. Positron emission tomography (PET) brain scans indicate that meditation stimulates the medial prefrontal cortex—the area of the third eye. Brain research shows that regular meditation alters the brain's neural anatomy to promote higher consciousness.

Neuroscientists have found the prefrontal cortex, connected with mental processing, can calm the limbic part of the brain. When a person is under stress, the amygdala initiates the fight-or-flight response, producing the hormone cortisol. This damages cells and shrinks the hippocampus. In contrast, meditation activates the prefrontal cortex, which reduces anxiety and trauma. Brain scans show that meditators shrink their amygdala and increase their hippocampus. This reduces stress and increases emotional stability and the ability to live in the present.

The hippocampus is one of the first regions of the brain to suffer damage in Alzheimer's disease. Meditation can reverse or repair some of this damage. It has been shown to calm the body-mind system and create a relaxed autonomic response. Such a tranquil state promotes and sustains healing.[11]

Revolutionary Pineal Gland Research

Since 1984, the *Journal of Pineal Research* has published hundreds of articles citing scientific studies on the pineal gland. Please refer to its online archive to read articles from 1984 to the present: *http://goo.gl/ IxThnt*. Many of its recent articles report the vast benefits of melatonin for health and anti-aging, and the detrimental effects of LAN (light-at-night pollution).

"We still lack a complete understanding of the pineal gland," states Jimo Borjigin, University of Michigan professor of physiology and neurology, and a pioneer in medical visualization (creating 3D computer images from medical imaging data) of the pineal gland's melatonin secretion.

Borjigin states, "Numerous molecules are found in the pineal, many of which are uniquely found at night, and we do not have a good idea of what their functions are. The only function that is established beyond doubt is the melatonin synthesis and secretion at night, which is controlled by the central clock in the suprachiasmatic nucleus [SCN] and modulated by light. All else is speculative."

Borjigin continues, "The central circadian clock controls timing of almost all aspects of our life, including physiology and behavior, and melatonin is the best marker to decode the fingerprints of circadian timing...[Melatonin secreted during sleep] helps the brain repair and sync our bodies to Earth's rotation. Melatonin is a stunning compound...a powerful antioxidant, its list of medicinal uses only seems to grow each year, as we learn more about its ability to help with immune disorders, chronic illnesses, and neurodegeneration.

"Pineal microdialysis [used uniquely in Borjigin's lab] allows us to monitor melatonin secretion closely under various conditions to simulate jet lag, shiftwork, light pollution, diet manipulation, and more to define the fingerprints of circadian response to environment," she adds. "It also allows us to discover animals with extreme chronotypes, like early-birds or night-owls, to understand how individuals with different chronotype respond to circadian challenges differently."[12]

One of Borjigin's studies discovered that pineal melatonin secretion is controlled by the superior cervical ganglion (SCG) and suprachiasmatic nucleus (SCN). When one of the two SCGs is removed, melatonin secretion is reduced by 50 percent initially, but fully recovers within 36 hours. It is not known how the pineal gland can recover so rapidly and completely.[13]

Electromagnetic Radiation Exposure

In 1989, S.G. Wang of China found that workers who were exposed to high amounts of RF/MW (Radio Frequency and Microwave) had an increase in serotonin and reduction in melatonin. Since that time, many scientific experiments have corroborated that ELF and RF/MW exposure reduces melatonin production in the pineal gland.[14]

Research in 2011 by Kavindra Kumar Kesari, Sanjay Kumar, and J. Behari at the School of Environmental Sciences, Jawaharlal Nehru University, New Delhi, India, has measured the effects of electromagnetic fields (RF-EMF) on the brain. In rodents, chronic exposure to 60-Hz electric fields (prevalent in our environment) lowers pineal melatonin levels by 40 percent. And 900 Mhz microwave radiation promotes oxidation in the brain. Mobile phone exposure and microwave radiation significantly decreases melatonin in the pineal gland and suggests a health risk.[15]

Barry W. Wilson, Cherylyn W. Wright, and other researchers from Battelle, Pacific Northwest Laboratories in Richland, Washington, and Rita Sommer-Flannigan of University of Montana in Missoula, discovered that human pineal function was adversely affected by continuous polymer wire electric blankets.[16]

At the University of Berne in Switzerland, the effects of exposure to 16.7-Hz magnetic fields on railway workers were studied. Those working on electrically powered engines or beneath transmission lines showed a decrease in melatonin production.[17]

Light at Night Risks

Research by Shu-qun Shi, Tasneem S. Ansari, Owen P. McGuinness, David H. Wasserman, and Carl Hirschie Johnson at Vanderbilt University in Nashville, Tennessee, showed that staying up late in artificial light curbs melatonin production. This is the first study to show that the body's circadian biological clock controls insulin activity. Eating habits correlated to disrupted sleep schedules and late work shifts led to obesity, diabetes, and risk of cancer and heart disease.[18]

"Our study confirms that it is not only what you eat and how much you eat that is important for a healthy lifestyle, but when you eat is also very important," explained Shu-qun Shi. "People have suspected that our cells' response to insulin had a circadian cycle, but we are the first to have actually measured it," reported Owen McGuinness. "The master clock in the central nervous system drives the cycle, and insulin response follows."[19]

Research at the Department of Natural Resources and Environmental Management, University of Haifa, Israel, indicated that the "modern urbanized sleeping habitat" is a massive, hormone-based cancer risk. From 2008 to 2011, Itai Kloog, Richard G. Stevens, Abraham Haim, and Boris A. Portnov published a series of studies on the risk of "light at night" (LAN).[20]

Kloog was quoted as saying, "Light at night has been proven on many levels, by our group and many others, to definitely contribute to higher risk of developing hormonal cancer." Kloog's team found that breast cancer rate increased significantly in women who were exposed to light at night more often.[21]

Kloog stated, "Up until around 120 years ago, humans were basically exposed to 12 hours of sunlight and 12 hours of darkness on average, seasons and latitudes permitting of course. But since the invention of the light bulb, we've artificially stretched the day. We go to sleep late at night, we have lights on while we sleep, we have a shorter sleep duration. We have a lot of factors stretching out our days, relative to the light period we experienced during millions of years of previous evolution."

Kloog's suggestion is to "go to sleep in a dark room. Use less light. Close the shutters. Circadian disruption is carcinogenic to humans."[22]

Dr. Alfred J. Lewy of Portland's Oregon Health and Science University, Dr. Josephine Arendt of University of Surrey, UK, and many others have conducted research to delay or advance onset of sleep. They found that animal and human circadian rhythms could be reset with light therapy directed at the eyes (for wakefulness), and with oral administration of melatonin (for sleepiness).

In 2012, David W. Frank, Jennifer A. Evans, Jeffrey A. Elliott, and Michael R. Gorman, of University of California, San Diego, discovered that low-level light at night accelerates circadian re-entrainment of hamsters of all ages by 50 percent. The dim light is intended to simulate moonlight.[23, 24]

According to the World Health Organization, circadian disturbances such as jet lag, nighttime work, and sleep disorders affect 40 percent of the world's population. These disruptions have caused the body mass index to rise above recommended levels in 50 percent of Europeans, as well as behavioral disorders that affect 25 percent of the population at least once in their lifetime in which melatonin levels are related.[25]

Calcification of the Pineal Gland

Babies and children have large, pristine pineal glands. As they approach puberty, the gland shrinks. With that contraction, the childlike sense of wonder also diminishes. Clairvoyant experiences of children disappear with age. This might be the result of pineal gland calcification, which begins as early as 5 years of age.

Over time, the pineal gland accumulates calcium deposits: *corpora arenacea (acervuli*, or "brain sand"). These are composed of calcium phosphate, calcium carbonate, magnesium phosphate, and ammonium phosphate, and have been linked with aging.[26] Research shows the degree of pineal gland calcification is significantly higher in patients with Alzheimer's disease versus other types of dementia.[27]

The pineal gland calcifies with the introduction of halides, such as bromide, fluoride, and chlorine. Thus, pineal gland calcification and decreased enzyme production has been linked to sodium fluoride, which is added to 90 percent of United States drinking water, bath water (absorbed by our skin), beverages, food, toothpaste, Prozac (fluoxetine), fluoroquinolone antibiotics, and nonstick cookware.

In 1997, Jennifer Anne Luke of the School of Biological Sciences, University of Surrey, Guildford, UK, The Royal London Hospital, was first to study the effects of fluoride on the pineal gland. Fluoride does not accumulate in the brain, and the blood-brain barrier obstructs fluoride from passing into the central nervous system. However, the pineal gland is not part of the brain. It is outside the blood-brain barrier.

In Luke's study on elderly pineal glands, she showed for the first time that fluoride accumulates in the pineal gland, and by old age an average pineal contains 300 mg per kilogram, as much fluoride as in teeth (300 mg in dentine and 100 mg in enamel). The pineal has the highest concentration of fluoride in the body—enough fluoride to inhibit enzyme production.

Luke found that high fluoride levels in the pineal are due to the large surface area of calcium phosphate (hydroxyapatite) crystallites both inside and outside its cells. The pineal has the highest calcium concentration of any normal soft tissue. Plus the pineal has profuse blood flow and high capillary density—second only to that of the kidney.[28]

Most developed countries do not allow fluoride in their drinking water. However, more people in the United States drink fluoridated water than the rest of the world combined. Countries with high fluoride levels in the water are now taking measures to remove the fluoride because of potential health problems. Check the website *www.fluoridation.com* for 50 reasons to eliminate water fluoridation.[29]

In 2006, the National Research Council (NRC) released a study titled "Fluoride in Drinking Water: A Scientific Review of EPA's Standards." Here is an excerpt: "Fluoride exposure results in altered melatonin production and altered timing of sexual maturity.... Recent information on the role of the pineal organ in humans suggests that any agent that affects pineal function could affect human health in a variety of ways, including effects on sexual maturation, calcium metabolism, parathyroid function, postmenopausal osteoporosis, cancer, and psychiatric disease."[30]

Decalcifying Your Pineal Gland

You can well imagine what effect calcification of the pineal gland has on your third eye. Therefore, you may use some of the following methods to decalcify your pineal gland.[31]

IMPORTANT: Check with a physician before ingesting any of the following and before following any of this advice.

Diet

Some foods reported to aid in pineal gland decalcification include: garlic, lemons, Braggs raw apple cider vinegar, natural butter oil, raw cocoa, garlic, tamarind, goji berries, cilantro, watermelon, bananas, honey, coconut oil, hemp seeds, nigella sativa (black seed), seaweed, chaga mushroom, and noni juice.

Avoid the following: processed foods and drinks, GMO foods, pesticides, artificial sweeteners, mouthwash, cleansers, refined sugar, sodas, caffeine, alcohol, tobacco, mercury in fish, tooth fillings, and vaccines.

Water

Drink fresh, pure water that has not been fluoridated. That includes fresh spring water, distilled water, and reverse osmosis water. Most water filters do not remove fluoride. Avoid tap water and cooking with tap water.

Supplements

Recommended supplements include hydrilla verticillata (freshwater plant), chlorella (green algae), spirulina (blue-green freshwater algae), ginseng, Vitamin D3, Vitamin K1/K2 (Jarrow Formulas), MSM, bentonite clay, chlorophyll, skate liver oil (Blue Ice), ratfish liver oil, cod liver oil, iboga root bark, wild oregano (OregaMax), and neem extract. Avoid calcium supplements.

Boron

Boron can effectively remove accumulated fluoride. It naturally occurs in organic beets. The Homeopathic company Boiron also makes a completely safe Borax medicine. Or make a concentrated solution by dissolving 1/4 teaspoon or less of Borax in 1 liter of pure water. Start with a dose of 1 tablespoon per day mixed with drink or food, and continue with 1 to 2 doses daily. Keep out of reach of children.[32]

Minerals

Iodine (Lugol's iodine solution) helps to remove fluoride from the pineal gland, and magnesium helps to flush out fluoride from your body. Iodine naturally occurs in seaweed. Zeolite (Zelite Pure) and black mica extract (Adya Clarity) are effective toxin removers.

Toothpaste

Avoid fluoride in toothpastes to avoid further pineal gland calcification.

Yoga

The yoga practices in this book, including khechari mudra, help to awaken and decalcify your pineal body.

Sleep Cycles

Sleeping in the dark stimulates melatonin production in the pineal gland. Get an effective, comfortable eye mask and use it every night for deeper sleep and wellness.

Sun Gazing

Under the guidance of a qualified guru, build up slowly, starting with a few seconds, until you can gaze at the sun for a few minutes, during the first 15 minutes after sunrise and last 15 minutes before sunset. Do not attempt this without permission from your physician.

Essential Oils

Recommended oils include lavender, sandalwood, frankincense, parsley, davana, pine, pink lotus, and mugwort. These can be inhaled directly (except mugwort), burned in a diffuser or nebulizer, and added to bath water.

Meditation

Meditation on the third eye will fill it with prana and increase its health and size. See how to meditate in Chapter 14.

Affirmation

Using affirmative prayer can help you decalcify your third eye. Please see Chapter 13 of this book.

For more detailed information and product recommendations to help you decalcify your third eye, please visit *http://decalcifypinealgland. com/how-to-decalcify-the-pineal-gland*.

Scientific Evidence of the Third Eye

Professor Robin Dunbar from the University of Oxford, Dr. Joanne Powell and Dr. Marta Garcia-Finana at the University of Liverpool, Dr. Penny Lewis at the University of Manchester, and Professor Neil Roberts at the University of Edinburgh, found in a 2012 study that people need specific cognitive skills in order to hold conversations, maintain multiple friendships, and handle a complex social world. The skill of "mentalizing" or "mind-reading" is defined as the ability to understand what people are thinking. It was found that those with a greater capacity in this area have larger frontal lobes (the third eye region: orbital prefrontal cortex).[33]

Dr. Joanne Powell said: "We have been able to show that the relationship between brain size and social network size is mediated by mentalizing skills. What this tells us is that the size of your brain determines your social skills, and it is these that allow you to have many friends."[34]

In 1993, Serena M. Roney-Dougal of Psi Research Centre, Glastonbury, Somerset, Great Britain, summarized research that connects the pineal gland with a psi-conducive (psychic) state of consciousness, and its link with the earth's electromagnetic field (EMF).

The pineal gland produces an endogenous hallucinogen 6-MeOTHBC (6-Methoxytetrahydrobetacarboline), known as pinoline, which is almost chemically identical to harmala alkaloids occurring in the vine *Banisteriopsis caapi,* used by Amazonian tribes for psychic purposes. The pineal enzymes act on serotonin to produce several possible hallucinogens. The production of melatonin, 6-MeOTHBC, and serotonin is affected by variations in the EMF. This could be related to variations in a psi-conducive state.

Roney-Dougal suggests any strong change in the Earth's ambient magnetic field can produce a rush of natural bodily hallucinogens, enabling people to be more psychically receptive. Parapsychologist Stanley Krippner's studies showed a connection between EMF and geomagnetic activity and an increase in dreams or psychic activity.

When people visit certain places on earth known as sacred sites, psi experiences heighten. This suggests that sensitivity to psi experiences is somehow affected by EMF. The pineal production of melatonin and possibly psi-conducive beta-carbolines is affected not only by light and stress, but also by EMF.[35]

Eyeless Sight

Bio-introscopy is the term used by parapsychologists in Russia for "eyeless sight," "skin vision," "dermo-optical perception," or "paroptic vision." The term simply means seeing things hidden from view—presumably with the third eye.

Rosa Kuleshova (1955–1978) could read printed words with the fingers of her right hand when her normal vision was completely blocked. She could also determine color tones on paper and objects by touch. She underwent experiments at the Biophysics Institute of the Soviet Academy of Sciences in Moscow.[36]

Tania Bykovskaia was tested by a commission from Kuban Medical Institute in Krasnodar, which reported her ability to distinguish colors of two balls hidden from view.[37]

Dr. Abram Novomeisky of the psychology lab at the Nizhne-Tagil Institute studied a metallurgist named Vasily B., who had been totally blind for seven years. He could distinguish colors by touch and at a distance. His eyeless-sight ability diminished in dim light or darkness. Bright electric light enhanced his faculty, and specific colors were associated with unique sensations.[38]

In 1960, fourteen-year-old Margaret Foos of Ellerson, Virginia, underwent elaborate tests. Securely blindfolded, Margaret read randomly selected passages of print, identified colors and objects, and even played a game of checkers.

Yakov Fishelev of the Sverdlovsk Pedagogical Institute, with subjects at the Pyshma school for the blind, experimented with eyeless sight through recognizing color with fingertips and distinguishing shapes of letters.

In 1965, at the Scientific Conference of the Ural Division of the Society of Psychologists in Perm, Dr. S.N. Dobronravov of Sverdlovsk stated that 72 percent of children had "skin sight" potential, especially between the ages of seven and twelve.

Anatoly Rodionov, researcher at Voronezh State University in Russia, has studied eyeless sight for more than 40 years. He found that animated objects have biomagnetic fields, and under some conditions these fields can be seen with the third eye.

For many years, Rodionov worked as head consultant for the Russian gymnastics team. With his talent of "diagnostic imaging" (medical clairvoyance), he helped well-known athletes return to sports after physicians had declared they would never recover. Rodionov devised a medical rehabilitation plan for a famous gymnast, Lyubov Burda. She revived and won titles of both Soviet and Olympic champion.

Also, experimental bio-introscopy was able to effectively diagnose, recommend treatments, and reduce traumas suffered by hockey players from the Soviet hockey squad.

Rodionov says that almost anyone can learn to perceive subtle bioenergetics processes invisible to normal eyesight. In Russia, diagnostic imaging has become a university discipline, and scientists are publishing works on the subject. At Voronezh State University, Rodionov trains students to master this ability.[39]

Pineal Meditation Research

Beverly Rubik of the Institute for Frontier Science in Oakland, California, researches the biofield, the life-force energy that surrounds living organisms. Rubik says the biofield is the "the next step" in science, which would "explain more deeply how the mind works and how the body responds to various types of alternative therapies."

Rubik, who believes the human body is more than "just a bag of biomolecules," studies clairvoyance, Qigong, psychic healing, and "high-frequency brainwaves that may be involved in higher states of consciousness." Using Neurotek neurofeedback devices, Rubik measured the brainwave patterns of habitual meditators and found that meditators' brains produce higher frequencies than the brains of non-meditators.

Rubik found that the frontal portions of the brains of Tibetan Buddhist meditators, just above the third eye area, consistently measure at a speed of 40 hertz. Her research indicates this high frequency is associated with feelings of love, joy, gratitude, clairvoyance, and childlike wonder.[40]

In 2005, Sara Lazar, along with her colleagues at the Massachusetts General Hospital in Boston, used magnetic resonance imaging (MRI) to compare the brains of Buddhist insight meditation practitioners (with experience ranging from 1 to 30 years) with those of non-meditators. She found that meditation increases the thickness of the cortex in the prefrontal area (third eye) and the right anterior insula. This supports studies showing that accomplished musicians, athletes, and linguists have thickening in relevant areas of the cortex. It is further evidence, says Lazar, that yogis "aren't just sitting there doing nothing."

Differences in prefrontal cortical thickness were most pronounced in older, more experienced meditators, suggesting that meditation might offset age-related cortical thinning. This data provides the first structural evidence for experience-dependent cortical plasticity associated with meditation practice.[41]

In 2007, at National Taiwan University, Chien-Hui Loou, Chang-Wei Hsieh, Jyh-Horng Chen, Si-Chen Lee, and Chi-Hong Wang studied the correlation between pineal activation and meditation, using MRI brain scans. Their findings indicated that, together with other brain regions, the pineal body exhibited significant activation during meditation, supporting the long-lasting speculation that the pineal plays an important role in the intrinsic awareness that might concern spirit or soul.

Jyh-Horng Chen of the National Taiwan University in Taipei, co-leader of the study, stated, "Our results demonstrate a correlation between pineal activation and religious meditation, which might have profound implications in the physiological understanding of mind, spirit and soul."[42]

Please refer to my books *The Power of Auras* and *The Power of Chakras,* where you will find reports of extensive scientific research on clairvoyance and the biofield—the invisible energy body that pervades, permeates, and surrounds the physical body. In the next chapter, we will turn to the time-tested wisdom of the East to deepen our understanding of the third eye.

Anatomy

of the

Third Eye

PART II

5

| Your Subtle Body |

*Glory, glory to Mother Kundalini, who through
her Infinite Grace and Power, kindly leads the
Sadhaka from Chakra to Chakra and illumines
his intellect and makes him realise his identity
with the Supreme Brahman.*

—Sri Swami Sivananda

As you have discovered in this book, Western minds have devised many theories about the third eye. But in the Far East, the Earth's crown of profound wisdom—that is where you will find truth rather than speculation. As long as history has existed, the East has been the fountainhead of truth about subtle energies. And the third eye *(ajna chakra)* is part of subtle human anatomy. This energy center, situated in the middle of the head, is mentioned in ancient literature throughout the Orient. It is invisible to human eyes, and is not found in any cadaver, because it is not physical.

The Key to Life

The Sanskrit word *prana* derives from roots *pra* ("first," "primary," "before," or "forth") and *an* ("breathe," "move," "live"). So *prana* means "breathing forth." However, prana is much more than breath. It is the energy that gives life to your body, and life to all matter in the universe.

Known as *chi* in China, *ki* in Japan, *ka* in ancient Egypt, and the *biofield* to modern researchers, prana is life-force energy—the power within all things and all beings, from elementary quantum particles to the most complex life forms. As the finest vital force in everything, prana manifests on the physical plane as motion and on the mental plane as thought.

Prana is in the air, yet it is not any physical constituent of air. All living beings absorb prana with every breath. Both oxygen and prana are required to keep you alive. Oxygen flows through your circulatory system to build and replenish your blood. Prana moves through your subtle body to bring strength and energy. Prana resembles electric currents flowing through your body, transmitting commands from your brain through your nerves. Pranic energy is crucial to your body's homeostasis, and if pranic flow is blocked, disease or death occurs.

Without prana, you could not move or breathe. Your blood would not circulate, your lungs would not move, and your body would be stiff and cold. It is said in the ancient scripture of India, *Hatha Yoga Pradipika*, "When there is prana in the body it is called life; when it leaves the body it results in death."[1]

Your Energy Field

Your physical form is just one of your bodies. You are a multidimensional being with both a gross physical body and a subtle body, which in the West we call an *aura* or *energy field*. Your physical body is visible to your physical eyes. Your subtle body is invisible to physical eyes, but visible to your third eye. With developed subtle perception and spiritual sight, you can view this auric field.

According to the wisdom of ancient India, you have a threefold body: gross physical body, subtle body, and causal or seed body. Within these three bodies are five sheaths: food sheath (gross physical body), vital sheath, mental sheath, intellect sheath, and blissful sheath or causal body. These five are termed sheaths because, like veils, they hide your luminous *atman* (higher self). Your subtler bodies and sheaths permeate and surround the grosser ones. Therefore, you inhabit all these bodies simultaneously and multidimensionally.

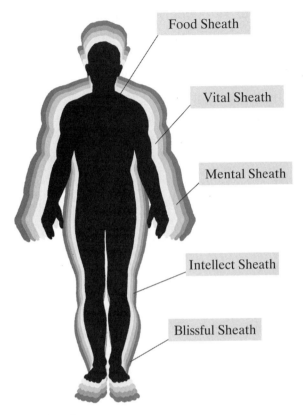

Image 5a. *Fivefold Sheath*

Your vital sheath (*pranamaya kosha*), often called etheric or astral body, breathes life into your body, animates it, and gives it expression. Your food sheath (physical body) engages in all activities as if alive, but without the vital sheath, your food sheath would be a corpse.

Your vital sheath is made of prana. Intensifying pranic energy increases vitality, health, power, influence, charisma, willpower, and supernormal powers. Pranic energy is continually drained by every thought, word, and action, and consistently replenished with every breath. Other sources of prana are sunlight, water, air, and food.

Thought is the most refined, potent form of prana. Therefore, when your mind is relaxed and expanded during deep meditation, pranic energy is boosted exponentially. In fact, meditation is the single most powerful way to increase pranic energy.

Speech vibrates with pranic energy, and certain forms of speech, such as prayer and affirmation, increase pranic energy. Positive, powerful statements of truth vitalize and expand your aura. But negative, damaging speech diminishes and shrinks your aura.

Gopi Krishna says prana "energizes, overhauls, and purifies the neurons and maintains the life-giving subtle area [soul] of the body much in the same way as the blood plasma maintains the grosser part."[2]

Moderate exercise, such as walking, bicycling, swimming, and yoga postures (*asanas*), along with proper breathing and yogic breathing exercises (*pranayama*), oxygenates blood and revitalizes pranic energy.

Pranic energy is undetectable by scientific measurements. Yet, the subtler, more elusive, and more abstract this energy is, the more potent it is. When you learn to control the tiny currents of prana working in your mind, the secret of controlling universal prana is also unlocked. Once this secret is revealed, you fear no power, because you have mastered all the powers in the universe.

The Serpent Power

Your subtle body's vital sheath (pranamaya kosha) consists of a vast complex of *nadis* (energy conduits) and *chakras* (plexuses of subtle energy), through which prana circulates and energizes your body. This system is like a computer board—intelligence underlying the growth, health, and maintenance of your body.

In the form of vital currents, prana flows through fixed pathways—subtle energy tubes called *nadis* (conduits or channels). According to ancient scriptures of India, there are 72,000 nadis in your pranic body. Some of these are known in Chinese medicine as acupuncture meridians.

Your pranic body contains numerous centers of concentrated vital energy, called *chakras*. They appear as vortexes of pranic energy at specific points in your subtle body. Their main function is to control pranic circulation throughout your system. Some of these are known as acupuncture points.

The Sanskrit word *chakra* means "wheel." This is because it is a circular concentrated plexus of pranic energy—an energy center with a hub and spokes. The hub is where many nadis (conduits of pranic energy) intersect, and the spokes are radiations of pranic energy.

The ancient scriptures count hundreds of such energy centers. However, seven primary chakras are responsible for maintaining life in your body and for sense perception, mental activity, and higher awareness. These seven correspond to glands, organs, and nerve plexuses in your physical nervous system. Though they sustain and govern your physical body, the nadis and chakras are by no means physical. If you dissected a corpse, you would detect no nadi or chakra anywhere.

The three most important nadis through which prana flows are called *sushumna, ida,* and *pingala.* Of all the nadis, the most essential to spiritual development is sushumna nadi. The ancient scriptures call sushumna the "royal road" (*rajapath*), because it is the conduit through which kundalini (the serpent power) flows. Sushumna is the median channel running from the base of your spine, near the tailbone, through your vertebral column, all the way up through the top of your skull.

The caduceus, symbol of the American Medical Association, is a depiction of ida and pingala coiling around the central canal, sushumna. Although most medical doctors have no knowledge of nadis, the ida and pingala govern the parasympathetic and sympathetic aspects of your autonomic nervous system, respectively. See an image of the caduceus on page 50 of this book.

Only the most rarefied, refined, subtlest form of prana, known as *kundalini,* can force sushumna to open and flow through it. Kundalini is the cosmic pranic energy that remains dormant until it is awakened, usually through spiritual practices. Raising kundalini up through the chakras progressively awakens consciousness.

The word *kundalini* derives from Sanskrit roots, *kundala* ("curled up") and *kunda* ("pit," "depression," "deep place"). Referred to as "serpent power," "mystic coil," or "primal power," kundalini is likened to a coiled snake or serpent residing at the base of your spine. In ordinary humans, this energy remains dormant, coiled up below the root chakra. As it wakes up and rises up the spine through sushumna, it opens the chakras, bringing health, well-being, energy, and, ultimately, spiritual enlightenment.

Image 5b. *Kundalini Coiled at Base of Spine*

The great yoga text *Light on Yoga*, by B.K.S. Iyegar, states,

"The human body is a miniature universe in itself.... The solar and lunar energy is said to flow through the two main nadis, Pingala and Ida, which start from the right and the left nostrils respectively and move down to the base of the spine. Pingala is the nadi of the Sun, Ida is the nadi of the Moon. In between them is the Sushumna, the nadi of fire. Sushumna Nadi is the main channel for the flow of nervous energy and it is situated inside the spinal column. Pingala and Ida intersect each other and also Sushumna at various places. These junctions are called Chakras or wheels and regulate the body mechanism as fly-wheels regulate an engine."[3]

The refined prana of kundalini can only flow through sushumna when you attain a subtle level of awareness. In deep meditation, as you achieve *samadhi* (equanimity of mind and body), your breath becomes so rarefied that it is imperceptible. Then your mind and body settle to quietude, and your breath becomes so fine that it is suspended between in-breath and out-breath.

The most refined prana flows when this most delicate form of breathing occurs. Rarified breathing is sublime, blissful, and spiritually enriching. You are then breathing the breath of God, the holy breath.

The Chakra System

To write my award-winning book *Exploring Chakras,* and its later edition *The Power of Chakras,* I researched the Vedic and Tantric scriptures of ancient India to find the most authentic information about the subject. In that book I cover the 14 chakras mentioned in the scriptures: seven major chakras that you may already be familiar with, and seven others that you might not be aware of. Many of the lesser-known chakras are in your skull or above your head.

According to the wisdom of ancient India, each sound or vibration in the universe is the precursor of a corresponding form. The letters of the Sanskrit alphabet are believed to be the primal sounds from which the universe springs. And the fundamental seed sound that underlies and gives rise to the entire cosmos is said to be *OM*—the hum of creation.

The seven major chakras are vibrational plexuses, like lotus flowers with a seed sound (*bija mantra*) at the core of each lotus, and other seed sounds on the radiations—the lotus petals. The vibrations of the entire Sanskrit alphabet, consisting of a total of 50 letters, are the seed sounds on the lotus petals of the first six major chakras, and all the 50 seed sounds radiate on the petals of the seventh chakra.

Kundalini traveling up the spine awakens the chakras and vibrates the 50 seed sounds as it flows through sushumna nadi. The Sanskrit letters appearing on the petals of the chakras give rise to the forms of presiding deities in each chakra.

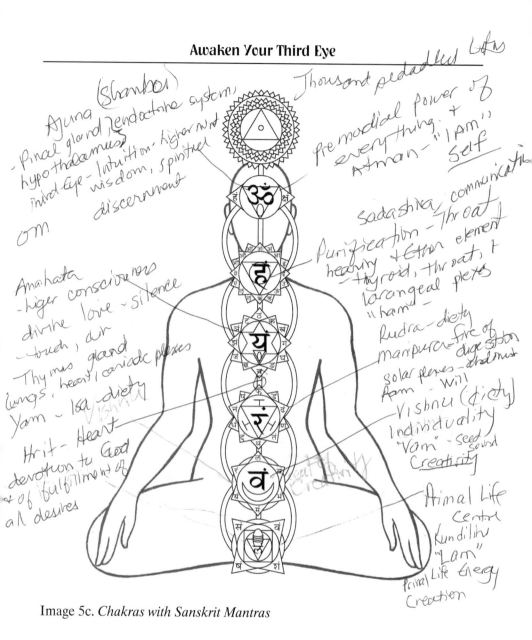

Handwritten annotations on the image:

Ajna (Shambari)
- Pineal gland - endocrine system, hypothalamus
- Third Eye - Intuition - higher mind, wisdom, spiritual discernment
- OM

Thousand pedadded Lotus
- Premordial power of everything +
Atman - "I AM" Self

Sadashiva, communication - Throat
Purification + ether element
heavy + thyroid, throat, +
larangeal plexus
"ham"

Anahata
- higher consciousness
- divine love - silence
- touch, air
- Thymus gland
- lungs, heart, cardiac plexus
- Yam - Isa - diety Vishnu
- Hrit - Heart
- devotion to God
+ of fulfillment of
all desires

Rudra - diety
manipura - fire of digestion
solar plexus - about trust
Ram - Will
Vishnu (diety)
Individuality
"Vam" - seed sound
Creativity

Primal Life
Center
Kundilitu
"Lam"
Primal Life Energy
Creation

Image 5c. *Chakras with Sanskrit Mantras*

The third eye is the only chakra with the vibratory sound *OM* at its nucleus. This means the third eye holds the primordial seed sound whose vibration is the precursor of all of creation. It is the primal pulsation out of which the entire universe springs. Thus the third eye is called *ajna chakra* ("command center").

There are seven major chakras generally familiar to people. These chakras have specific functions affecting both your subtle body and your physical body. In addition to these seven, there are another seven mentioned in the Vedic and Tantric scriptures of ancient India. Here is a brief description of all 14 chakras:

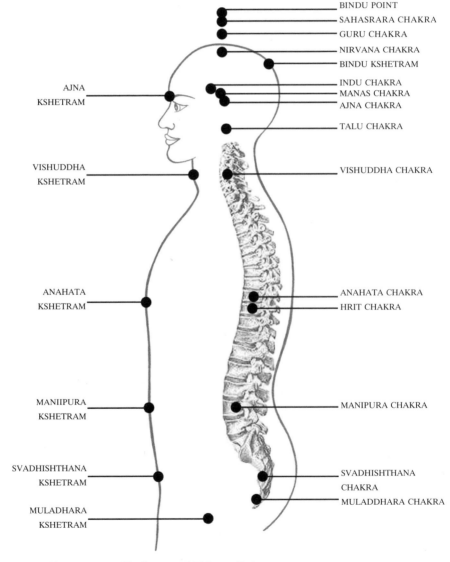

Image 5d. *Fourteen Chakras and Trigger Points*

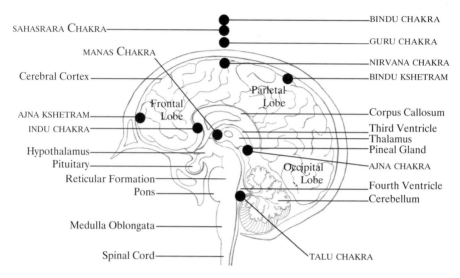

Image 5e. *Chakras In and Above the Head*

1. ***Muladhara:*** *Mula* means "base" or "root," because it is at the base
   of your spine near the tailbone. This first chakra is responsible for
   excretion, sense of smell, and earth element, and it is associated
   with the adrenal glands. The seed sound (*mantra*) of this chakra is
   lam. Its form is a four-petaled lotus and a triangle with kundalini
   in its center. The Sanskrit letters on its petals are semi-vowels: *vam*
   and sibilants: *sham, shham, sam.* Brahma, the Creator, is its deity.
   This center is the seat of primal life energy—kundalini.

2. ***Svadhishthana*** means "one's own self," because it is where
   individuality comes into embodiment through procreation.
   The second chakra, in the sacral region, governs sexuality,
   reproduction, sense of taste, and water element. It is associated
   with the gonads and prostatic plexus. *Vam* is its mantra. Its form
   is a circular moon with a six-petaled lotus. Its letters are labials:
   bam, bham, mam, and semivowels: *yam, ram, lam.* Vishnu is the
   presiding deity. A bright crescent moon is in its center. This center
   is the seat of creativity.

3. ***Manipura*** means "city of jewels," where 101 conduits of pranic energy intersect and where the fires of digestion burn. The navel chakra, in the lumbar region, oversees digestion, sense of sight, and fire element. This third chakra is associated with the pancreas and abdominal organs, the navel, and solar plexus. Its form is triangular, its mantra is *ram,* and its deity is Rudra. It has ten petals. Its letters are cerebrals: *dam, dham, nam,* dentals: *tam, tham, dam, dham, nam,* and labials: *pam, pham.* This is the seat of ego, will, determination, and persistence.

4. ***Anahata*** means "unstruck sound," because a sound that is "unstruck" is the soundlessness of silence in the seat of divine love. The heart chakra, in the thoracic region, is the gateway to higher consciousness. This fourth chakra manages the sense of touch and air element, and is associated with the thymus gland, lungs, heart, and cardiac plexus. Its mantra is *yam,* its deity is Isa, and its form is a six-pointed star with twelve petals. Its letters are gutturals: *kam, kham, gam, gham, nam,* palatals: *cham, chham, jam, jham, nam,* and cerebrals: *tam, tham.*

5. ***Hrit*** means "heart." Right below the *anahata chakra,* it is the seat of devotion to God and of fulfillment of all desires, and some people believe it to be a sub-center of the fourth chakra (anahata).

6. ***Vishuddha*** means "purification." The throat chakra, in the cervical region, is associated with sense of hearing and ether element. It is associated with the thyroid gland, throat, and laryngeal plexus. Its mantra is *ham,* its deity is Sadashiva, and its form is a triangle with sixteen petals. Its letters are vowels: *a, aa, e, ee, u, uu, kr, kree, lre, lree, ye, yai, o, ow, aam, ah.* This fifth chakra is the center of creative expression and communication.

7. ***Talu,*** the nectar chakra, in the medulla oblongata, is related to the uvula, the flow of *soma* (nectar of immortality), and the current of pranic energy.

8. ***Ajna*** means "command center" and is situated in the glands that regulate the entire endocrine system, including the pineal

gland and hypothalamus. Known as the third eye, and associated with the cavernous plexus, this sixth chakra is the seat of higher mind, wisdom, clairvoyance, knowledge, divine experiences, intuition, spiritual discernment, and higher voice. Ajna is the center of *sukshma prakriti* (primordial power of everything) and *atman* ("I AM" self). Its form is a triangle with two petals with Sanskrit letters *ham* and *ksham*. Its mantra is *OM*, and its deity is Paramashiva (Shambu).

9. *Manas* means "mind." In the upper part of ajna chakra, it is the center of your lower mental vehicle: instincts, sensory impressions, and habits.

10. *Indu* means "moon." In the front part of the brain, it is the seat of intellect and higher mind.

11. *Nirvana* means "dissolution." At the top of your brain, it is associated with the annihilation of your ego.

12. *Guru* means "light/darkness" or "teacher." Above your head in the lower part of sahasrara chakra, it is the center in which divine light dispels the darkness of ignorance.

13. *Sahasrara* means "thousandfold." The thousand-petaled lotus above your head, it is the center of divine union, integration, and spiritual enlightenment. In this chakra the primordial *OM* sound, the source of all mantras, splits into 50 mantric units—the 50 letters of the Sanskrit alphabet, in 20 different strengths, which forms a thousand-petaled lotus—1,000 light radiances. When Shakti (kundalini) unites permanently with Shiva in this seventh chakra, you become a perfected liberated soul, dwelling in eternal bliss, possessing all powers.

14. *Bindu* means "point." In the upper sahasrara chakra, it is the center of infinitely concentrated energy, the fountainhead from which your entire energy system springs.

Pathway of Kundalini

Usually kundalini is asleep, coiled near the tailbone. As kundalini wakes up and moves up the spine, it pierces through six of the seven major chakras: root, pelvic, navel, heart, throat, and brow chakra. Finally kundalini reaches the crown chakra, which is outside sushumna nadi, above the skull.

Sushumna is usually closed at its lower end in a nadi center called *kanda mula* (root bulb), which lies just below the root chakra, below the coccyx (tailbone). In most people, no prana ever passes through sushumna, and kundalini remains dormant. Some ways to activate kundalini are meditation, devotion, worship, willpower, discernment, knowledge, breathing exercises, and body purification. Any manifestation of spiritual gifts or supernormal powers indicates kundalini is awake to some degree.

In India, kundalini is personified as the Divine Mother: Shakti Ma, Kali Ma, or other goddesses. She is the feminine power at the base of the spine, which travels up the spine to unite with the masculine power, her consort, Lord Shiva (Shakta), in the crown chakra. This union of opposites is a powerful symbol depicted in all cultures.

Shakti is the link to higher awareness and the eternal source of bliss. As she ascends from the base of the spine, she becomes subtler. During her homeward journey, she removes the veils of illusion, which evaporate like a mirage. As she rises up sushumna, mental limitations are gradually removed so consciousness can shine in its pristine glory. Mental fluctuations settle down and the mind becomes serene. Awareness flows smoothly and the mind becomes a vehicle for bliss and happiness.

As she ascends, Shakti energy kindles spiritual awakening, freedom, and wisdom. The rising kundalini opens the chakras and awakens dormant supernormal powers. When she finally reaches sahasrara chakra (thousand-petaled lotus), then the goal of yoga—divine union—is achieved, and limits of time, space, and causation are transcended.

Swami Harinanda, author of *Yoga and the Portal,* states that meditation and pranayama can awaken the vital force, kundalini Shakti, at the base chakra. Kundalini moves up through sushumna nadi when you neutralize the polarizing effects of ida and pingala nadis. When Shakti reaches the head, it stimulates the pineal and pituitary glands to secrete hormones. The pineal secretes a white, milky fluid, and the pituitary secretes a yellowish, creamy fluid. When the two fluids meet, there is a flash of light so bright that the third eye ("Star of Bethlehem") opens.

Then, the two fluids, known as the land of Milk and Honey in Biblical terms, begin to flow down the pancreatic nerve (the holy river Jordan) to the third energy center (navel chakra), which is known as the manger, where Christ consciousness is born within you. This potent state of consciousness illumines your entire body. This light energy is lifted to the top of the head, where you unite with God ("I and the Father are one").[4]

More about Chakras

Eleven of the 14 chakras are located along the corridor of the energy tube sushumna nadi, your subtle body's main conduit of pranic energy, which runs through the center of your spine from your tailbone to your head. The other three chakras are above your skull.

Your chakras are generally located near the area governing the activity represented by that chakra. For instance, your navel chakra is near the solar plexus, which governs digestive functions.

In addition to actual chakra points within sushumna nadi, there are frontal trigger points called *chakra kshetram*—physical counterparts lying directly in front of corresponding chakras on the same horizontal plane. Images 5d and 5e on pages 89 and 90 depict the chakra points and frontal trigger point locations.

Each chakra indicates specific subtle frequency levels and progressively higher states of consciousness, from basic survival instincts, associated with muladhara (root chakra), to intuitive powers in ajna (third eye area), and finally spiritual enlightenment in saharara (crown chakra).

Thus, the three lower chakras (root, pelvic, and navel) are concerned with material life and bodily survival. The upper chakras (throat, third eye, and crown) deal with spiritual life and higher creative expression. The key that unlocks this entire system is the middle chakra—heart chakra. It is the gateway to higher consciousness.

The chakras embody your spiritual path. These seven gates to higher consciousness open your ascent from limited awareness to expressing your full potential. The first three states are sleep, dreaming, and waking, depicted by the three lower chakras. The transcendental state is pure consciousness—the key to unlock spiritual awakening. This is seated in your heart chakra. Three higher states of consciousness—cosmic consciousness, God consciousness, and Brahman consciousness—are represented by the three upper chakras. For more information about these states of consciousness, read my books *Divine Revelation* and *Exploring Meditation*.

Third Eye Teachings of Jesus

The great yogi Paramahansa Yogananda believed that Jesus taught methods of yoga and the deeper mysteries to his closest disciples who were ready to receive them.[5] In *The Second Coming of the Christ*, Yogananda describes the seven major chakras, and the light of consciousness in the third eye:

"Man's body, unique among all creatures, possesses spiritual cerebrospinal centers of divine consciousness in which the descended Spirit is templed. These are known to the yogis, and to Saint John—who described them in Revelation as the seven seals, and as seven stars and seven churches, with their seven angels and seven golden candlesticks. When one is baptized by immersion in the light of Spirit, the microcosmic spiritual eye in the body may be seen in its relation to the light of descending Spirit as the Cosmic Trinity."

He continues,

"The seven centers are divinely planned exits or "trap doors" through which the soul has descended into the body and through which it must reascend by a process of meditation. By seven successive steps, the soul escapes into Cosmic Consciousness."[6]

"The light of the body is the eye: if therefore thine eye be single, thy whole body shall be full of light."

—Jesus Christ.[7]

Russia physician Nicolas Notovich wrote *The Unknown Life of Christ* in 1894. During his extensive travels, he visited a Buddhist convent in Himis, near Leh, capital of Ladakh, India. There he found two ancient volumes, containing more than 200 verses titled "The Life of St. Issa," which describe the travels of Jesus during his "lost years," between ages 13 and 29. This was later confirmed by both Swami Abhedananda and Nicholas Roerich, who independently traveled to Himis and found the same text.

According to the text, Issa spent six years in Varanasi, Rajagriha, the temple of Jagganath in Orissa, and other holy cities, where he studied the ancient knowledge of the Vedas. Then he traveled into Nepal, Tibet, and Persia, teaching monism and denouncing idolatry. He returned to Jerusalem at age 29. Fascinating details of his life and teachings, missing from the Bible, are described in this ancient text.

You can learn much more about your subtle energy system, chakras, kundalini, and pranic energy by reading my books *The Power of Auras* and *The Power of Chakras,* where you will find profound information not found in any other book. In the next chapter, we will explore the ajna chakra, seat of the third eye.

Ajna: Your Third Eye Chakra

*I venerate the Supreme Creator of bliss
situated in your Ajna-Chakra—between
the eye brows—resplendent like millions of
suns and moons, adorned on his side by the
Supreme Power, meditating on whom with
devotion, one lives in the effulgent world
which needs no light and is beyond the
reach of the sun, moon, and fire.*

—Adi Shankaracharya[1]

The third eye is one of the seven major chakras (energy centers) in your subtle body. The chakras have been depicted in many traditions and cultures. Often chakras are symbolized by lotus flowers, representing the ascent of human consciousness from ignorance to enlightenment. The first lotus grows in mud, representing ignorance. It seeks to grow out of the water through effort and aspiration. Finally, the lotus reaches the direct sunlight, symbolizing illumination. When the lotus blossoms, even though mud is all around, the flower remains untouched. This is higher awareness, unsullied by the mud of material life.

The Command Center

The ajna (third eye) chakra, meaning "command center," is the hub of wisdom, higher consciousness, self-realization, and self-authority.

Here, awareness opens to the divine. Opening the ajna chakra develops intuition, insight, super-sensory perception, clairvoyance, telepathy, direct revelation, higher voice, divine experiences, and spiritual powers.

Because ajna is the seat of purified *buddhi* (intellect), when it opens, mental fickleness and fluctuations disappear. The mind becomes a perfect instrument of spiritual discernment. In this elevated state of awareness, vestiges of imperfection burn away. Ajna is associated with the "I AM" self (*atman*), which brings God-realization.

Ajna is the place within your subtle body where illumination occurs. It is the center of divine light, spiritual awakening, true wisdom, and supreme knowledge. Divine light pours into and radiates out of your third eye. It is a lighthouse that shines light upon your pathway. It points the way to your divine purpose and destiny. It illuminates the divine plan for your life. Its light guides you through the darkness. It brings you to your true destination, through all the pitfalls and potholes that you might encounter on the way. The third eye is your way home.

The *ajna* (command, order) chakra is so-named for several reasons. As the distribution center for transmitting prana to various areas of the body, it regulates the flow of prana. It is the key to the yoga technique *prana vidya* (healing through vital energy). When this chakra is awake, willpower is intensified and desires are fulfilled almost instantaneously. The transference of guru's *ajna* (order) occurs in this chakra.

This is the third eye (*tisra til*) of higher mind, the eye that looks inward rather than outward, the eye of Shiva (higher consciousness). Ajna is the seat of the primordial power of everything and the *atman* (higher self).

Whereas the five major lower chakras are associated with the five elements (earth, water, fire, air, and ether), ajna chakra is the seat of the mind. The planetary ruler of ajna chakra is Jupiter. The Sanskrit name for this planet is *Guru* ("the light that dispels darkness"). In the ancient Vedic scriptures, ajna is symbolized by *Brihaspati,* the *guru* (preceptor) of the deities (*devas*). Its day of the week is Thursday, and its esoteric color is blue. The astrological house ruled by ajna is the ninth house of wisdom, higher education, spiritual teaching, and learning, ruled by Sagittarius.

Ajna chakra is located in the center of the skull, in the region of the pineal gland. Directly in front of ajna chakra, on the same horizontal plane, is the *ajna kshetram* (trigger point)—between the two eyebrows in the forehead at the center called *bhru madhya* (brow center). The ajna chakra in the pineal area is directly connected to the ajna kshetram in the forehead through a *nadi* called *mahanadi* (great nadi). By placing a dab of tiger balm or camphor between your two eyebrows, you can increase sensitivity and intensify perception of the third eye.

Hexagonal Region

An excellent fluid, namely, the nectar of immortality, known as *soma* or *amrita,* is said to abide in the hollow of the brow center. There the three major nadis (ida, pingala, and sushumna) meet together at a junction that forms a red hexagonal region. In fact, the ida and pingala nadis terminate in the brow center, at the point where they conjoin with sushumna, the central median axis of your subtle body.

Because these three nadis join there, the brow center is termed *mukta triveni* (three strands where liberation is attained). It is also called Prayag, the ancient name for Allahabad, India, where the three rivers Ganges, Yamuna, and the mythical underground river Saraswati meet. The Ganges represents ida, Yamuna symbolizes pingala, and Saraswati indicates sushumna. In Allahabad, a special festival called *Kumbh Mela* (festival of the pot of nectar of immortality) celebrates bathing in the nectar of this chakra at the juncture of these three sacred rivers.

Another symbol for the meeting of these three nadis is the Christian cross, where ida is balanced with pingala. The left side of the cross is ida, the right side is pingala, and the vertical line is sushumna, which continues upward to sahasrara. The three lines meet in ajna chakra, the egoless state, where you die (are crucified) to your old self.

Image 6a. *Ajna Chakra Lotus*

Triangular Region

Within the hexagon is a triangle, which is a *yoni* (female genitalia)—the receptacle of the *linga* form (phallus) of Lord Shiva. This linga is the power of Shiva, representing full control over his desires in meditation. It is described as red, golden, or shining white.

The triangular yoni, seat of Lord Shiva, is the supreme *shakti kundalini.* Her energy, like streaks of lightning flashes, radiates as the mantra *aing* (the seed mantra of the *guru*), which generates the manifestation of the primal *bija* (seed sound) *OM*, fundamental source of the Vedas, where kundalini is in its radiant sound-form *OM*.

Two Lotus Petals

Two petals radiate from ajna chakra, which are described by the ancients as vibrating with nectarous, cool rays and of intensely white or lightning-like color. The two petals of ajna represent the sun nadi (pingala) and moon nadi (ida), which merge in ajna chakra. The Sanskrit letters on these petals are the shining bright white letters *ham* and *ksham,* or the mantras of Shiva (*hang*) and Shakti (*kshang*).

The two petals of ajna are two radiations of power. One of these radiates downward through the five lower chakras. The other moves toward the upper chakras. These radiations of *hang* and *kshang* are white, pure, and powerful. In the radiations are the five vital airs, five divine powers, and kundalini power.

The white color indicates a preponderance of *udana vayu*, one of the five vital airs—aspects of pranic energy. Of special significance to spiritual practice, udana is upward-moving breath, which directs pranic flow from lower to higher planes of consciousness. The ascending and radiant force udana delivers prana to energy centers in the brain. Kundalini energy, which ascends through sushumna nadi, is a form of udana vayu.

Udana vayu arouses the five elements and five sense objects in the five lower chakras and the threefold mental capacity in the *manas* (mind) and *indu* (intellect) chakras. When *hang* and *kshang* merge during meditation, the lower radiation stops, and power is concentrated in the upper radiation. Then the forceful upper radiation does not stop at manas or indu, but instead passes directly to nirvana chakra, which brings forth *samadhi*, transcendental consciousness.

Bija Mantra Om (Ong)

Within the triangular region of ajna chakra is the moon-white, shining, splendorous, imperishable seed mantra *OM*. The vibration of *OM* is believed to be the primary source of the Veda, and Veda is the precursor of the entire universe. Therefore, *OM* is considered to be the primordial seed mantra.

Image 6b.
OM: Precursor of the Universe

Ajna chakra is the seat of kundalini as splendorous, pure, aroused inner consciousness. She emerges from her subtle form through the first sounds that form the *OM*. The coils of kundalini are described as a luminous circle of light.

Shiva and Shakti

Every sound or vibration in the universe is the precursor of a corresponding form. From each Sanskrit seed sound or mantra, a corresponding deity form arises. In the hub of each chakra is a Sanskrit letter, which gives rise to a specific form of Lord Shiva presiding over that chakra.

Also, a particular form of Shakti (the divine mother) is the doorkeeper of each chakra. The Shaktis control the chakras and only admit practitioners who are qualified to experience them. The fierce appearance of the shaktis is a deterrent for the neophyte. The Shaktis in the chakras are various forms of kundalini.

In the ajna chakra, a form of Lord Shiva known as Parashiva dwells in the *bindu* (point) above the mantra *OM*. He represents the subtle form of Brahman (absolute consciousness) as the golden egg of creation, characterized by the seed mantra *OM*. Because he is beyond manifest creation, he is without attributes. Therefore he is unmanifest, unfathomable, nameless, formless, timeless, spaceless, beginningless, endless, limitless, and infinite.

The power (*shakti*) and doorkeeper of ajna is the goddess Hakini, who is white like the moon. With six beautiful, moon-like faces, curly hair, six arms, and three eyes in each face, her awareness is in supreme consciousness. Her eyes, beautifully painted with kohl, are said to roll like a moving black bee. Her upper garment is white and her lower garment is red. She sits on a white lotus, and her white body symbolizes her rarified, pure form.

The third eye of Hakini is the light of deep meditation, while the other two eyes represent knowledge gleaned through sensory input and thought. The six faces of Hakini represent the five elements centered in the five lower chakras and the mind located in ajna chakra.

In one of Hakini's hands is a book, which is the highest supreme wisdom translated into understandable words. In another hand, she holds a skull, which is the perpetuation of spiritual consciousness developed through meditation, even after death. Her third hand holds a drum, symbolizing the silent mantra sounds transformed into audible sound. Hakini's fourth hand holds a *rudraksha* bead rosary (holy seeds used in meditation practices), indicating the spiritual practice of mantra repetition (*japa*). Her fifth hand is in the gesture of granting boons, which imparts spiritual knowledge. The gesture of dispelling fear removes all obstacles to meditation.

Ajna Subcenters

In addition to the two-petaled *ajna chakra* (third eye wheel), three other chakras exist within the brain in the area of the third eye: *manas chakra, indu chakra,* and *nirvana chakra.* According to ancient scriptures of India, there are three seats in the forehead region. They are called *bindu* (point), *nada* (crescent moon), and *shakti* (power). The bindu point is the dot above the mantra *OM* in ajna. The nada is manas chakra, and the shakti is indu chakra.

Manas Chakra: Sensory Mind

Manas (mind) chakra, your mental vehicle, consists of three parts: conscious mind or lower, instinctive mind (*manas chitta*); subconscious, emotional, or impression mind (*sanskara chitta*); and habitual, patterned mind (*vasana chitta*). This chakra is ruled by the planet Mercury, which governs mental activity, the sign Gemini, ruler of lower mind, and the third house of the astrology chart.

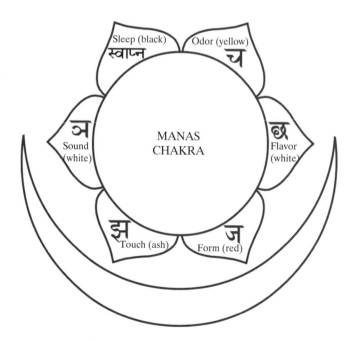

Image 6c. *Manas Chakra Lotus*

Also known as sensory or lower mind, manas is responsible for perceiving sensory impressions through seeing, hearing, tasting, smelling, and feeling. More powerful and rarified than your physical senses, it makes your senses operate by transporting sensations to your higher chakras in the brain.

Sense operations such as seeing or hearing are dependent on bodily eyes or ears, but manas can operate independently of the sense organs, even after death. Manas is not only responsible for outer sensory perception, but also awareness of subtle sense perception, such as clairvoyant sight or clairaudient hearing, independent of physical eyes or ears.

The location of manas chakra is a sub-center within ajna. It is found above ajna chakra, above the bindu of OM, in a second nada (crescent moon shape). This corresponds to the front part of the brain's third ventricle.

Indu Chakra: Intellect

Image 6d. *Indu Chakra Lotus*

The Sanskrit term *indu* (meaning "drop," or "moon") refers to drops of nectar of immortal life that drip from the moon region in your subtle body. Indu chakra is also called wheel of Brahma, moon circle, and nectar wheel. This chakra is ruled by the planet Uranus, which governs the intellect and higher mind, the sign Aquarius, and the 11th house in astrology.

Indu chakra is located in the brain, just above ajna chakra, in the front part of the brain's third ventricle, in the region of the *lamina terminalis* and *commissura anterior*.

Indu chakra is the seat of *buddhi* (intellect). This aspect of mind gains higher knowledge than *chitta*, the sense mind located in manas chakra. Chitta, responsible for sensory perception, can only derive sensory knowledge. In contrast, the knowledge obtained by buddhi is intellectual knowledge. The primary functions of buddhi are higher intellection, thought, insight, and retention.

Nirvana Chakra: Concentrated Mind

Nirvana (meaning extinguishing or dousing a flame) chakra is where your ego, along with its cravings and defects, is annihilated when kundalini passes through it. This chakra is ruled by Neptune, planet of ego dissolution, the sign Pisces, and the 12th house in astrology, which connotes absorption and loss.

Nirvana chakra is also known as "highest brahma wheel," "hundred-petaled lotus," "lotus of peace," "wheel of time," and "hollow of brahma."

Nirvana chakra is the highest chakra in sushumna nadi, so subtle that it does not manifest until kundalini reaches it. As kundalini ascends through sushumna nadi, it travels up the spine through the vertebral column all the way to the top of the brain. It then terminates at a point called *brahmarandhra*.

Nirvana chakra is located in the upper portion of the cerebral cortex, about five fingers back from the hairline at the soft spot where the skull bones come together in infancy, called the *anterior fontanelle*.

Image 6e. *Nirvana Chakra Lotus*

Nirvana chakra is the seat of the focused mind (*dhi*), as well as the center of the ego or "I-ness." Dhi is the part of your mind that sifts through innumerable sensory objects and focuses on a particular object. By concentrating on one object, your mind develops clearer thought, greater intellection, and better retentive power. Thus, dhi is responsible for arousing deeper thought intellection (*manisha*).

The main function of dhi is the ability to concentrate. The bindu point is the symbol of the highest form of concentration, in which consciousness is centralized in oneness. You can read more about how to develop dhi through Trataka meditation on page 214.

In the next chapter, we will learn how to heal the three granthis, which are psychic knots that block the flow of kundalini through the chakras.

7

| Overcoming Psychic Blocks |

*The wise one, who continually [contemplates]
this Ajna lotus, becomes free from the mighty
chain of desires, and enjoys happiness. When, at
the time of death, the Yogi contemplates on this
lotus, leaving this life, that holy one is absorbed in
the Paramatma (supreme soul).*

—Shiva Samhita

The yogis of ancient India discovered three *granthis* (knots) in
the pranic energy body, which are storage areas for psychic blocks,
attachments, and delusions that prevent kundalini from flowing freely
through sushumna nadi. These psychic knots are traps blocking you
from ascending higher and ultimately achieving spiritual enlightenment. One of these knots is in the third eye area.

In these three regions, the power of *maya* (illusion), ignorance, and
bondage to the material world is particularly strong. The granthis are
located in the chakras where there is a convergence of the three major
nadis: ida, pingala, and sushumna.

Brahma Granthi

Brahma granthi, seated in the root center (*muladhara chakra*), is the
knot of attachment to material life (*samsara*), which binds the mind to
base desires and cravings for physical pleasures through sensory stimuli

and sexual contact. This knot obscures the truth and ensnares the intellect. This granthi's predominant drives are self-preservation, producing offspring, and acquiring material objects. The outer world is viewed as a means to obtain security. Brahma granthi is the seat of instinctive cravings and appetites welling up from unconscious depths.

This trap is not easy to escape from, because many people are unaware of anything more to life than the material world. The vast majority of humanity, which gives no credence to the spiritual world, is stuck at this self-centered level.

However, once this blockage is removed, survival instincts are transmuted into creative impulses. The primal energy of kundalini then rises, and awareness becomes interested in higher pursuits, rather than base desires.

Vishnu Granthi

Vishnu granthi in the heart center (*anahata chakra*) is the knot of attachment to emotions, which binds the mind to love, sentimentality, nostalgia, loyalty, attachment, sympathy, pity, and pride about a cause. Emotional attachment is a strong pull that ensnares the mind and blocks it from spiritual awareness. Those stuck in Vishnu granthi might label true spiritual adepts as cold, heartless, and selfish, because they do not understand that true spirituality transcends earthly love.

Vishnu granthi may foster control and domination, which satisfies egoic needs by coercing and manipulating situations and people. This is expressed in motives to gain wealth, prestige, status, and recognition. The world is seen as an object for gaining personal power and fulfilling worldly ambitions. Selfishness, arrogance, anger, hostility, and resentment are the result.

Once the Vishnu granthi blockage is removed, emotions are purified and transmuted into devotion to God. The emotion of love is no longer misused in order to feed and glorify the ego. Instead, people are viewed as unique embodiments of perfection, expressing their true nature. Vishnu granthi is the gateway to higher awareness, and its opening is effected through unconditional love, understanding, and acceptance.

Rudra Granthi

Rudra granthi in the third eye center (*ajna chakra*) is the energetic knot of attachment to the mental world. It binds the mind to intellectual pride, tenacious beliefs, habits, conditioning, and brainwashing. It ensnares the ego with arrogance about spiritual experiences, psychic powers, and supernormal abilities.

Spiritual development can be the ultimate liberation, or an alluring trap. If individuals develop psychic powers without ego transformation, they may fall under the spell of spiritual materialism, where the ego is fed by attachment to self-importance and specialness.

Under the glamour of Rudra granthi, people might feel superior to so-called lesser-evolved souls, and may develop spiritual arrogance—self-righteousness and excessive pride in intellectual capacities. They might misuse their abilities to lord over others. In extreme cases, they may withdraw and dwell in a world of illusion, as they suffer from hallucinations, with little connection to reality.

In Rudra granthi, your ego awareness, mental awareness, and physical awareness are dissolved. Your sixth sense or eye of intuition develops. Once the knot of ego-awareness and intellectual pride is broken, your spiritual energy transcends duality and sees the truth. Your consciousness is lifted, and your individual soul merges with the universal, cosmic soul.

Removing the Granthi Blockages

The three granthis prevent prana from flowing freely through sushumna nadi. All three knots must be released in order for kundalini to awaken, open sushumna nadi, and complete its ascent through the chakras to the crown chakra, where spiritual enlightenment occurs.

Among the ancient practices of the yogis are methods that effectively release the granthis (psychic knots). *Bandhas* (muscular locks) and *mudras* (gestures) can open these blockages, awaken kundalini, and increase pranic flow.

The Sanskrit word *bandha* means "to hold, lock, or tighten." Thus, while practicing bandhas, you will contract and hold specific muscles.

Among the most powerful practices for awakening kundalini through the chakras, these should be practiced after yoga asanas (yoga postures) and before pranayama (breathing exercises).

IMPORTANT: Please consult with your physician before attempting to practice any of the exercises in this book.

Jalandhara Bandha: Throat Lock

Jalandhara bandha is a physical lock that binds a plexus of nadis in your neck and directs prana into sushumna nadi. *Jala* refers to the nadi passing through the neck to the brain. *Dhara* means upward pull. *Bandha* means lock. This bandha blocks the immortal nectar, produced in the chakras in your head, from flowing down your throat and burning up from digestive fires in your stomach. In addition, this bandha slows down your heart rate due to compression of carotid sinuses. The scriptures of India claim this bandha can prevent old age and death.

How to Practice

Sit in a comfortable position. The best positions are *padma asana* (lotus pose: see page 181), siddhasana, or *siddha yoni asana* (perfect pose: see page 180). It can also be done in a standing position. If seated, place palms on your knees.

Close your eyes. Relax your entire body. Inhale deeply and retain your breath. Bend your head forward and press your chin tightly against your sternum. Straighten your arms and lock your elbows. Keep your hands on your knees. Locking your elbows will intensify the pressure applied to your neck. Simultaneously hunch your shoulders upward and forward. This keeps your arms straight and elbows locked. Stay in this position as long as you can hold your breath. Maintain your attention on the area of your throat. Then, relax your shoulders, bend your arms, slowly raise your head, and exhale slowly. Breathe normally. Repeat this as many times as is comfortable.

If you have high blood pressure or heart ailments, do not practice this bandha.

Uddiyana Bandha: Abdominal Lock

The Sanskrit word *uddiyana* means "to raise up, to fly upward." This physical lock, which causes your diaphragm to rise upward, directs prana into the sushumna nadi and moves kundalini upward through the chakras. This is why the ancient scriptures claim *uddiyana bandha* expands higher awareness, reverses aging, and promotes longevity. This bandha acts directly on the navel chakra, the storehouse of prana. It stimulates and distributes prana throughout your body.

How to Practice

Uddiyana bandha can be practiced in vajrasana (see page 177), padmasana (see page 181), siddhasana or siddha yoni asana (see page 180), or standing. Let us learn how to do it in standing position.

Stand with your feet about 18 inches apart. Bend forward at the waist and bend your legs slightly. Place palms on your thighs near your knees and place pressure on your thighs with your arms

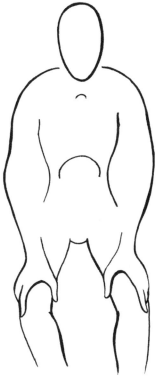

Image 7a.

Abdominal Lock

straight. Exhale completely and empty your lungs as much as possible by blowing out repeatedly.

Then make a false inhalation, by performing the same action of an inhalation without actually pulling any air into your body. Keep the glottis closed and expand the chest, as though breathing in but not actually taking in air. That means tighten your glottis, neck muscles (*sternocleidomastoids,* or SCM), and respiratory muscles and expand your chest as though you are ready to take in air through your nose. But stop any air from entering your nose or lungs. This will automatically raise your diaphragm, and your abdomen will take a concave shape, inward and upward. It is the false inhalation that raises the diaphragm—not active contraction of the abdominal muscles. Hold this position as long as you can hold your breath.

To release the bandha, exhale slightly to release the lock on the lungs and finally breathe in. This will automatically allow your abdomen to resume its normal shape. Relax your arms and gradually stand up. This is one round. Practice several rounds and gradually increase the number of rounds over several weeks or months.

Practice uddiyana bandha early in the morning before breakfast. Your stomach must be empty, so wait four hours after your previous meal. Also, evacuate your bowels before this practice.

Pregnant women and those with heart problems, ulcers, colitis, or other serious abdominal problems should not practice uddiyana bandha. After childbirth this practice will help new mothers reshape and strengthen their abdominal area.

Mula Bandha: Root Lock

The Sanskrit term *mula* means "root." Here it refers to muladhara kshetram, at the perineum. Therefore, *mula bandha* is the "perineum contraction lock." In this bandha, the area contracted is the physical trigger point of muladhara. This is different in males and females. In the male it is at the perineum between the anus and genitals. In the female it is at the cervix, where the vagina meets the uterus. Many people practice mula bandha incorrectly by only contracting the sphincter muscles.

How to Practice

The best positions for practicing this bandha are siddhasana or siddha yoni asana (see page 180). If you cannot sit in these postures, then sit in any comfortable seated position. You can even practice it while standing.

Place your palms on your knees. Close your eyes and relax your entire body. Inhale deeply. Apply firm pressure in the region of muladhara trigger point with one heel. This will strengthen the physical contraction.

Inhale deeply and hold your breath. Strongly contract your muscles at the muladhara trigger point. Draw up your muscles maximally but without excessive strain. Hold your attention at the point of contraction. Remain in this bandha as long as you can hold your breath. Then let go of the contraction and breathe out. This is one round. Practice several more rounds as is comfortable.

If you are not quite sure how to practice mula bandha, imagine you are urinating and then stopping the flow in midstream. That is the same muscular contraction performed in mula bandha.

This supreme age-reversing bandha awakens the root chakra and draws up the downward-moving vital air (*apana,* which exhales and expels bodily waste materials), to unite with the upward-moving vital air (*prana,* which inhales and supplies energy and bodily upkeep). Mula bandha balances prana and apana, providing equilibrium to the incoming and outgoing energies. It is one of the most potent practices to rouse kundalini, because it forces sushumna nadi to open.

Maha Bandha: Great Lock

Maha bandha is a powerful bandha combining the three major locks. The Sanskrit word *maha* means "great."

How to Practice

Inhale slowly with your attention on muladhara (root chakra), imagining the luminous form of kundalini in awareness. At the same time, practice uddiyana bandha (abdominal lock) and contract your perineum in mula bandha (root lock). Once you have inhaled completely, bend your head downward and press your chin against your chest in jalandhara bandha (throat lock), and suspend your breath.

Maintain these muscular contractions while continuing to imagine kundalini. Hold your breath as long as comfortable. Then release mula bandha, uddiyana bandha, and finally let go of jalandhara bandha.

This powerful bandha is key for awakening kundalini.

Mudras to Open Your Third Eye

Taraka yoga is a highly esoteric yoga practice. Since it is virtually absent from books in English, it is nearly impossible to locate a spiritual master who teaches it. The Sanskrit word *taraka* means "cross over," "liberate," or "deliver." What is being liberated? The goal of all yogic practice is to liberate your soul from the bondage of this relative world—the dualistic field of suffering and ignorance—and to realize the true self.

Taraka yoga consists of five *mudras* ("seals" or "closures"), which are physical gestures that powerfully affect your body's energy flow. Taraka yoga comprises the five mudras *khechari, bhuchari, madhyama, shanmukha,* and *shambhavi.* These work specifically to awaken kundalini and to cleanse, heal, energize, and open your third eye.

If your third eye chakra is closed, unhealthy, or blocked by negative emotions or toxic substances (such as drugs, alcohol, cigarettes, or GMO foods), you might experience headaches, dizziness, insomnia, sinusitis, or poor eyesight. In extreme cases you may suffer brain hemorrhage, stroke, tumor, Alzheimer's disease, or epilepsy. You could develop a learning disability, dyslexia, autism, ADD, frequent nightmares, or forgetfulness. Even mental illness is related to contamination of ajna chakra.

While practicing these five mudras, you might see divine visions, hear celestial sounds, smell sweet fragrances, taste delicious flavors, or feel ecstatic sensations. This is in indication that kundalini is moving through sushumna nadi and ajna chakra is opening.

Here is how to practice the mudras:

Khechari Mudra: Tongue Lock with Ujjayi Pranayama

Khechari means to roll back the tongue and focus on the *bhrumadhya* (*ajna kshetram,* the point on the forehead between the eyebrows), either with eyes closed or open. The *ujjayi pranayama* breathing method is often practiced simultaneously.

The purpose of khechari mudra is to raise kundalini and access the stores of immortal elixir produced in the chakras in the head. This elixir floods the body and brings health, well-being, spiritual awakening, and, ultimately, immortality.

Khechari mudra can be a long, complicated practice involving several surgical operations to the membrane under the tongue. However, the simple method given here requires no preparation and is for everyone.

How to Practice

Roll your tongue upward and backward, so the lower surface of your tongue comes into contact with your upper palate. Stretch the tip of your tongue backward as far as possible, without straining. At the same time, focus your attention on the third eye at the bhrumadhya point between the eyebrows, without straining, with eyes closed or open.

Ujjayi Pranayama

This breathing technique, combined with rolling back the tongue in *khechari mudra,* places slight pressure on your carotid sinuses. Therefore, it reduces heartbeat and blood pressure. This technique produces mental and physical calm. It soothes and harmonizes your body, brain, and subtle body.

How to Practice

Sit in any comfortable position with spine and head upright. It can even be practiced in *savasana* (see page 182) to promote greater relaxation. Roll your tongue back into khechari mudra. Closing your eyes, relax your body and breathe slowly and deeply. Partially close the glottis by slightly contracting your throat muscles. Simultaneously, your abdominal muscles will slightly contract automatically. Keep your facial muscles relaxed.

As you breathe in this position, you will notice a quiet rasping sound coming from your throat. This sound, caused by the air passing through the restricted glottis, is similar to the sound of a sleeping baby.

Bhuchari Mudra

Bhuchari mudra ("gaze into the void") is a powerful psychic cleanser that enhances powers of concentration and stimulates ajna chakra. It is practiced by focusing attention at the tip of the nose without blinking.

How to Practice

Remove any glasses or contact lenses. Sit comfortably in a relaxed position, with spine and head upright. It is better if your field of vision is free from distractions. Therefore, if possible, face a wall painted one single color—preferably white.

Place the thumbnail of your right hand just above your upper lip. Lift up the pinky finger of your right hand, and allow your index, middle, and ring fingers to relax and curl over. Then stare at the tip of pinky finger with a steady gaze, trying not to blink, for two minutes. Do not strain.

Then drop your hand and continue to gaze at the blank point in space where your index finger had been. Continue to gaze at this void for a few more minutes. Gradually build up to five minutes for the first part of the practice and 15 minutes for the second.

If you become tense, or if your eyes start to tear during this practice, just close your eyes and imagine the image of your pinky finger in your mind's eye.[1]

Madhya Lakshyam

Madhya lakshyam ("to attain the center") relates to focusing attention at the bhrumadhya (point on your forehead between your eyebrows) with eyes closed and concentrating on your inner vision.

How to Practice

Sit comfortably, preferably in a dark room. Close your eyes, and, keeping your eyes closed, fix your gaze on the spot between your eyebrows, without moving your eyelids or allowing your eyes to tremble. With practice, a microscopic hole will eventually appear in your third eye.

When you enter your focus of awareness inside that tiny pore, you will see visions in your inner eye. Lightning, stars, illumination of sun and moon, and colors of the five elements will appear.

You might view five skies of magnificent radiance: an infinitely extending sky, dark-colored infinite sky, sky resembling fire, brilliantly shining sky like a void, and a sun-sky that shines with the radiance of a billion suns. The sight of these divine skies will bring great bliss.[2]

Shanmukha Mudra

Shanmukha mudra ("attitude of the seven gates") is a profound practice to help you hear the inner *nada*, known as the sound of sounds, sound of silence, music of the spheres, or hum of creation. In this mudra, the seven doors of outer perception are closed, and awareness turns within. The best time to practice is late night or early morning, when fewer external noises interfere with subtle sensory perception.

How to Practice

This can be done in any comfortable seated position or even standing. Relax your entire body and hold your spine and head upright. Raise your hands in front of your face with elbows pointed sideways.

Then plug your ears with your thumbs. Place your index fingers lightly on your eyelids. Do not press against your eyes. Close your nostrils tightly with your middle fingers. Encircle your mouth, pressing above your upper lip with your ring fingers and below your lower lip with your pinkie fingers.

Then perform *kaki mudra* (crow's beak gesture). Here's how: pout your lips in a small circle, as though you were going to whistle. Relax your tongue. Suck in air vigorously through your mouth with sibilance and blow out your cheeks so they puff out. Retain your breath.

Now, as you keep your nostrils tightly closed, pretend you are blowing your nose, just as you would do on an airplane to equalize air pressure in your ears. This will force air into the eustachian tubes.

Then perform jalandhara bandha, lowering your head to the sternal notch (see page 110). Hold your breath as long as is comfortable without straining.

Meanwhile, notice any sounds you perceive in the region of the top of your head, middle head, right ear, or heart chakra. Keep your attention on the inner nada. If you perceive a sound with a subtler sound in the background, then switch awareness to the fainter sound. Continue to move to subtler regions of sound as you travel deeper inside. Do not dwell on any one sound but continue to move within.

When you can no longer hold your breath, raise your head, release your fingers from your nose, and exhale slowly through your nose. This is one round.

Practice several rounds, as is comfortable. After practicing yoni mudra for at least a month, then add mula bandha (see page 112) during the practice. After another month, also add uddiyana bandha (see page 111).

Do not try to hear any sounds. By letting go, the sounds will come to you naturally. This mudra will reveal deep mysteries of your inner being.

Shambhavi Mudra

Shambhavi mudra is so-named because the legend is that Shambhavi (Shakti) taught it to Shambhu (Lord Shiva). Also called *bhrumadhya drishti* ("brow center gazing") this practice stimulates and opens your third eye. This mudra, which fixes your mind constant, removes distractions by focusing attention inward.

The fundamental experience of *shambhavi mudra* is that your eyes roll up and back into your head. When your third eye opens to genuine spiritual sight of divine light, this happens automatically.

How to Practice

Here are various ways to practice shambhavi mudra:

Version 1

Close eyes and relax entire body. Then open eyes and focus on a spot in the center of your forehead, between your eyebrows. Direct eyes inward and upward as much as possible in that direction. You should see two curved images of the eyebrows merging with each other, making a V-shape. Do not strain your eyes. If you feel any strain, stop immediately and lie down.

If you find this difficult, place a fingertip on the tip of your nose and focus both eyes intently on it. Then slowly move your finger up the nose to the center of eyebrows while keeping eyes firmly focused on your fingertip.

Version 2

Keep your eyes half-open and focus all internal attention on the same spot, but without rolling your eyes upward. In this case, the focus is entirely mental.

Version 3

Remain in a transcendental state inwardly, in deep meditation, while keeping your sight directed to external objects, without blinking your eyes. Remain inwardly attentive to absolute bliss consciousness, keeping your mind and breathing still. In that state, keep your sight steady, as if seeing everything, while in reality seeing nothing outside, below, or above.

Version 4

Once you have mastered this technique, you can practice it with eyes closed. The inner light will dawn, and visions of celestial beings and divine lights will occur in your inner eye.

Breathing Like Bellows

Bhastrika, which means "bellows" in Sanskrit, also known as *kapalbhati,* is a pranayama (breathing exercise) that involves a rapid succession of forcible exhalations. This powerful method cleanses your nadis and your lungs. Just as bellows are used rapidly to fan a fire, so you exhale and inhale rapidly in this exercise.

How to Practice

Sit in a comfortable position, or practice while standing. Keep your mouth closed as you forcibly exhale through your nose quickly, like a bellows. When you practice this pranayama, a puffing sound is produced. Start with forcible expulsions of breath following one another in rapid succession. After ten expulsions, take a deep inhalation and retain the breath as long as is comfortable. Then slowly exhale.

While inhaling, distend your abdomen. While exhaling, contract it. Place your hand on your abdomen to make sure you are doing it correctly. Placing attention on the exhalation will allow the inhalation to occur by itself. Contract your abdominal muscles with a backward push while you quickly, forcefully exhale. Your abdomen will naturally distend during inhalation.

Begin with 10 expulsions for one round and increase it gradually to 20 or 25 for one round. The period of retention of breath at the end can also be gradually and cautiously increased. Rest a while after one round before beginning the next. Do three rounds in the beginning and gradually increase until you can do 20 rounds. Advanced students practice this pranayama after partially closing the glottis.

The most effective of all pranayama exercises, bhastrika enables prana to break through the three granthis.

Rise of Kundalini

The practices of bandhas, mudras, pranayama, and meditation should be performed daily. Then your mind becomes quiet, and breath becomes refined. As your practice progresses, mental impurities are removed, and kundalini awakens. First it pierces sushumna nadi, normally closed at its lower end. It is said in the ancient scriptures that it flashes like lightning at the mouth of sushumna as it breaks through Brahma granthi.

Then kundalini rises up through sushumna to pierce Vishnu granthi at the heart. It continues above the heart to the middle of the eyebrows to pierce Rudra granthi. The agitated kundalini moves upward, and the shower of nectar from the brain flows more copiously.

When nectar flows, you will lose much of your desire for sensual pleasures. You will become absorbed in the atman (higher self), partaking of the sacrificial offering of ambrosia. You are then established in the self. Enjoying this highest state, you become devoted to atman and attain peace.

By using the methods in this chapter, and by practicing deep meditation, which you will learn in Chapter 14 of this book, you can awaken kundalini, open your third eye, and attain the state of no-mind.

In the next chapter, we will learn about opening the third eye to develop supersensory perception and other spiritual gifts.

Treasures

of the

Third Eye

8

| Developing Your Super-Senses |

*The common eye sees only the outside of things,
and judges by that, but the 'all seeing eye' pierces
through, and reads the heart and the soul, finding
there capacities which the outside didn't indicate or
promise, and which the other kind couldn't detect.*

—Mark Twain

Do you want to open your third eye? Do you want to receive clear intuition and know for certain it is real? It is not only possible to do this—anyone can, *at will*, anytime. Even if other people claim you are incapable, unworthy, or undeserving to open your third eye, you have the power to do it right now.

You may believe the only individuals worthy to open their third eye are highly evolved spiritual masters who reside in remote monasteries, caves, or ashrams—or great, holy, exalted beings, such as saints, sages, prophets, holy men (I emphasize the word "men") and other saintly beings who lived at least 2,000 years ago in a faraway land.

Contrary to this notion, I affirm that everyone is born with the ability to listen to the "still, small voice" of inner wisdom and develop innate spiritual gifts. The methods revealed here are simple and easy to master. Anyone can open and develop the inner eye of wisdom, the third eye. You can have direct spiritual experiences and two-way conversations with your inner divine guidance.

The Secret Now Revealed

It might be difficult to imagine opening your third eye. Perhaps you believe that unless you spend decades in serious spiritual study, you do not have a chance of receiving genuine spiritual experiences. But I strongly disagree. You can experience your third eye, and I am going to tell you right now how you can do it.

Here is the big secret, now revealed:

Just sit down in a chair. Close your eyes. Get comfortable, quiet, and still. Take a few deep breaths and let go. Get quieter. Take some more deep breaths and give up even more. Go deeper. Get even quieter, more centered and balanced. Take more deep breaths and let go. Give up even more. Get into a state of inner peace, relaxation, and deep meditation.

Once you have attained a state of pure serenity, it is time to do something that people generally never do while in a deep state of meditation:

ASK.

Ask Spirit to help you open your third eye. Or ask for a spiritual experience. Ask for a divine being, deity, or being of light to appear. Call upon that being by name. Ask for inner guidance. Or ask for healing, for love, for light, for inspiration. Ask a question.

Then take some more deep breaths and do what I call the "do-nothing program." That means do nothing, nothing, and less than nothing. In other words, stay in a neutral state of awareness, without expectation, strain, or concentration. Be open to receive, but without seeking any outcome. Place no effort or exertion into your awareness. Just do nothing.

As you remain in this neutral state, you will receive the outcome you asked for. If you asked to open your third eye, you will receive an experience. If you asked for healing, you will receive healing energy.

If you asked a question, you will receive an answer. Within your heart an answer will come from the deep part of your being that is connected to Spirit. You will see a vision, hear some words, or get a feeling.

The message will occur to you, just like any other thought in your mind. You will see it, hear it, or feel it. You will hear the "still, small voice" of inner wisdom within.

That is it.

How to experience Spirit in one easy step: *"Ask, and it shall be given you."*[1]

Subtle Sense Perception

Any spiritual experience or the answer to any question comes by merely asking for it. It is just that simple. The trouble is, we do not realize we can ask, or we do not believe we can receive, or we forget to ask. Just ask, and, according to the promise ("Ask, and it shall be given you"), you will receive. There is nothing you cannot experience or receive. Just ask.

Once you ask, let go and let Spirit give you the result. Do not try to hold onto the question; do not seek the answer. After you have asked, engage in the do-nothing program. In that quiet state of mind, your answer comes.

Messages from divine Spirit appear in one of three basic ways:

1. You might see an inner vision with your inner eye.

2. You may hear an inner voice with your inner ear.

3. You could receive an inner feeling, like a gut feeling.

In other words, you will contact Spirit through one of your subtle senses.

What are subtle senses? Usually your senses are projected outward, toward material objects. You see, hear, feel, taste, and smell the pleasures and pains of earthly life. However, during meditation, senses turn inward. In fact, as soon as your eyes close, your outer senses shut down and inner senses take over.

For example, your eyes see the outer world. But with your third eye, you can see the inner world. Your inner eye sees with a subtle sense mechanism that does not normally operate in waking life. However, it is fully active at night as you dream. Through meditation, your subtle senses can be developed.

Every person has one subtle sense more developed than the other senses. You might naturally be more visual (seeing), more auditory (hearing), kinesthetic (feeling), gustatory (tasting), or olfactory (smelling).

"Extrasensory perception" is a misnomer. Subtle perceptions are not actually "extrasensory," because nothing can be perceived without using the senses. It is impossible to experience anything without seeing, hearing, tasting, smelling, or feeling it. Your subtle senses are used during ESP experiences, so they are more properly called "subtle-sensory" or "supersensory" experiences.

What is it like to use your inner senses? It is rare to see, hear, or feel ESP experiences while engaged in everyday activities. In most cases, these experiences will appear during meditation, with eyes closed.

Receiving Inner Guidance

1	CLAIRVOYANCE	Visual
2	CLAIRAUDIENCE	Auditory
3	CLAIRSENTIENCE	Kinesthetic

Image 8a. *Supersensory Perception*

Clairvoyance

Your subtle sense of sight is called *clairvoyance. Clair* is French for "clear," and *voyance,* French for "sight." By virtue of your gross physical eyes, you can see a rainbow of colors and shapes of objects in your environment. But when you open your inner eye, you receive insight and inner seeing. This might look like a motion picture playing on the inner screen of your mind, also called your "mind's eye." Generally, subtle visions appear with eyes closed, rather than open.

Clairaudience

Clairaudience means "clear hearing." Gross hearing, such as listening to music through headphones, uses your ears. In contrast, subtle auditory messages are usually inaudible. They are rarely heard externally. They seldom sound like someone speaking. More likely they sound just like any other thought passing through your mind. For example, you might receive the thought: *I love you; I am with you always.* Whenever words pass through your mind, your inner ear "hears" them. Thus, the experience is defined as auditory: "clairaudience."

Clairsentience

Inner gut feelings come kinesthetically through *clairsentience,* "clear feeling." You would receive these as feelings in your subtle body, rather than gross feelings of outer sense perception in your physical body. For example, a gross feeling might be a breeze blowing across your face, the warmth of sunshine, or the prick of a bee sting, all felt by nerves under your skin. In contrast, here are examples of subtle sense perceptions: you might get a subtle sensing about which direction to take; a feeling of great love or peace may overtake you; the boundaries of your body might seem to dissolve.

How can you receive divine intuitive messages? Ask. That is how. Ask your higher self for a message. Ask for an answer to a question. Ask for healing, for love, for inspiration. Ask to know your true purpose. "Ask, and it shall be given you."

Clairvoyance, clairaudience, and clairsentience are not the only means of receiving intuition. Other ways to get an answer or message from Spirit include: serendipity or coincidence, a flash of insight or direct cognition, revelations in dreams, warning signals, telepathic communication, divine messengers in physical form, and divination or devices.

Although you can receive intuition and communication from Spirit through these other channels, they are not consistent or reliable. Therefore, opening your third eye reigns supreme, because it allows you to get messages anytime you want. And how does that occur? Simply by asking, "Ask, and it shall be given you."

What if You Do not Receive?

What happens when you try to ask, and you do not appear to get the experience you seek? In such a case, some teachers have been trained to help you get the experience known as the Divine Revelation® Breakthrough Session.

Breaking down the wall to the divine presence at the center of your being—that is how you might define the breakthrough. The wall may be made of gossamer for some or brick for others. It consists of habits, beliefs, and thoughts that have convinced you that you are separate from divine Spirit. These thoughts of fear, judgment, guilt, and confusion have coagulated into solid form.

There is a "façade barrier," "ego-façade," or "veil of unbelief," which seems to separate you from God. It is an illusory division between matter and Spirit—a false barrier of error-thoughts that cuts you off from your true nature. This veil of subconscious beliefs prevents you from experiencing Spirit, from opening your third eye, and from developing your natural intuitive abilities. This façade-barrier is not designed by God, but by human free will, which builds a wall of illusory thoughts so crystallized that they become things. Your habitual thoughts can become so deeply entrenched that they become defensive armors covering your clear, radiant, true self.

With this protective façade-barrier, you could feel so comfortable and secure in old habits that you have no incentive to change. You may resist healing old fears and worn-out beliefs. This barrier is made of memories stored in your subconscious mind. These memories comprise your ego identity—who you think you are. Who-you-think-you-are and who-you-really-are, most likely, are two different things, for you probably identify yourself as your limited ego based on past history.

"Breaking through" means walking through the façade barrier and experiencing who you really are. When you experience your break-through, the divine self that you contact is so different from your ordinary human self that you might think it is another person! But this perfect spiritual being is the real you, the true self beyond boundaries.

When you lift above false human beliefs and penetrate the barrier, you return to a state of pure innocence—the original divine being you were intended to be, living in paradise, heaven on earth. At that moment you are one with Spirit and your own love-nature. You find no limitation, fear, frustration, or confusion there—only peace, love, truth, and wisdom.

Each time you break through your ego-façade and experience the true nature of your being, you identify more deeply with your divine self. By contacting your higher self daily, you gradually develop a rapport and a deeper identification with it. Eventually the day dawns when you come to the realization, **"I AM that oneness, I AM that wholeness, I AM that God-being. THAT is who I AM!"**

In the next chapter, you will learn how to break through this ego-façade and attain the experience of your divine self.

9

| The Seat of Siddhis |

*By practicing samyama on the light in the
skull, siddhas [perfected beings] in the
celestial realms can be seen.*

—Patanjali, *Yoga Sutras* 3:32

The term *Yoga* is fraught with misconceptions. Although a Yogic path called Hatha Yoga does teach specific physical postures, the Sanskrit word *Yoga* does not mean "exercise." The word comes from the root "to yoke." In other words, Yoga means "unity" or "integration." But this unity does not refer to union of the nose with the knee or the forehead with the floor. It is union of the individual soul with supreme Spirit—union of individuality with universality.

The state of Yoga can be attained by anyone from any background, not just mystics from the East. Anyone who wants divine contact and divine love, light, power, and energy can experience this. There is not one sole way to experience Yoga. People from every culture seek unity with the divine, and all religions and spiritual paths have validity.

What Yoga Really Is

Yoga, which is one of the six main systems of philosophy in India, originated from two main sources:

1. The *Bhagavad Gita,* a section of an ancient history book called the *Mahabharata* (Great India), written by the seer Veda Vyasa in approximately 3129 BC.

2. An ancient philosophical text called *Yoga Sutras,* written by a great sage named Patanjali in approximately 250 BC.

The *Bhagavad Gita* ("song of God"), the most revered scripture of India and the kernel of Eastern philosophy, is a dialogue between Lord Krishna, a divine *avatar* ("incarnation of God"), and his disciple Arjuna. In this dialogue, Krishna describes the *state* of Yoga (a state of consciousness—not an exercise program) to Arjuna:

"When the mind, thoroughly settled, is riveted in the higher self, then the person, free from yearning for all enjoyments, is said to be established in Yoga. As a lamp in a windless place does not flicker, such is like the subdued mind of the yogi absorbed in the self. The state in which the mind finds rest, stilled by the practice of Yoga, is the state that, seeing the self by the self, finds contentment only in the self."[1]

Here Krishna is often misunderstood as advocating austerity and renunciation as a means to attain Yoga. But he is describing the *destination* rather than the *process* of attaining that goal. The goal is *samadhi* (equanimity of mind and body)—the fulfillment of all seeking and source of satisfaction, beyond which no greater goal exists. When you achieve that state, you are free from longing. Your mind is steady, like a "lamp in a windless place" or a honeybee enjoying nectar.

Yoga is a complete science of mind, body, and Spirit. Its holistic approach can help anyone become happier, in tune with natural life, free from habits that cause disease. It heals your body, clarifies your mind, and strengthens your spirit. Practicing Yoga can purify and balance your life. It improves health, develops mental concentration, and promotes inner peace.

Yoga practices include the following:

1. *Yoga asanas* (postures), stretch the muscles, lubricate joints, improve flexibility and posture, increase circulation, enhance concentration, and reverse aging.

2. *Pranayama* (yogic breathing) awakens the flow of *prana*—the life-force energy, which reverses mental illness and increases alertness, rejuvenation, and spiritual awakening.

3. **Deep relaxation** recharges the body, reduces stress, reverses aging, and improves health. Physical, mental, and spiritual relaxation conserve *prana.*

4. **A healthy diet** consists of natural organic foods—unprocessed, free from chemicals and pesticides. Such a diet, along with regular fasting, promotes longevity, robust health, and disease prevention.

5. **Meditation** is the key to achieving Yoga. Exercise, breathing, relaxation, diet, and positive thinking are just preparations for meditation, which is the crown jewel of Yoga.

To learn about the eight pathways of Yoga—Hatha Yoga, Raja Yoga, Karma Yoga, Gyana Yoga, Kundalini Yoga, Bhakti Yoga, Tantra Yoga, and Integrated Yoga—please read my book *Exploring Meditation.*

Eight Limbs of Yoga

The definitive Yoga philosophy, the *Yoga Sutras* ("threads"—aphorisms of divine union), was written by the ancient seer Patanjali in approximately the second century BC. The sutras help seekers unify *atman* (individual consciousness) with *Brahman* (divine consciousness).

Patanjali defines Yoga as "the restraint of the modifications of the mind-stuff (*chitta vrithri*)." He says that once that restraint is accomplished, "then the Seer (self) abides in his own nature."[2] Patanjali's *Ashtanga Yoga* ("eight limbs of Yoga") are considered by most commentators as steps along the pathway to Yoga. But they are not steps. They are limbs. Limbs of a tree are not paths to the tree. The trunk of the tree is *kaivalya* ("singularity" or "oneness"). Limbs are branches of the tree, upheld by the trunk.

Here are the eight limbs of Yoga:

1. Yama: associated with universal life

The first limb is *Yama* (abstinence), which upholds the laws of Yoga. The five aspects of yama are:

a. *Satya* means truth. The non-changing absolute is eternal truth. A yogi, therefore, knows truth, lives in truth, and speaks only truth.

b. *Ahimsa* signifies non-violence. A yogi perceives only a state of oneness. Therefore, to harm others would be to harm your own self.

c. *Asteya* is non-covetousness. To covet is to possess property that is not yours. When objects overtake the senses, those objects possess the self. In contrast, nothing can overtake the self of a yogi in perfect unity.

d. *Brahmacharya*: means living (*charya*) the absolute (*Brahman*). A yogi dwells in a state of divine unity in perfect contentment. Brahmacharya also signifies conserving sexual energy, which increases spiritual radiance.

e. *Aparigraha* means non-accumulation, freedom from sensory objects. A yogi "content with whatever comes unsought"[3] seeks nothing from objects of perception.

2. Niyama: link between universal and individual life

Niyama (observances) are laws of Yoga, rules that connect individual life to universal life. There are five:

a. *Shaucha* means purity, attained by releasing tension and toxins from the body and false beliefs from the mind.

b. *Santosha* is contentment. The only unshakable state of complete fulfillment and satisfaction is absolute pure consciousness.

c. *Tapas* ("heat") is defined as asceticism. But it really means turning senses inward during meditation, away (abstaining) from sensory objects. Turning your senses within increases the heat of spiritual fervor.

d. *Swadhyaya* ("opening the chapter of the self") signifies opening awareness to the self. When your mind turns inward, the chapter of the outer world closes, and the inner world opens.

e. *Ishwar-Pranidhan* ("bringing divinity into breath") means imbibing the divine presence when breath is suspended in the state of Yoga. That is surrender to the divine.

3. Asana: associated with body

Asana (seat) indicates stability, established in absolute pure consciousness, stable, unshakable—the ultimate state of Yoga. You will learn some Yoga asanas in Chapter 12.

4. Pranayama: associated with breath

Prana (life force in breath) and *ayama* (coming and going) indicate movement of breath. Pranayama controls life energy, which harmonizes all movement. A yogi's breath in transcendental consciousness achieves a state of suspension (see Chapter 12).

5. Pratyahara: associated with senses

Pratya ("direction") and *ahara* ("food") mean introspection: reversing the outward direction of the senses and turning inward, toward ultimate fulfillment. In the Bhagavad Gita, Lord Krishna said, "When, like a tortoise draws in its limbs from all directions, he withdraws his senses from the sense-objects, then the mind of the yogi is stable."[4]

6. Dharana: associated with mind

Dharana ("hold" or "grasp") signifies the mind held on a fixed point or strong intention.

7. Dhyana: associated with intellect

Dhyana ("meditation") is flow of the mind in an inward direction.

8. Samadhi: pure consciousness

Sama ("stable") and *dhi* ("intellect") signify the state of evenness of mind and stillness of body in transcendental awareness.

Patanjali's Supersensory Powers

Patanjali's *Yoga Sutras* explains how Yoga, integration of individual spirit with universal spirit, is achieved. The goal is *kaivalya,* which literally translates as "isolation." However, in reality, kaivalya means identifying yourself as supreme Spirit rather than as matter. This means total detachment from the material world, even while busily engaging in worldly activities.

Patanjali's method to attain kaivalya is a meditative technique called *samyama,* a practice that comprises the three final limbs of Yoga, described in the previous section: dharana, dhyana, and samadhi.

The Sanskrit term *siddhi* ("perfection") is a supernormal power achieved by practicing *samyama.* Some siddhis are levitation, walking through walls, supernormal strength, disappearing from view, seeing hidden objects with your third eye, supersensory perception, traveling in a subtle body, making the body very small, large, light or heavy, appearing in physical form in several places at once, walking on water or hot coals, omnipotence, omnipresence, omniscience, and acquiring hidden knowledge.

The premise of samyama is that you can manifest anything, even supernormal powers, through your power of intention. You can open your third eye and see things at great distances. You can develop intuition and gain hidden knowledge. You can see stars, planets, and cosmic regions. You can communicate with divine beings. All this and much more is possible for anyone.

The siddhis are supernormal powers that average individuals could never imagine as possible. Yet they are real and attainable. The recipe for creating the impossible is simple—and surprising: take one male, one female, mix well, and let go. How do living beings create offspring? A male element projects into a female element, lets go, and voila—new life appears, a miraculous gift from the Creator.

Miracle-Making

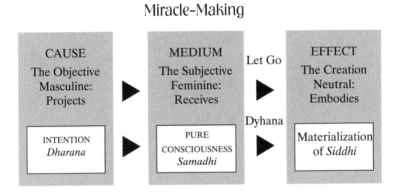

Image 9a. *Samyama Practice*

In Patanjali's practice of *samyama,* the masculine element, which sets the goal, is called *dharana* ("holding"). The feminine element, the state of perfect equipoise, pure consciousness, is called *samadhi* ("evenness"). The third element, *dhyana* ("meditation"), is a flow of movement or letting go.

Patanjali's key to unlocking the mysteries of manifestation is based on universal principals. It reveals the secret of how any goal can be attained. The answer is to let go. The most potent part of any prayer, any intention, or any meditation, is to simply give up. Have you noticed that when you are overly attached to an outcome, and you put excessive effort into chasing it, that goal seems to elude you? Yet, when you give up on ever getting the goal, and you just let it go, that is when your goal is achieved.

Attaining Miraculous Powers

The practice of *samyama* cultivates higher consciousness and manifests miraculous siddhis through a three-part practice: intention (dharana), wholeness (samadhi), and movement between them (dhyana), which unites the first two elements.

1. **Dharana** (concentration) is holding the attention of the mind (chitta) fixed on a particular object or point of space. In simple terms, that means stating your intention.

2. **Dhyana** (meditation) is the continuous, unbroken flow of the same knowledge. Here the mind lets go of the object and allows it to be absorbed or disappear into wholeness. In plain language, that means letting go or giving up your intention.

3. **Samadhi** (evenness of intellect) is the transcendental state of pure awareness, the experience of wholeness in absolute bliss consciousness (*satchitananda*). Here even "I-ness" gets absorbed into oneness. In simple words, that means being at peace.

The perfections (*siddhis*) of supernormal powers described in *Yoga Sutras* are accomplished through the process of samyama. Although is it believed that samyama cannot be taught in a book, I will describe some of its methods now, so you can begin to practice it in your endeavor to open your third eye.

Here is a description of how to practice samyama:

Step 1

In order to successfully practice samyama, the fundamental requirement is your capacity to attain a state of tranquility, perfection, and oneness. This is called samadhi ("even intellect" or "integration")—evenness of mind and stillness of body, in quietude, deep relaxation, and inner peace.

This state is accomplished by going into deep meditation. In case you are inexperienced in achieving this state of perfect wholeness, here are a few simple steps:

1. Sit comfortably and close your eyes.

2. Call upon a divine being or deity by name, and ask to be taken into deep meditation.

3. Take a few deep breaths and settle down to deep relaxation.

4. Take more deep breaths and become quiet, still, and centered.

5. Take more deep breaths and allow the mind and body to be at peace.

6. Take more deep breaths and completely let go. Be at peace.

7. Give up and give over to Spirit, and settle down to perfect wholeness.

Step 2

After you have attained the state of samadhi, set your intention. That means stating clearly what you want to accomplish. This step is called *dharana* ("holding")—stating your intended goal in your mind. In *Yoga Sutras,* Patanjali states these goals plainly in his aphorisms. These are used in the practice of samyama. So, to accomplish one of the siddhis, all you need to do is use a particular aphorism.

Step 3

Let go of the intention. In this third stage, called *dhyana* ("meditation"), just allow your mind to release its grasp on the goal and return to the state of samadhi. That means to simply let go and let your mind relax into inner peace again.

The sutras in Patanjali's text are used during the practice. For example, here is the sutra for the siddhi of physical strength: "By practicing samyama on physical strength, the strength of elephants can be acquired."[5]

After you have attained the state of perfect relaxation and wholeness (samadhi), briefly hold on to the sutra (dharana). That means you consciously state your intention by thinking a portion of the sutra in your mind, such as "strength of an elephant," along with visualizing the elephant in your mind. Then you drop the sutra and let it go completely (dhyana), and you return to the state of samadhi. Then the cycle is repeated.

As a result, by practicing this particular sutra on a regular basis, greater physical strength is acquired. The wonderful side effect is that you establish yourself more profoundly in the state of samadhi, also known as *satchitananda*—absolute bliss consciousness.

Since this book is about awakening your third eye, I recommend you begin the practice of samyama by using some sutras that might help you further this particular goal. You may experiment with the following sutras that I have selected from the *Yoga Sutras*. When you use the sutra in your practice, just use a portion of the sutra that encapsulates what you want to achieve. I have stated that shortened version in brackets after each sutra.

To begin, choose three to five sutras to work with, and then practice samyama for about five minutes per sutra.

1. "By practicing samyama on friendliness, love, and compassion, and other similar virtues, strength is obtained therein."[6] ["Friendliness, love, and compassion"]

2. "By practicing samyama on the effulgent light of the higher sense-perception (*jyotishmati*), knowledge of subtle objects, or things obstructed from view, or placed at a great distance, can be acquired."[7] ["Inner light" while visualizing light in your heart]

3. "By practicing samyama on the sun (the point in the body known as the solar entrance) the knowledge of the cosmic regions is acquired."[8] ["Sun" while visualizing the warming pranic energy in pingala nadi, which flows through the right nostril and raises metabolism. This does not refer to the actual sun in the sky.]

4. "By practicing samyama on the moon (the lunar entrance) the knowledge of the arrangements of stars is acquired."[9] ["Moon" while visualizing the cool pranic energy in ida nadi, which flows through the left nostril. This does not refer to the actual moon in the sky.]

5. "By practicing samyama on the polestar, motion of the stars is known."[10] ["Polestar" while visualizing the bindu point at the top of the skull]

6. "By practicing samyama on the plexus of the navel, knowledge of the bodily system is derived."[11] ["Navel" while visualizing the navel chakra]

7. "By practicing samyama on the coronal light (light in the pineal gland), *siddhas* (perfected celestial beings) can be seen."[12] ["Coronal light" while visualizing the center of the head, at pineal gland]

8. "By practicing samyama on knowledge known as *pratibha* (intuition), everything becomes known."[13] ["Intuition" while visualizing the center of the head, at the pineal gland]

9. "By practicing samyama on the heart, knowledge of the mind is acquired."[14] ["Heart" while visualizing the heart chakra]

10. "By practicing samyama on the distinction between *buddhi* (intellect) and *purusha* (higher self), a knowledge regarding purusha is acquired."[15] ["Distinction between intellect and higher self"]

11. "From the knowledge of Purusha arise Pratibha (prescience), Sravana (supernormal power of hearing), Vedana (supernormal power of touch), Adarsa (supernormal power of sight), Asvada (supernormal power of taste), and Varta (supernormal power of smell)."[16] ["Subtle smell"] ["Subtle taste"] ["Subtle sight"] ["Subtle touch"] ["Subtle hearing"] Each of these five super-senses should be practiced separately.

Please send me an email at divinerev@aol.com, and let me know about your experiences with practicing the siddhis. In the next chapter, we will learn about Taoist alchemical practices for opening your third eye.

10

| Third Eye Alchemy |

*People often ask how you become a Taoist,
what books do you read, what temples do
you attend? The sage replies that you don't
become a Taoist, you just realize that Taoist
is a name for what you already are.*

—Lao Tzu

In ancient traditions of the Far East, the chakras are viewed as essential elements of the subtle energy system. The third eye is known as *ajna chakra* to the yogis and Buddhists of India, Tibet, Japan, and Indonesia, and the *upper dantian* (also *dan tien* or *tan tien*) to the Taoists of China. Nearly every spiritual tradition of the Orient recognizes three major subtle energy centers along the central median channel that runs through the spine in your subtle body. According to the Taoists, these three centers are spiritual transformers.

The Three Dantians

The three *dantians* (also *elixir fields* or *cinnabar fields)* of ancient Chinese Taoist philosophy are situated along the Tai Chi ("great pole," known as *sushumna nadi* in India) in the area of the sacral chakra, heart chakra, and third eye chakra. The Tai Chi extends from *baihui* acupuncture point at the crown of the head (named *bindu point* in India) down to the *huiyin* point at the perineum (named *mula kshetram* in India).

The three dantians gather, store, transform, and project life force energy. Their purpose is to facilitate alchemical energy changes in your subtle body. The Tai Chi pole enables communication among the three dantians and facilitates flow of life force energy.

The three dantians are centers that transmute the "three treasures of the human": *jing, qi,* and *shen.* Since antiquity, Chinese medicine defines these "treasures" or "jewels," which are essential energies sustaining human life. Taoist practices transform the tree treasures through practices of inner alchemy.

Chinese alchemy is an ancient Taoist tradition of body-mind-spirit purification and cultivation. There are two main branches of alchemy—*Waidan* (outer alchemy) and *Neidan* (inner alchemy).

Waidan

Waidan is the practice of changing the mortal body into indestructible matter through external alchemy by using breathing techniques, sexual practices, physical exercises, yoga, herbal and chemical elixirs, special diets, and medical skills.

Waidan is the forerunner of modern chemistry. Alchemists from both the West and Far East experimented with minerals, animals, and plants with the goal of turning base metals into gold. But their ultimate objective was to produce the philosopher's stone—a golden elixir that would bestow immortal life. While experimenting, the ancient Chinese alchemists discovered potent herbal medicines, in addition to other chemical formulas, such as gunpowder.

Neidan

Neidan, also known as *jindan* ("golden elixir"), is a spiritual discipline used by Taoists to transmute subtle body energies and thereby build an immortal spiritual body that survives death. Meditation, visualization, breathing, and bodily postures transform the inner being. Inner alchemy purifies and transforms practitioners to express their pure and radiant potential—without the use of external agents.

In the practice of Neidan, the three dantians are considered cauldrons, crucibles, or stoves that purify and transform the three treasures. These methods take the practitioner to the unity of the Tao and, ultimately, to immortality.

The three treasures cultivate and transform energy by the process of *lianjing huaqi* ("refining essence into breath"), *lianqi huashen* ("refining breath into spirit"), and *lianshen huanxu* ("refining spirit and reverting to emptiness"). The action of the three cauldrons is like heating ice to transform it into liquid and vapor.

Taoist Qigong exercises and meditations gather and circulate these three treasures, also known as "inner elixirs," of *jing, qi,* and *shen* at the dantian points.

Jing at Lower Dantian

Jing or *ching* means, "essence," "primal energy," "spark of life," "sexual energy," "refined," "perfected," "extract," "spirit," "vitality," "excellence," "purity," "skill." It is the densest physical matter in the body and is yin in nature. Associated with the lower dantian, located about two inches below the navel at the qihai (Ren 6) acupuncture point, it is also called *shenlu* (the "sacred furnace"). The lower dantian is called the "golden stove" where jing is refined, purified, and finally transmuted into qi. In Japan, the lower dantian is known as *hara*.

Qi at Middle Dantian

Qi, chi, or *ki* means, "breath," "spirit," "air," "gas," "steam vapor," "vitality," "energy," "vigor," "attitude." It is the life force energy obtained from air, food, water, and cultivated through thought. This is named *prana* in India and *ki* in Japan. Qi is associated with the middle dantian, or heart chakra, which transforms qi into shen. The middle dantian is located at hanzhong (Ren 17) point, midway between the two nipples.

Shen at Upper Dantian

The upper dantian is the third eye, at *yintang* point, also called *meijian* ("between eyebrows") or *xuanguan* ("gate of mysteriousness"), in the middle of the forehead, above and between the eyebrows. This is the seat of *shen,* which means, "spirit," "soul," "mind," "god," "deity," "supernatural being," "awareness," "spiritual energy."

Shen is the purest, most refined and rarified vital energy. In upper dantian, shen transforms into *wuji* (or *wu wei*—the absolute openness of infinite space, ultimate nothingness, beinglessness, limitless infinite). Finally, wuji gets absorbed into Tao, the underlying natural order of the universe—eternally nameless and formless, the nondual unmanifest absolute.[1]

Power of the Dantians

The three dantians are vital centers for energy cultivation, diagnosis, and healing. Your health and strength of your energy field depend on the amount of qi (life energy) present in the three dantians.

When you place focused attention on increasing qi energy in the lower dantian, the result is an elevated feeling of power and stability. Focusing intention to increase qi in the middle dantian will heighten emotional awareness. Focus on increasing qi in the upper dantian will enhance spiritual awareness and connection to your higher self. The body relates to jing, breath relates to qi, and mind and spirit relate to shen.

Taoists believe the amount of jing you are allotted at birth is finite, and when it gets depleted, the body dies. Jing can be preserved through conserving sexual fluids. Depletion of jing results in poor concentration, memory lapses, dizziness, and absentmindedness. Deficiency of prenatal jing causes mental retardation and attention deficit disorder (ADD).

Yogis of India believe preserving sexual fluids transmutes these substances into marrow, then blood, then *ojas*—the material equivalent of prana. Ojas is a sweet, oily substance that covers the skin, imparting divine radiance and charisma.

Taoist alchemy teaches aspirants to use the jing's generative force, usually discharged through ejaculation, to instead renew the body. Jing is retained, conserved, and drawn upward from lower dantian through the spine to bathe the energy centers (chakras) and nourish the brain ("sea of marrow").

Qi moving through the meridians (known as nadis in India) is stored in lower dantian. Its energy flow then nourishes the whole body and radiates into the *wei qi* field—your protective energy field that projects several feet from your body. Qi can be cultivated through Qigong (Chinese martial arts), Tai Chi Chuan (Chinese exercises), and pranayama (yogic breathing exercises).

Upper dantian is the generator and storehouse of heavenly qi, which is subtle, ethereal, and vapor-like. Opening the upper dantian (known as "crystal room") awakens supersensory perception, spiritual intuition, higher awareness, and perceptions outside time and space.

The head is the most yang part of the body, because it closest to heaven. Therefore, the qi in upper dantian is yang. It is possible to consciously absorb the yang qi of heaven, which flows into the upper gateway (baihui GV-20) from the celestial bodies: sun, moon, planets, and stars. This clear yang qi enables mental clarity.

Location of the Upper Dantian

The upper dantian, seat of shen (Spirit), is located in the center of the brain, in the area of the pineal, pituitary, thalamus, and hypothalamus glands. It is said to have an upright-pyramid shape in order to assist in storing light and gathering energy from the heavenly realm (sun, moon, and planets).

The upper dantian is known as "muddy pellet" (*niwan*) or "palace of qian." Qian refers to one of the eight trigrams or eight *bagua* (commonly known in Feng Shui). These represent fundamental principles of nature in Taoist cosmology. Each trigram consists of three lines, either broken (yin) or unbroken (yang). The trigram *qian* (three unbroken lines), signifying upper dantian, represents pure yang and heaven.

The upper dantian is divided into nine palaces or chambers arranged in two rows. When the inner elixir moves to the upper field, the third and last stage of the Neidan process ("refining spirit and reverting to emptiness") is complete.[2]

There are four major points in the upper dantian, identified by the Taoists—front, back, top, and center. Here is more information about these four points:

Yintang (Hall of Impression)

The front point of upper dantian is known as *yintang* point, third eye and seat of wisdom and enlightenment, at the middle of the forehead—the size and shape of a large almond, in a chamber glowing with spiritual light. It is known as the front gate of the sixth major chakra, called *ajna kshetram* or *bhrumadhya*.

Taoists believe you can communicate with the spirit world by rolling your eyes upward and focusing one inch behind the yintang point. This is *mingtang* ("hall of light") point. Taoists believe that the crossing of the eyes to focus at mingtang (a practice known as *Shambhavi Mudra* in India) allows the soul to unite with Tao. (See page 118 to practice.)

Fengfu (Wind Palace)

The back point of upper dantian is located at the external occipital protuberance, at the back of the skull, just above the neck. It is the back gate of the sixth major chakra (ajna chakra). This point (Fengfu GV-16) is believed to act as an antenna, tuning in to various frequencies in the sea of consciousness and thereby receiving spiritual impressions through clairvoyance, clairsentience, and clairaudience.

The Fengfu point is believed to affect the flow of qi and blood to the brain, and is used to treat shen disturbances and astral entity possession. A prominent occipital protuberance indicates a tendency toward clairvoyant sight and the ability to receive psychic impressions.

The Celestial Pillar points (UB-10), to the sides and below Fengfu, are associated with trance mediumship. Gateways to spiritual communication with other-dimensional beings, these points receive qi and shen from spiritual beings.

Baihui (One Hundred Meetings)

The highest point of upper dantian is at the apex of the crown, baihui (GV-20) point. This is the same location as the *bindu point* in the chakra system, at the top center of *sahasrara chakra*. The Baihui is at the upper gate of the Tai Chi pole (sushumna nadi).

According to the ancients, you can access spiritual planes and ascend to higher consciousness through this point. Taoists believe that baihui directs heavenly qi into the "chamber of mysterious elixir," located in the brain's third ventricle. All the body's major channels of energy (nadis or meridians) connect to Baihui, so, at death, the shen can leave the body through this upper gate and ascend to the heavenly realms. Taoists believe the eternal soul enters the body through the Tai Chi pole at conception, and exits through the Tai Chi at death.

According to Kabbalah, nine *sephiroth* evolve from kether (bindu). These sephiroth are chakra points on the tree of life. Thus kether, source of the light of consciousness, progressively filters down to the other sephiroth (chakras).

The key to achieving Yoga is to return to bindu. Rather than continually vacillating between external sensory pleasures, the mind draws inward and returns to concentrated focus of such intense one-pointedness that it becomes a point (bindu). When all mental fluctuations (internal chatter) cease, then Yoga (integration) is attained.

Center of Upper Dantian

The center of upper dantian ("original cavity of spirit") is located at ajna chakra, in the pineal gland. This gland is large in children but shrinks in adults, and is more developed in women than men. As the organ of telepathic communication, it receives impressions through thought vibrations, waves, and impulses projected from other people's auric fields. The pineal gland is considered the place where shen transcends the limitations of form and merges with the infinite space of *wuji*. From wuji, shen reunites with Tao.

Cultivating Upper Dantian

Medical Qigong practitioners cultivate upper dantian and strengthen intuition through *Shengong* meditations. Qi is absorbed from the celestial realms and the environment into upper dantian through the baihui point (crown of head), the yintang (between eyebrows), and the *tianmen* ("heaven's gate," middle of forehead) points. Qi can then be directed outward as healing energy through the same three points.

Medical Qigong practitioners gather and balance yin (female) and yang (male) energies within upper dantian. This is called "The union of husband and wife in the bed-chamber." The primordial deities of Taoism, who represent yin and yang, are Hsi Wang Mu (Queen Mother of the West), and her consort, Tung Wang Kung (Lord King of the East). In the Yoga tradition, the same mystical union occurs in crown chakra (sahasrara) at the bindu (baihui point). The female goddess Shakti (kundalini) rises up the spine and unites with Shiva at crown chakra. Shakti is the yin energy, and Shiva is yang.

Taoists believe the primordial breath or life-force energy appears as a blue-green luminous mist, residing within the nine chambers of *niwan palace* (pineal gland area). In advanced Neidan practice, the nine chambers open. Then nine small spheres appear, revolving around a large ball of light. The large light ball corresponds to the sun and the nine smaller light balls parallel the nine planets.[3] The solar system resides within your multidimensional energy field, in the crystal chamber of your third eye.

Taoists believe gods reside within the dantians, and practitioners perceive them during meditation and while practicing embryonic breathing (*taixi*), known as "breathing of the cinnabar field" (*dantian huxi*).[4] The yogis of India concur. Male and female deities reside within each chakra, and they appear to adepts during meditation.

Practicing the Microcosmic Orbit

The "microcosmic orbit" or "self-winding wheel of the law," a practice originating in India, is a circuit of energy used in Taoist meditation. Meditating with the microcosmic orbit prevents the body's jing from depletion through loss of sexual fluids. This method circulates and refines qi via a circuit, from perineum up to head, and then from head back down to perineum.

The usual downward outlet of jing, or essence (to create offspring), is upturned into a channel starting at the base of the spine (the "first gate," *huiyin*), rising up the spine to the coccyx, then to the spot between the kidneys (the "second gate," *mingmen*), to the back of the head (the "third gate," *yuzhen*), and reaching up to the top of the brain (*baihui*). Then it flows back down the front of the body to the third eye (*yintang*), heart (*shanzhong*), navel (*duqi*), and perineum (*huiyin*).

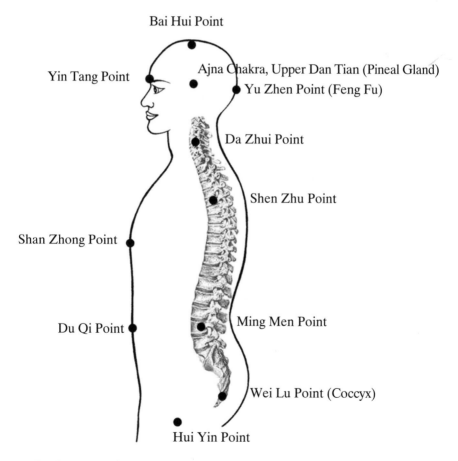

Image 10a. *Points on the Microcosmic Orbit*

This circuit is created by first taking a deep inhale into the lower dantian, forcing kundalini fire (life energy at base of spine) and jing (generative force) to rise up the spine through the chakras to the head through the "governing vessel" or "channel of control" (*dumai*, known as back midline channel—*sushumna nadi*), which connects all the yang vessels (meridians) in the body.

Then an exhalation relaxes the lower abdomen so the kundalini and jing sink into the "conception channel" or "channel of function" (*renmai*, known as front midline channel), along the front of the body, which connects all the yin vessels (meridians) in the body, through the chakra trigger points (*kshetram*).

Thus completes a full rotation of the circuit.[5]

Here is a way to practice the microcosmic orbit:

Sit down or lie on your back with eyes closed. If sitting, stay upright with feet flat on the floor, sitting forward, so only your buttocks are on the chair.

Focus attention on your lower dantian, about two inches below the navel, and visualize a small, luminous golden or white energy ball, bright and pure. Maintain your attention on lower dantian until you feel the ball. This could be heat, vibration, warmth, or a sensation of its presence.

Start practicing abdominal breathing as follows: Close your mouth and inhale through your nose. Draw air into your belly, and your abdomen will expand. Slightly open your mouth and exhale as you lift your tongue to the palate with the tip of the tongue touching the back of your upper front teeth. As you exhale, your abdominal muscles will contract.

Now, using this same abdominal breathing process, take a deep breath into the belly and imagine the small ball of energy passing down from the lower dantian, past the huiyin at the perineum, up the spine through the weilu (coccyx). Then imagine the ball rising up the spine to the mingmen (navel chakra point in spine) and then up to where the ribs meet the spine, and next to the back of the head, where it joins the neck at dazhui point (throat chakra point in spine).

Then visualize or imagine this qi ball in the center of your brain, at the pineal gland (crystal palace), absorbing healing energy through the baihui point (bindu point), which is at the top of your head. Next, focus your attention on the yintang point, at the center of your forehead just above your eyebrows, and draw energy into the ball from the yintang point, as the ball passes to the roof of your mouth. You may feel a tingling or throbbing sensation in your mouth.

This ends your inhalation.

(For beginners, taking a breath or two while the energy ball is still in your mouth can help you focus on the ball.)

Then, as you exhale through your mouth, let the energy ball sink down through your palate and tongue (which is still lightly pressed against your palate), into your throat to the heart (shanzhong point). From the heart, draw it down through your solar plexus, past your navel, and down into the lower dantian, where energy gathers, mixes, and is reserved for internal circulation.

Then begin another cycle. You can practice this orbit several times.

As the qi is circulating, your breathing will become refined, rarefied, and smooth, rather than ragged or irregular. This meditation may cause your head to rock or body to tremble. Qi circulation harmonizes and transmutes the vital fluids to produce true vitality.

If you have any discomfort in your body while practicing the orbit, stop the circulation and focus qi at the uneasy point. Allow it to pulse there until any agitation subsides. This will heal the body and improve energy flow.

You can use this beneficial meditation during the day to reduce stress. You can also practice it lying down before sleep. If you have trouble imagining the flow, try visualizing a golf ball or Ping-Pong ball. You can even use a finger to trace the flow during the practice.[6]

In the next chapter, we will explore the legendary nectar of immortality, also known as ambrosia, elixir, or soma—the eternal fountain of youth.

11

| Nectar of Immortal Life |

*Keep the pineal gland operating and you
won't grow old—you will always be young.*

—Edgar Cayce

The ambrosial elixir of life is a potion that, when ingested, is believed to grant eternal life. In myths of Enoch, Thoth, Hermes Trismegistus, and Al-Khidr (the Green Man), the immortal white drops, liquid gold, or dancing water is drunk. In Homer's poems, nectar is the drink of the gods, and ambrosia is their food. *Amrita* is the equivalent in India, which is consumed by the gods. In the myth of the Holy Grail, its magical nourishment sustained Joseph of Arimathea for 42 years.

In the Zoroastrian and Mithraic cults, the substance *haoma*, equivalent to the Sanskrit *soma*, from the roots *su* or *bu* ("squeeze" or "pound"), is the name of a yellow plant whose juice is extracted for sacramental ceremonies.

The Nordic god Wotan, Woden, or Odin possesses a magic goat that fills the never-ending pitcher of poetic mead—the most precious drink in the universe, which imparts secret wisdom and inspiration. The golden apples of immortality bestow strength, health, and eternal youth to Germanic and Norse gods.

In Mesopotamia, winged genies hold a pinecone (symbol of the third eye or pineal gland), which is used to drip a magical potion or immortal elixir upon the king or upon the sacred tree of life. The bucket of tonic is held in the genie's hand.[1]

Image 11a. *Assyrian Blessing Genie*[2]

Seeking the Philosopher's Stone

The vast writings of Hermes Trismegistus appeared in the Roman Empire in the second century AD. In the Middle Ages and Renaissance, Hermeticism and the Hermetic Tradition became popular among alchemists. The Emerald Tablet, known as Smaragdine Table or the Secret of Hermes, was the bible of the alchemists' craft and was said to reveal the secret of the Philosopher's Stone.

The word "alchemy" has its roots in Arabic: *al-kimia* (the art of transformation). Therefore, by definition, alchemists attempt to transmute one material into another, such as base metal into gold. In India and China, alchemists sought the Philosopher's Stone, the "water stone of the wise," in the fourth century BC. Alchemists in Europe attempted to discover the Stone for five centuries. This miraculous tincture or powder was believed to reverse aging and grant eternal life.

The hundreds of names for the Philosopher's Stone include the Sanskrit *soma rasa* (soma juice), *maha rasa* (great juice), *amrit rasa* (nectar of immortality juice) and *amrita* (nectar of immortality); and the Arabic *aab-i-hayat/aab-i-haiwan* (water of life), and *chashma-i-kausar* (fountain of beauty, located in Paradise).

An entire chapter of the most ancient scripture of India, *Rig-Veda*, is devoted to a mysterious substance called *soma* (also *Soma Pavamana* or *Indu*), which promises eternal life. From the Sanskrit root *sav* ("press" or "squeeze"), soma is a drink of living drops produced by pressing stalks of the legendary soma plant.

Here are a few verses from *Rig-Veda*, written by the seer Rishi Kashyapa, which invoke Soma Pavamana and its properties of immortal life:

"Flow Soma, in a most sweet and exhilarating stream, effused for Indra to drink. The all-beholding destroyer of Rakshasas has stepped upon his gold-smitten birthplace, united with the wooden cask. Be the lavish giver of wealth, most bounteous, the destroyer of enemies; bestow on us the riches of the affluent."[3]

"Where light is perpetual, in the world in which the sun is placed, in that immortal imperishable world place me, Pavamana; flow, Indu, for Indra. Where in the third heaven, in the third sphere, the sun wanders at will, where the regions are filled with light, there make me immortal; flow, Indu, for Indra. Where there is happiness, pleasures, joy and enjoyment, where the wishes of the wisher are obtained, there make me immortal; flow, Indu, for Indra."[4]

There are many legends associated with soma. Many believe this chemical is extant in a rare Himalayan plant. It might be the potent antioxidant resveratrol, which is scientifically proven to slow aging and increase lifespan. The knotweed vine (*polygonum cuspidatum*), a natural source of resveratrol, is known in China as the anti-aging remedy *Fo Ti Tieng* roots (*Ho Shou Wu*) or Tiger Cane (*Hu Zhang*). This has been used as an herbal remedy in China for 1,500 years.

For more detailed information about these herbs and the illustrious beings who used them to attain extraordinary longevity, please read my book *Ascension*.

Nectar in Your Third Eye

Many yogis believe the legendary soma substance to be self-generated, in the pineal gland, where it programs the body to rejuvenate itself indefinitely. My personal experience is that when deep meditation is practiced for long periods of time, soma juice trickles down the back of the throat and can be tasted as a sweet liquid.

Yogic and Taoist practices stimulate the production and conservation of this precious immortal nectar, which is believed to flow from the pineal gland. One of these is *khechari mudra*. This dangerous technique should never be attempted without guidance from a physician, and under the direction of a genuine yogic master. Otherwise, severe speech impairment will result.

The membrane under the tongue, *frenulum linguae*, which attaches the tongue to the floor of the mouth, is cut, only "a hair's breadth" daily, and treated with rock salt and herbs. The tongue is stretched and lengthened. After about six months, the membrane is completely cut away. Then the yogi curls up the tongue and thrusts it back toward the uvula at the back of the throat, to seal off the esophagus, windpipe, and palate. *Hatha Yoga Pradipika* states:

"If the Yogi drinks Somarasa (soma juice) by sitting with the tongue turned backwards and mind concentrated, there is no doubt he conquers death within 15 days. As fire is inseparably connected with the wood and light is connected with the wick and oil, so does the soul not leave the body full of nectar exuding from the Soma."[5]

A modified form of khechari mudra can also be practiced without cutting the membrane, and many people have reported positive results from the practice. See page 114 in this book for instructions.

Kaya-Kalpa

In India, the ancient medical practice is called Ayurveda, "the science of life." One branch of Ayurveda specializes in longevity—*kaya-kalpa*. *Kaya* means "body" and *kalpa* means "end" or "dissolution." The treatments for kaya-kalpa are described in *Siddha's Science of Longevity and Kalpa Medicine of India*, by Dr. A. Shanmuga Velan. They are:

1. Preserving vital energies by diverting the internal secretions of the body through pranayama (breathing exercises).

2. Transmuting the sexual energy and conserving the sperm by celibacy and Tantra Yoga practices.

3. Taking three consolidated mineral salts, known as *muppu*, which are elaborately prepared.

4. Taking calcined powders prepared from mercury, sulphur, mica, gold, copper, iron, and other minerals.

5. Using drugs prepared from rare Indian herbs, including Fo Ti Tieng and hydrocotyle asiatica.

Sushruta Samhita, an ancient Ayurvedic text, describes kaya-kalpa as a ritual of entering a chamber for seven days after detoxifying the system through purgatives, enemas, and sweat baths. The soma liquid is carefully prepared and administered by the physician. The patient then vomits blood, breaks out in swellings, and defecates worms. The muscles wither and fingernails and hair fall out. The body expels all undesirable toxic matter accumulated through errors in diet and conduct. On the eighth day the rejuvenation process begins. The hair and nails grow back, muscles regain their vitality, skin assumes a new luster, and body emerges new and youthful.

For more information about kaya-kalpa and the elixir of immortal life, please read my book *Ascension*.

Doctrine of the Golden Elixir

Taoists are vitally interested in attaining longevity and physical immortality. Taoism is the only religion that places as much emphasis on the deathless body as other religions place on the deathless soul. Ko Hung (288–343 AD) wrote the original textbook on Taoist alchemy: *Pao P'u Tzu Nei P'ien* ("he who holds to simplicity"), circa 320 AD.

According to Taoism, the "original cavity of the spirit" is in the center of the brain, in the area of the pineal gland. Lao Tzu (circa 604 BC to 531 BC), founder of the Tao chia school of Taoism and author of the Tao Te Ching, called it "the gateway to heaven and earth." He advised people to concentrate on that gateway in order to realize the oneness. This is the key to immortality, as it is where the golden elixir arises.

Taoists believe there is a pearl, the size of a grain of rice, which is that gateway. It is there in the "cavity of one true prenatal vitality," that the wondrous light of essential nature dwells. It is symbolized by a circle, which Taoists call the elixir of immortality or spiritual light.

Confucius calls it "virtuous perfection" (*jen*). *The Book of Changes* (*I Ching*) calls it *wu chi* ("ultimateless boundless infinite"). Buddhists call it "perfect knowledge" (*yuan ming*). It is believed that anyone who really knows this cavity can prepare the golden elixir of immortality. It is said: "When the One is attained, all problems are solved."[6]

The great ancient sages perfected the art of inner alchemy. Through their secret practices, the physical body transmutes into the Christian resurrection body or glorified body, the Sufi most sacred body or supra-celestial body, the Taoist diamond body, the Buddhist light body or rainbow body, the Indian siddha body of bliss, or the Hermetic immortal body. Read my book *Ascension* for more information.

Is DMT the Nectar of Immortality?

Scientific research has recently found that the hallucinogenic chemical DMT (N-dimethyltryptamine) is produced by the pineal gland (see page 60). Rick Strassman, MD, author of *DMT: The Spirit Molecule* (2000), described the compound as "the first endogenous human psychedelic." Terrance McKenna, advocate of psychedelic drugs, called DMT "the most powerful hallucinogen known to man and science."[7]

We might wonder whether the ancients knew the properties of this chemical—whether naturally generated in the pineal gland, found in a plant, derived from substances, or synthetically produced. In ancient meditative practices, the ajna chakra, seated in the pineal gland, is involved in raising kundalini and developing clairvoyant sight. The chemical DMT, produced by the pineal, might be a generator of spiritual or mystical experiences.

The body produces more DMT in extraordinary conditions, such as birth, sexual ecstasy, childbirth, extreme physical stress, near-death, death, and meditation.[8] Such life-changing milestones are often described in terms that resemble psychedelic "trips" on drugs such as DMT.

Author and physicist Cliff Pickover, from the IBM Thomas J. Watson Research Center, Yorktown, New York, was elected as a Fellow for the Committee for Skeptical Inquiry and has been awarded more than 170 U.S. patents. He states, "DMT in the pineal glands of Biblical prophets gave God to humanity and let ordinary humans perceive parallel universes."[9]

Pickover conjectures that prophets of old were more in touch with God, angels, miracles, and visions because their pineal glands produced more DMT than ours do today. He blames electric lighting for today's reduction in pineal gland DMT production. (See page 66 for more information.)

DMT advocates maintain the burning bush of Moses was actually a shamanic herb, and Moses imbibed it through smoking the leaves. The theory is that the bush may have been any of the following ancient sacred herbs: *cannabis sativa*, acacia *sant*, Assyrian rue (*pegunam harmala*), *asena* (*hoama* in Persian and *essene* in Egyptian), Gnostic *besa*, Etruscan *phallaris arundanacia*, Sumerian tree of life, or North African acacia tree.

Assyrian rue (*esphand*) was sacred to Mohammed, to Zoroaster, to the Petra mystery rites and alchemy schools, and to Egyptian mystery schools. Mohammed imbibed the holy *esphand* before receiving the Koran. The herb, associated with angels and casting out evil spirits, was known to cure fever and malaria.[10]

The Essenes were named after the *asena* plant, which is used by shamanic Bedouins to create "Egyptian Eucharistic Bread of Light," when mixed with ground meteorite and North African acacia. It is said this concoction was also imbibed by Leonardo da Vinci and Michelangelo for inspiration.

The Pot of Nectar of Immortality

Every twelve years, like clockwork, tens of millions of pilgrims and thousands of holy men and women from India meet at the extraordinary Maha Kumbh Mela ("great festival around the pot of nectar of immortality"). A staggering 80 to 100 million people attended the 2013 Kumbh Mela—the "greatest recorded number of human beings assembled with a common purpose," according to the *Guinness Book of Records.*

The bathing event at the holy confluence of three sacred rivers at Allahabad, India, is the central feature of the festival. The Kumbh Mela occurs during an auspicious planetary position believed to transmute the Ganges River into flowing nectar. Millions are purified through holy bathing rituals that wash away karmic consequences from past deeds.

Kumbh Mela celebrates a sacred legend about the retrieval of the *kumbh* (pot) of amrita (nectar of immortality), which lay buried in the depths of the primeval ocean. The gods conspired with the demons to recover the nectar by churning the entire ocean, which they did for a thousand years. Finally Dhanvantari, the divine physician and founder of Ayurvedic medicine, surfaced from the primordial sea, bearing the coveted pot of nectar and the sacred book of Ayurveda.

Both gods and demons tried to seize the pot. For 12 years they wrestled. The gods eventually took possession of the ambrosia and ingested it, while the demons were distracted by the whiles of the most beautiful goddess Mohini.

I have personally led several tour groups to the Kumbh Mela. I can attest that when bathing at that holy time and place, the river is like nectar, the experience is ambrosial, the result is blissful, and the transformation on mind, body, and spirit is dramatic and permanent. For information about how you can experience this blessing, visit our Kumbh Mela website: *www.kumbhmela.net.*

In the next chapter, we will learn traditional yogic practices from antiquity that will help us awaken our third eye.

Opening

the

Third Eye

12

| Third Eye of the Yogis |

He who always contemplates on the hidden Ajna lotus, at once destroys all the karmas of his past life, without any opposition… All the fruits…resulting from the contemplation of the other five lotuses, are obtained through the knowledge of this one Ajna lotus alone.

—Shiva Samhita

The yogis of ancient India developed specific techniques that help individuals open the third eye. In this chapter you will learn a few simple, safe, effective Yoga practices that do not require any previous skill or training. Although it is recommended to learn these methods from a live teacher, you can follow the instructions in this book successfully. Only the practices pertaining to opening the third eye are taught here. To learn more Yoga methods, please read my books *Exploring Meditation, The Power of Auras,* and *The Power of Chakras.*

IMPORTANT: Please consult with your physician before attempting any of the techniques in this book.

Conserving Pranic Energy

Have you ever noticed that your breathing is irregular, broken, and heavy when you are under stress, yet it is regular, smooth, and slow when you are at peace? Breath control is a key for opening the door to your third eye.

When you inhale, prana enters your body and your subtle energy centers (*chakras*). These chakras store and emit energy the way a battery does. The more pranic energy you absorb, the more vitality rushes to every cell. Yogic breathing methods (*pranayama*) collect and conserve pranic energy in your solar plexus (navel *chakra*), your pranic storage battery.

By practicing pranayama, you can collect and conserve pranic energy, tap into the vast power within breath, and use it for self-healing, healing others, even healing the entire planet. The more prana you receive, the more vital you become. Yogic breathing saturates your physical body with pranic energy, preventing disease and augmenting willpower, concentration, self-control, and spiritual awakening.

Deep meditation automatically controls breathing, which becomes slow, regular, and quiet. As mental activity becomes subtle and quiet, physical activity relaxes, and metabolic functions decrease. Energy is conserved. Heart rate slows. Breath rate lessens. In the state of *samadhi* (equanimity of mind and body), your breathing becomes so refined that it is imperceptible. You appear to be holding your breath, but you are not. Your breath is in suspension—neither breathing nor not breathing.

Sun and Moon Breaths

Hatha Yoga uses pranayama to optimize the prana in breath. The Sanskrit word *hatha* means solar and lunar breaths, which refers to two major nadis, *ida* and *pingala*. These run alongside sushumna nadi to the brain. Ida emanates from the left side of *kanda mula* (root bulb) at the base of your spine and ends at the left side of ajna chakra (third eye). Pingala begins at the right side of root bulb and ends at the right side of ajna chakra.

Unless kundalini is somehow awakened, prana normally only flows through ida and pingala. However, pranayama can force prana to withdraw from ida and pingala, open sushumna nadi, flow into it, and travel up the spine, awakening kundalini.

Ida, the left nadi, represents the female, moon, and your subjective nature. Connected to the breath flowing through your left nostril, it operates the parasympathetic area of your autonomic nervous system. The right nadi, pingala, connected to the breath flowing through your right nostril, symbolizes the male, sun, and your objective side, and operates the sympathetic area of your autonomic nervous system.

For optimum health, the energies governed by ida and pingala must be balanced. Too much objectivity, dynamism, and physical activity stress the body beyond its limits. Too much subjectivity, passivity, thought, and internal brooding can cause neurosis, depression, even insanity.

It is significant that kundalini, unifier of all divergent energies, rises up sushumna nadi, the middle path, balanced between ida and pingala, inner and outer, absolute and relative, yin and yang, nirvana and samsara.

Ida and pingala nadis represent time and duality, but sushumna nadi devours time and leads to oneness in timeless eternity. Thus ida and pingala bind you to material life, while sushumna is the path to freedom (*moksha*), full integration, and balance. Through pranayama and meditation, when ida and pingala become balanced and prana enters sushumna, you enter the timeless state.

Please read my books *The Power of Auras* and *The Power of Chakras* for more information about the nadis and kundalini.

> *One should control the sun (pingala) and moon (ida)*
> *because these are the day and night of time; the secret is that*
> *the sushumna (passage of kundalini) is the eater of time.*
>
> —Hatha Yoga Pradipika[1]

Three Styles of Breath

Yogic breathing is complete breathing. What does that mean? Your chest and abdomen are separated by your diaphragm. As you inhale, your ribs move outward and the diaphragm contracts and moves downward.

This movement expands the lungs. Therefore, your diaphragm is the key to absorbing maximum pranic energy during breathing.

Now try an experiment:

1. Sit up straight. Take a big deep breath while moving the diaphragm downward. Do not raise your chest or shoulders. If you are doing this right, your belly will distend as you inhale.

2. This time take a big, deep breath while expanding your chest, but do not let your diaphragm move or allow your belly to distend.

3. Now try to take a breath without moving the diaphragm or chest. Do this by sniffing in through your nose and raising your shoulders.

The first way of breathing, called "deep breathing," "low breathing," or "diaphragmatic breathing," brings significantly more air into the lungs. The second, "chest breathing," brings less. The third, "high breathing," the worst, is the breathing habit of people under stress.

Now try another experiment:

Sit up straight. Put your left hand on your belly and right hand on your upper chest. Take three deep breaths. Notice whether your belly distends as you inhale (as it should) or contracts (which it should not), and whether your shoulders rise while breathing (which they should not).

Although diaphragmatic breathing is the best of these three styles of breathing, it is still not complete breathing. During low breathing, the lower and middle parts of the lungs expand. In chest breathing, the middle and part of the upper lungs expand. In high breathing, only the upper lungs expand. However, in yogic breathing, the lungs expand entirely.

Ordinary exhalation releases just a small pocket of air from the upper part of the lungs. But yogic breathing releases a maximum quantity of stagnant air from the lungs to allow more prana to enter.

Practicing Yogic Breathing

Sit up straight. Put your left hand on your belly and right hand on upper chest. Take five deep breaths. As you inhale, first expand your belly, then your chest, and finally your upper chest, using deep breathing, chest breathing, and high breathing. As you exhale, your belly and chest contract. Do not raise your shoulders at any time.

Now repeat the exercise, only this time, count the seconds as you breathe. Count three seconds as you inhale and six seconds as you exhale. Take five deep breaths like this. Do this exercise for a week.

During the second week, take ten deep breaths and increase the number of seconds to four for inhalation and eight for exhalation. During the third week, take fifteen deep breaths and practice five seconds to inhale and ten to exhale. During the fourth week, six seconds to inhale and twelve to exhale.

By doing this exercise, you will learn to breathe properly, expand your lung capacity, and purify your nadis. Once you have practiced this exercise for a month, discontinue it and begin the next exercise: Yogic alternate breathing.

Alternate Breathing Exercise

Have you ever noticed when one of your nostrils is more open and the other more blocked? You will recognize this if you sleep on your side, because you will breathe mostly through one of your nostrils during sleep. Clear breathing automatically switches from one nostril to the other periodically. If you are in excellent health, this alternation takes place regularly, approximately every 110 minutes.

Your right nostril's breath, connected to pingala nadi, is believed to be hot. So its breath is called "sun breath," which generates body heat, raises metabolism, and accelerates your organs. Your left nostril's breath, said to be cool, is "moon breath," connected to ida nadi. Its energy cools your body, lowers metabolism, and inhibits your organs.

If your breath flows through one nostril for more than two hours, your body is unbalanced—too much heat or cold. If ida is overactive, mental activity wanes and lethargy increases. If pingala is overactive, nervous activity rises and mental disturbances result.

Yogic alternate breathing, *anuloma viloma pranayama,* equalizes the sun and moon breaths. By breathing through one nostril and then the other, you will create equilibrium in body metabolism and purify your nadis. With purification of your nadis, your third eye awakens.

Anuloma Viloma Pranayama

Sit up straight. Close your right nostril with your right thumb. Inhale noiselessly and completely through your left nostril, taking a full yogic breath, for six seconds. Begin that inhalation by expanding your belly, then chest, then upper chest. Then immediately close your left nostril with the middle and ring fingers of your right hand. Now exhale for twelve seconds, fully and noiselessly, through your right nostril, contracting your belly and chest. Without stopping, close your right nostril again with your right thumb and repeat the process. Do this fifteen to twenty times.

Once you have mastered six seconds to inhale and twelve to exhale, gradually increase to seven and fourteen seconds, then eight and sixteen. Do this only after practicing several months.

By practicing this pranayama, your breathing becomes regular and deep, health improves, body becomes lighter, and eyes shine. These changes indicate the nadis are purifying. Health benefits include stress reduction, calmness, slower heart rate, and lower blood pressure. Spiritual benefits include purifying and awakening your third eye.

Having mastered the alternate breathing pranayama, you can practice a more advanced version after a few months:

Practice the same alternate breathing exercise, but add retention of breath. Inhale for four seconds, hold your breath for eight seconds, and exhale for eight seconds. After one month, increase the ratio to five seconds to inhale, ten to retain, and ten to exhale. Gradually increase until you attain eight, sixteen, and twenty-four seconds.

Jala Neti

If the nasal passages or sinuses are obstructed, the natural alternation of breath through ida and pingala is disturbed. *Jala* (water) *neti* (nose) is a yogic method for cleansing these passages with salt water. This purification procedure should be done before you practice pranayama (yogic breathing).

You have a powerful internal purification system that conditions the air before it enters your lungs: your nasal passages. If your nose is blocked, you are forced to breathe through your mouth. This is dangerous, because your mouth and throat do not possess the filtration system of your nose. That is why jala neti is essential.

Practicing jala neti removes impurities, stimulates various nadis, and clears your brain and other organs. Jala neti also stimulates your ajna chakra (third eye).

IMPORTANT: Be sure to consult your physician before practicing this.

Practicing Jala Neti

Take a *neti lota* (pot designed for jala neti) or small teapot with a spout that fits comfortably into your nostril. Mix about a pint of pure boiled or distilled lukewarm water with one teaspoon of pure sea salt, or 1/2 teaspoon of pure sea salt and 1/2 teaspoon of baking soda. Dissolve the solution completely. Fill the neti pot with the solution.

Bend over a sink and tilt your head toward the right. Gently insert the end of the spout into left nostril with a tight fit. Continue to tilt head to the right while raising the neti pot until saline solution flows into your left nostril, up through nasal passages, and out your right nostril. While doing this, open your mouth so you can breathe.

If you tilt your head too much, water will enter your throat instead of the other nostril. If you tilt the pot too much, water will overflow from the pot. Adjust your head and the pot until the water flows correctly.

If jala neti is performed correctly, water will not enter your mouth or throat. However, if it does, just spit it out. Allow the solution to flow through your nostrils ten to twenty seconds. Then remove the neti pot and blow your nose.

Next, repeat the entire process, this time placing the spout of the neti pot in your right nostril, and tilting your head toward the left. After completing jala neti, dry your nostrils by blowing your nose to expel any moisture.

This entire procedure takes less than five minutes. Once a day is enough, unless you have a cold or nasal blockage.

Alternate Method Without Neti Pot

Make the saline solution as previously described. Cup your left palm and pour some solution into your palm. Close your right nostril with right thumb, place your left nostril close to your left palm, and sniff the liquid up into your nose, through your nasal passage, and spit it out. Do the same with the other nostril.

Do not try either of these methods without the salt or with water that is too cold or too hot. With proper temperature and correct amount of salt, there is little or no discomfort. If you suffer from chronic nose-bleeds, do not practice jala neti.

Jala neti is excellent for preventing or healing colds, sinusitis, ailments of eyes, nose, or throat, tonsillitis, cataract, asthma, pneumonia, bronchitis, tuberculosis, and inflammation of the adenoids and mucus membranes. It can remove headaches, insomnia, migraine, epilepsy, tension, depression, and tiredness. It has a subtle effect on various nadis that end in the nasal passages, such as the olfactory bulb and nerves associated with eyes and ears. An added benefit is it purifies, cleanses, and opens your third eye.

Yoga Asanas

The Sanskrit word *asana* means "posture." These are traditional physical postures that bring greater energy to your body, mind, and spirit. The asanas taught here are specifically designed to help you open your ajna chakra (third eye).

The way to perform these postures is to assume the described position and then hold your body steady in that pose for a few seconds. Do these to the best of your ability. Stretch only to the point where you feel your muscles stretching. Then stop and hold the pose for the time allotted. Keep breathing slowly, through your nose, as you hold the posture (unless otherwise specified). Do not ever push further than your body wants; otherwise you might strain or injure yourself.

In addition to the benefits described for each posture, all the postures have the following advantages: improve circulation, flexibility and posture; lubricate joints; increase longevity and alertness; massage internal organs; stimulate nadis; stretch and strengthen muscles; and promote health and well-being.

IMPORTANT: Be sure to consult your physician before practicing any yoga asanas.

Vajrasana (diamond pose)

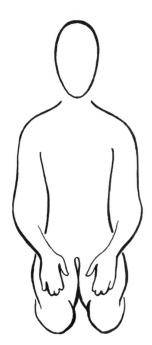

Kneel down. Sit on your heels with spine erect, gazing forward. Hold for ten seconds while breathing slowly. Say the following affirmation aloud (or something similar): "Radiant light and energy flow through my being now."

Take a deep breath. While exhaling, gradually lean forward until your forehead touches the floor, while still sitting on your heels. Stretch out your arms in front with palms down. Hold for five seconds. Then inhale and slowly return to upright position.

Image 12a.
Diamond Pose

Image 12b. *Diamond Pose Bending Forward*

Body Tone-up

Sit in Vajrasana (diamond pose). Massage your entire body, step-by-step, by pressing and releasing. Begin by placing your hands, palms down, on top of your head. Press and release, moving your hands down over your forehead, eyes, cheeks, front of neck, and chest, as though moving your blood toward your heart. Then, starting at the top of your head, press and release gradually. Move your hands over the top of your skull, back of head, back of neck, around the top of your shoulders and toward your heart.

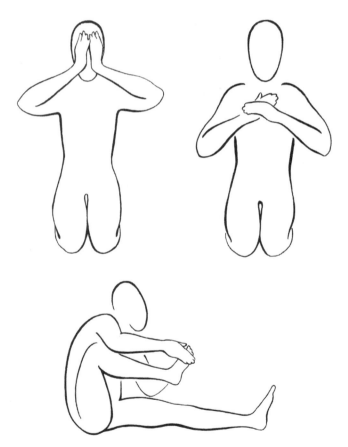

Image 12c. *Body Tone-up*

Place your hands on your lower abdomen. Press and release your abdomen and then move your hands upward, pressing and releasing, proceeding toward your heart. Then begin at the back of your waist, moving upward. Press and release your lower back, upper back, sides, and move gradually toward your heart.

Then squeeze your left hand with right hand, pressing and releasing. Move up the inside of your fingers, palm, wrist, lower arm, inside of elbow, upper arm, left armpit, and left side of chest, toward the heart. Then press and release the outside of your left fingers, back of left hand, wrist, lower arm, elbow, upper arm, shoulder, and chest. Do the same on your right hand and arm, while squeezing and releasing with left hand.

Next, unfold your legs. Grasp the left toes with your hands, right hand on the bottom and left on top. Squeeze your toes, pressing and releasing. Then move your hands up your left foot, ankle, lower leg, knee, thigh, buttock, abdomen, and back. Press and release while moving all the way to your heart. Do the same with your right toes and then press and release gradually, moving toward your heart.

This tone-up activates your acupuncture meridians, increases pranic flow through your nadis, and increases your life-force energy.

Urdhvasarvangasana (shoulder stand)

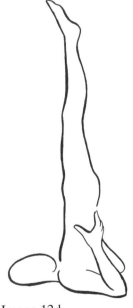

Lie flat on your back with arms at sides. Raise your legs slowly until toes point toward the ceiling. Then curl your spine upward gradually, vertebrae by vertebrae, as you support your back with your hands while elbows and upper arms rest on the floor, until finally your chin presses against your chest. Head, neck, and shoulders should touch the mat while doing this asana. If you cannot lift your trunk all the way up, lift as high as you can. Hold the posture ten seconds while breathing slowly. From this position, go directly into the next asana—plow pose.

Image 12d.

Shoulder Stand

IMPORTANT: High or low blood pressure or hernia patients must consult their doctor before trying such gravity-inversion postures.

Image 12e. *Plow Pose*

Halasana (plow pose)

While still in shoulder stand, bend at your hip joint. Keep your legs straight until toes touch the floor behind your head. Press chin against your chest. Place arms and hands in front of you with palms flat on floor. If you cannot touch your toes to floor, just go as far as you can. Hold this position ten seconds. Then bend your knees and gradually uncurl your spine, vertebrae by vertebrae, from neck to tailbone, while supporting your back with your hands, until buttocks return all the way to floor. Then straighten your legs and lower them slowly. Do this asana slowly and gracefully, without rushing. Do not shake or jerk your body.

IMPORTANT: Heart disease or high blood pressure patients must not attempt this.

Siddhasana (perfect pose or adept's pose)

Sit up and stretch your legs forward. Bend your left leg at knee and place left heel at perineum, the soft portion between anus and scrotum, or between anus and vagina. Then bend your right

Image 12f. *Perfect Pose*

knee and place your right heel against the pubic bone, just above the genitals. Adjust your body so that no pressure is felt on the genitals. Place toes of both feet between thighs and calves. Keep your spine straight and place hands on lap, palms up, right hand over left.

Close your eyes and say the following affirmation aloud: "I AM a perfected being of great power and energy" (or a similar affirmation). Hold the posture ten seconds and breathe normally.

Siddhasana is rated foremost of all 840,000 asanas. The best asana for meditation, concentration, prayer, self-realization, and worship, it awakens the third eye, helps attainment of *siddhis* (perfections or supernormal powers), promotes *Brahmacharya* (celibacy) and mental discipline, raises *prana* through the *nadis*, and awakens *kundalini.*

Padmasana (lotus pose or foot lock)

Sit on a mat with legs stretched forward. Grasp your right foot and place it onto your left thigh, near your hip. Then grasp your left foot and place onto your right thigh, near hip, with heels touching each other as close to navel as possible. Keep your head, neck, and trunk erect.

Place your hands between your heels, right over left, with palms up (to lighten the body). Or place hands on knees, palms up, touching tips of thumbs to tips of index fingers, allowing other fingers to relax (to ground the body). Keep both left and right

Image 12g. *Lotus Pose*

knees and thighs flat on the floor. If you have difficulty getting into lotus pose, then do "half-lotus," placing right heel against perineum and left foot on right thigh. Hold the posture ten seconds while breathing normally.

Image 12h. *Lotus Pose with Bending Forward*

Yoga Mudra (lotus pose with forward bending)

Sit in lotus pose (or half-lotus). Inhale deeply and then exhale while bending forward until your forehead touches the floor. Be sure to bend at your hip joint rather than just your waist. Stretch your arms out in front with palms down. Hold the posture for five seconds. Then inhale while uncurling your spine slowly, until you are once again sitting straight in lotus pose.

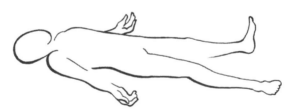

Image 12i. *Corpse Pose*

Savasana (corpse pose)

Lie down on the mat on your back, palms up, legs relaxed, toes pointed outward, eyes closed. Say the following affirmation aloud (or something similar): "I AM divine peace and harmony." Breathe slowly and rhythmically. Become aware of your body. Anywhere you feel a sensation of stress or tension, allow your attention to quietly rest on that place or places. Gradually your muscles will relax and become soft and pliable. Your mind will settle down. Your spirit will become tranquil and content. Stay in this pose for at least five minutes.

Subtle Body Exercises

These exercises belong to a category called *Yogic Suksma Vyayama,* meaning "easy, smallest movement Yoga." These can be practiced by people of all ages and states of health. Though simple and effortless, these practices produce highly beneficial, profound results. The exercises below are just a few of the Subtle Body Exercises found in my book *Exploring Meditation.* These have been chosen to include here, because they can help you cultivate your third eye.

Unless otherwise stated, these are done standing in an erect standing position, with mouth closed, arms at sides, palms open and fingers together, facing toward your thighs. Breathing is always done through the nose, unless otherwise indicated.

Medha-Sakti-Vikasaka (developing intellect)

Close your eyes. Lower your chin to rest on your sternal notch. This position, called *jalandhara bandha* (chin lock), creates an upward pull on your sushumna nadi and chakras. Place all attention on the depression at the nape of your neck. Keep your mouth closed and breathe in and out vigorously like a bellows at least ten times. (See page 119 to learn bellows breathing.)

Buddhi Tatha Dhrti-Sakti-Vikasaka (developing mind and will power)

Keeping eyes wide open, tilt your head back as far as possible. Place full attention on the crown of your head. Breathe in and out vigorously through your nose like a bellows at least ten times.

Smarana-Sakti-Vikasaka (developing memory)

Keeping eyes wide open and head upright, focus your eyes on floor at a spot five feet in front of toes. Place full attention on the point at the middle and top of your head (known as *brahmarandhra* or the *bai-hui* acupuncture point) and breathe in and out vigorously like a bellows at least ten times. This reverses mental fatigue, eliminates nervous exhaustion, and improves memory.

Visualizations to Accompany Pranayama

While practicing the inhalation and retention phases of pranayama, place your attention on the muladhara chakra at the base of your spine. During the exhalation phase, place your attention on bhrumadhya in the middle of your forehead.

After practicing these techniques, say the following affirmation:

"I AM filled with God's peace and grace. I AM a radiant being of beauty, power, and glory. I AM God's philanthropist, God's messenger, and God's ambassador on earth. My power is now used in God's service. Not my will but thy will be done. Thank you God, and SO IT IS."

In the next chapter, you will learn how to use the power of your word, through affirmation and prayer, in order to help you awaken your third eye.

13

| Third Eye Affirmations |

I quite admit the difficulty of believing that in every man there is an Eye of the soul which...is far more precious than ten thousand bodily eyes, for by it alone is truth seen.

—Plato

A powerful way to open your third eye is through a simple method known as "Affirmative Prayer." In 1986 I learned this amazing technique, whereby anyone can pray successfully and get startling results. This field-proven, practical, highly effective method has been tested and verified by millions of people from all backgrounds and religions, who have experienced significant positive results.

The method of Affirmative Prayer is a process of "treating" (healing and transforming) your mind until it realizes the truth of God's eternal good behind the appearance of false limitations. By changing your mind, you can change the outcome of actions previously set into motion by your former mind-set. By setting up conditions in your mind that allow God to work, your transformation occurs. When you accept with full faith that the desired goal is achieved, the power of intention helps you achieve it.

Although prayer and affirmation have become increasingly popular, many people do not know how to pray effectively. But this chapter makes it simple. The affirmations are already prewritten, easy to use, and they get results. Anyone can easily comprehend and apply these powerful methods.

Please study my books *Miracle Prayer* and *Instant Healing* for more information about how to compose and use Affirmative Prayer. To order a CD, downloadable files, or laminated cards of additional healing prayers, please visit *www.divinerevelation.org.*

Instructions for Affirmative Prayer

In this chapter, you will use specifically designed affirmations and prayers to help you open your third eye. These prayers are universal and can be applied to all religious paths and beliefs. You are welcome to change the words to fit your own spiritual affinities. For example, if you want to name the creator Goddess rather than God, please feel free to do so. If you prefer the name Hashem to the name Christ, please change it. If you desire to call upon Krishna, Buddha, or Allah, please do that. Any other name of God/Goddess you favor is acceptable in these prayers.

These prayers and affirmations are to be spoken in a strong, clear voice. Speaking audibly produces the greatest potency. You may repeat these prayers and affirmations as often as you like. If you want to manifest your desire more quickly, then say the prayer several times daily. Just keep repeating the prayer until you get results. Every prayer works. It either produces an instant result, or else it creates an instant healing that moves you toward your desired goal. So keep praying, and never, never, never give up.

Every time you say one of the prayers in this chapter, please speak the prayer as though your higher self were speaking through you. What does this mean? Your higher self has unlimited power and authority. It is the mighty "I AM" presence, your inner divinity—God within you. In India, this divine presence is called *atman.* If you speak with this kind of authority, your words will have potent manifesting power. Therefore, in your mind, just imagine your inner divine nature, your true higher self, is speaking the prayer. When you say the mighty words "I AM," speak those words with a commanding, authoritative voice. Know your inner divinity is at work, manifesting the desired outcome.

Affirmations for Protection

Divine protection is fundamental to all spiritual work. In order to begin opening the third eye and developing your spiritual energy, first affirm that you are protected by the presence of God within you.

Self-Authority Affirmation

Your ajna chakra (third eye) is the "command center." And awakening your third eye is associated with discovering your true self. To this end, the Self-Authority Affirmation can help you to realize who you really are and to decree yourself as the commander of your destiny.

This affirmation can transform your life instantly. With daily use, you can gain tremendous self-empowerment and confidence. This affirmation closes your energy field to lower levels of mind, and opens you to the spiritual world.

With this affirmation, you can heal oversensitivity to "environmental static"—negative vibrations and thought-forms in the mental atmosphere. If you tend to absorb vibrations as a sponge absorbs water, if you take on the ills of negative people in your proximity, or if lower vibrations of heavy environments weaken you, this affirmation can revive and restore your energy.

Use it whenever you feel weak, afraid, powerless, off-kilter, or intimidated. It is recommended before leaving your home, before meditation, and before sleep. Use it whenever you need protection, self-empowerment, and confidence, such as entering a crowded area, before meeting an authority figure, before and after meeting clients, and before tests, interviews, auditions, or meetings. When you feel drained by people or situations, or you feel an invasive or overshadowing energy, use this prayer, inside or outside of meditation.

I AM in control.
I AM one with God.

I AM the only authority in my life.

I AM divinely protected by the light of my being.

I close off my aura and body of light

To the lower astral levels of mind.

And I now open to the spiritual world.

Thank you, God, and SO IT IS.

Divine Armor Prayer

When you are filled and surrounded with the radiance of God's love, nothing and no one can invade or intrude upon your energy field. A divine armor of invincibility protects you in all places and circumstances. Allowing God to be your divine protector is the best way to become invulnerable to lower energies.

I now open my heart to the bright sunlight of God's love.

The radiant light of God now pours into my being.

God's grace now fills and surrounds my energy field

With great beauty, great light, and great wholeness.

I AM now enclosed in a divine bubble

Of beauteous, iridescent, shimmering, radiant light.

This divine bubble is a golden, multicolored sphere

Of white, luminous purple, pink, blue, green, and silver light,

Filling, penetrating, and surrounding my energy field.

This beauteous, invincible sphere of light

Now heals, protects, and seals me.

I know all seeming holes, punctures, and piercings,

Which have torn my energy field, are now sealed

With the pure white cleansing fire of the Holy Spirit

And the beauteous golden light of God's love.

Thank you, God, and SO IT IS.

Affirmations for Inner Light

Your subtle body can be transformed with two basic energies: light and sound. Your third eye is the center of light in your body, and the seed mantra in that chakra, *OM,* is the seed of all sounds in the universe. The following prayers increase your light, and speaking these affirmations positively affects your field through sound. Use them to heal, cleanse, clear, awaken, and lift your energy field to a higher vibrational octave, and connect with Spirit.

Rod of Light

You can invoke spiritual awakening and raise kundalini energy by visualizing God's light within you. The light rod of God is one of the ways God expresses through you.

> *A beauteous light rod of God is now established*
> *In the very center and midline of my body.*
> *This light rod extends from the top of my head*
> *To the bottom of my feet*
> *Right down the center of my body.*
> *This light rod of immeasurable beauty and glory*
> *Blazes with pure God love and God light.*
> *I AM centered, balanced, and protected*
> *By that light rod of God, and I AM at peace.*
> *Thank you, God, and SO IT IS.*

Divine Light Invocation

Invoke the light of God in order to experience awakening of your third eye. As you speak the affirmation, imagine God's light filling and surrounding you with divine power and glory.

> *I AM the divine light.*
> *I AM the light of God.*
> *The light of God fills and surrounds me now.*

The light of God permeates me and floods me with peace.

The light of God infuses my being with radiance.

The light of God lifts me with its power and glory.

I AM glorified by the light of God,

Which vibrates within me and all around me.

Thank you, God, and SO IT IS.

Clearing Your Third Eye Chakra

Affirmations can be a powerful way to heal your third eye and its seat, the pineal gland. These prayers can help you free your third eye from physical congestion, energetic blockages, and emotional limitations.

Unlocking Your Third Eye

This affirmation can help you open your third eye and release whatever is blocking it from opening.

I now invoke the holy presence of God

To lift my vibration and to open my third eye fully.

Anything covering or sealing my third eye,

Whether that be known, unknown, conscious, or unconscious,

Is now lovingly lifted, healed, released, and let go.

My third eye is now safely unlocked, loosed and fully opened.

My third eye now bursts forth in its glory

And floods my entire body with radiance.

My third eye now shines forth with luminous brilliance

And blesses me, and all those around me.

Thank you, God, and SO IT IS.

Cleansing Your Third Eye

This affirmation is for purifying, healing, and opening your third eye. When that inner eye is covered with limiting beliefs, it can atrophy and become calcified. The light that usually enters the third eye gets turned off, and the inner eye is blinded. This affirmation restores sight to a blind third eye.

I now call upon the Holy Spirit and the power of God
To heal, cleanse, and lift all seeming calcification of my third eye,
Whether that be spiritual, emotional, mental, or physical.
Any and all rigidity of my pineal gland is now dissolved
By the light of the Holy Spirit and the presence of God.
I now release, loose, and let go
Of all negative beliefs, habits, and conditions
That have been lodged and embedded in my third eye.
I now allow the third eye to lift, heal, and let go
Of all debris and dross that no longer serve me.
I call upon the Holy Spirit and the power of God
To fill my third eye with pure light, the light of God.
My third eye now opens to this light,
And it is filled with the radiance, beauty, and joy
That God is. I AM now lifted, healed, and blessed
By the power of God and by the soft, luminous glow
Of God's divine love.
Thank you, God, and SO IT IS.

Healing Your Ajna Chakra

This affirmation helps you to release the blockages of ego attachment that are connected to the third eye chakra.

God's grace and wisdom
Radiate and vibrate through me now.
I AM the eye of all-seeing, all-knowing wisdom.
I AM the wisdom that God is.

God's loving presence fills my being with light.

I AM now free from the bondage of ego-attachment.

I release the need to feel elite, singular, or misunderstood.

I let go of psychic powers and spiritual superiority.

I discharge all attachments to the mind.

I loosen all ties to the intellect.

I dissolve all beliefs and habits that have shackled me.

I surrender to God's grace

And I AM God's instrument of light.

Let God's will be done in all matters, now and always.

Thank you God, and SO IT IS.

Awakening Your Third Eye

Affirmations can be a powerful way to awaken and open your third eye. These prayers can help you cultivate the energy of your third eye.

Golden Healing Prayer

The golden healing substance is the elixir of immortal life, which is generated in the pineal gland, seat of the third eye. By invoking this substance, you are lifted into the light of God.

I AM now lovingly filled, lifted, and surrounded

With the golden healing substance of God consciousness.

I AM now filled with God's love, God's light, and God's truth.

God now fills my aura and body of light

With this golden healing substance,

Which closes the doors of both my physical and subtle bodies

To the lower astral levels of mind

And instead attunes me to God Consciousness.

This golden healing substance now heals and lifts me.

It awakens my awareness to God Consciousness within me

And within all of creation, now.

I AM now healed, and I AM more fully attuned

To God within me, and in all creation.

I lovingly awaken to greater awareness

Of God within me and around me, right now.

Thank you, God, and SO IT IS.

Stimulating Soma Production

This affirmation can help you awaken and stimulate the production of soma (nectar of immortality) in your third eye and pineal gland.

Flow, Soma, in a sweet and exhilarating stream.

Flow, Soma, elixir of the Gods, nourisher of humankind.

Flow, Soma, in currents of sweet honey from the moon.

Flow, Soma, in a flood of copious nectar.

Flow, Soma, in liquid light; flow throughout my body.

Flow, Soma, and make of my body a temple of God.

Flow, Soma, in an excellent stream of purity and wholeness.

Flow, Soma, and allow the floodgates to open and pour into my being.

Flow, Soma, and fill me with radiance, light, and glory.

Flow, Soma, and engulf me in God's immortal substance.

I surrender to God, and I AM at peace.

Thank you, God, and SO IT IS.

Absorption in Nirvana

The third eye sub-center of *nirvana chakra* is where kundalini is absorbed into absolute bliss consciousness. This affirmation asserts this experience of divine union and ultimate merging with God. Close your eyes and imagine that the subtle, yet powerful kundalini is slowly rising up your spine, piercing every chakra and absorbing each of the elements within the chakras. Finally, see kundalini arriving at nirvana chakra at the top of the skull. Then say the following affirmation aloud:

I AM absorbed in kundalini's all-consuming power.

I surrender to the will of God.

My being expands to touch the infinite

As my false ego disappears into wholeness.

I AM filled with the bliss of nirvana.

I now realize my true nature of being,

And I AM at peace.

Thank you God, and SO IT IS.

Third Eye Invocation

In this powerful invocation, you call upon divine beings of light and receive help in opening your third eye and experiencing spiritual awakening. Invoking divine beings in this way produces a profound and potent effect.

I let go and let God fill my third eye

With the brilliance of God's light.

I call upon all the divine beings of light

Who come in the name of God

To now fill my third eye with radiant blessings.

I call forth the beautiful Holy Spirit,

The Spirit of truth and wholeness,

To shine forth your beautiful, glowing white fire

To now fill and purify my third eye with blazing white light.

I call forth radiant Saint Germain

To now fill my third eye with your violet consuming flame

To cleanse, heal, and purify my third eye,

And to lift its vibration to the highest spiritual vibration

That I can comfortably enjoy at this time.

I call forth brilliant Jesus the Christ

To now fill my third eye with your dazzling golden light

Of the Christ consciousness

And to blaze that scintillating golden light

Through every atom of my body

And subtle bodies on all levels:

Spiritual, mental, emotional, physical, and material.

I call forth Kwan Yin and Mother Mary

To shine a beautiful, sparkling pink light

To now infuse and permeate my third eye

With divine radiance, softness, gentleness,

Peace, love, compassion, strength and wisdom.

I call upon Lord Buddha

To now vibrate the light of wisdom upon my third eye,

To allow me to attain spiritual enlightenment

And freedom from the wheel of samsara.

I invoke Mahamuni Babaji, the immortal sage,

To now blaze forth with glory

Your resplendent clear light of enlightenment

To lift, heal, cleanse, and transform my third eye.

I ask Babaji to now penetrate and suffuse my third eye

With the pure, clear light of enlightenment,

Opening me to realize the supreme truth,

Allowing my spiritual eye to see the ultimate reality

And lifting my vibration to the highest state of consciousness

That I can comfortably enjoy at this time.

I call forth all the divine beings of light

Who come in the name of God,

To now lift me into a new consciousness,

Where I now see the truth, know the truth, and live the truth.

Thank you, God, and SO IT IS.

Spiritual Mind Treatment

Prayer Treatments use a nine-step process that helps you convince yourself of the truth behind false appearances. This method is a very effective way to change your life by changing your mental state.

Treatment for Opening Your Third Eye

This is a treatment for myself,___(full name)___, for the perfect healing, awakening, and opening of my third eye, or better, now.

I now know and recognize that there is one power and one presence at work in the universe and in my life—God the good, omnipotent. God is the source of my good, the light of my life, the truth of my being. God is the one divine guide, the one divine intelligence, the one perfection of being. God is perfection everywhere now. God is perfection here now. God is the divine light within, the source of all wisdom, intuition, and supersensory perception. God is the all-seeing eye of truth and divine wisdom.

I AM now merged with and one with God, in a perfect seamless wholeness. God and I are one. We are one in Spirit. The in-house counselor that is God is within me. God is the lighthouse of my life, the wayshower, the one true guide along my pathway. God's divine light, wisdom, intuition, and supersensory perception is within me, at the very center of my being. I AM the all-seeing eye of truth and divine wisdom.

I therefore claim for myself,___(full name)___, that my third eye now awakens and opens as widely as I can comfortably enjoy at this time.

I now see, know, and accept that my third eye is open. I release, dissolve, loosen, and let go of all blockages that have kept my third eye closed. I let go of all tendencies to fear seeing the truth. I dissolve all beliefs that I must shut down supernormal powers because people would think I am not "normal." I release any ideas that I do not deserve to open my third eye. I dissolve all feelings of unworthiness. I let go of all ego-attachment, inferiority, and superiority.

I now welcome into my mind, heart, and spirit new beliefs that now serve me. I now accept thoughts that my third eye is now cleansed, healed, and purified. I accept that I am willing to see and know the truth. I now welcome my spiritual gifts and supersensory perception. I deserve to experience who I really am. I am worthy to open my third eye. I now accept the truth about myself as a divine being of light.

I now fully accept in consciousness that my third eye now awakens and opens as widely as I can comfortably enjoy at this time. I now release this prayer into the Spiritual Law, knowing that it does manifest right now, under God's grace, in perfect ways. Thank you, God, and SO IT IS.

For hundreds of more prayers and affirmations, please read my books *Miracle Prayer* and *Instant Healing.* In the next chapter, you will learn about breaking through barriers that have blocked your third eye and your intuitive gifts.

14

| Third Eye Meditations |

I want to know God's thoughts.
All the rest are details.

—Albert Einstein

In the session known as the "Divine Revelation® Breakthrough," you are guided into a deep meditation and receive direct contact with Spirit within you. During this session, remarkable experiences take place. Profound healing and lifting occurs. The vibratory level of your mind and body rises to a higher level. Energy, love, power, and light pour into your being. Inspiration flows.

Most people taking the Divine Revelation Breakthrough desire to develop their intuition. They may wish to open their third eye and develop their innate clairvoyance, clairaudience, and clairsentience. Some seek to directly communicate with their higher self, with God within, or with a guiding angel or ascended master, in whatever form they believe. They are often surprised at how easy it is to receive this blessing.

Communication with Spirit comes in three basic ways: 1) receiving inner divine visions, 2) hearing inner divine messages, 3) receiving inner divine feelings. For instance, you may see an angel or dazzling, brilliant light. You may hear words of comfort or wisdom with your inner ear. You might receive ecstatic feelings or promptings within. These are ways that Spirit communicates with your human self.

You can learn how to read these inner experiences and how to hear the divine voice. You can also learn to speak aloud while receiving the messages coming from within. This is called "speaking-through" messages from Spirit.

Comforting messages are accompanied by feelings of joy, happiness, peace, serenity, and ecstatic unity. Students are amazed at how inspiring and freeing this divine contact can be. They are astounded by the profundity of their thoughts and inspirations when they attune to Spirit.

In 1963, when my mentor Dr. Peter Victor Meyer first began to facilitate Breakthrough Sessions, a dense cloud of astral dust enveloped the earth with negation and pessimism. Because of the negativity present at that time, it took 18 weeks of classes before students were ready for their Breakthrough.

Today, much of this negative dross has been cleared as a result of so many people meditating, praying, healing, and clearing the atmosphere surrounding the earth. In 1963, there was "static on the line" preventing clear reception from Spirit. Today, students of every background can receive their Breakthrough within just a few minutes.

I personally possessed no special abilities in the field of intuition, clairvoyance, or clairaudience before I learned Divine Revelation, yet I learned to do it effectively. If I can learn it, then you can, too.

Goals of The Breakthrough Session

The Divine Revelation Breakthrough session includes a meditative experience in which you achieve the following four basic goals:

1. Inner Divine Contact

The first goal of your Breakthrough Session is to directly experience God's loving presence—a feeling of being at home in the heart of God. When I first learned Divine Revelation meditation, I found great comfort and solace, and I knew I would never be alone again.

When you are in contact with divine Spirit, you will receive ecstatic feelings and blessings, such as: unconditional love, peace, tranquility, serenity, comfort, protection, security, confidence, assuredness, joy, happiness, ecstasy, streams of divine light, waves of divine love, inner strength, power, energy, contentment, fulfillment, grace, blessings, glory, oneness, and wholeness.

The most important of these feelings are oneness and wholeness. Such feelings help you to identify that you are truly sitting in the lap of divine love.

2. Inner Vibrational Name

The second goal is to receive and verify at least one inner vibrational "name," which identifies an aspect of your higher self or a divine teacher within. Inner names are sound vibrations of various aspects of the divine. These might be deities, ascended masters, angels, archangels, or other divine beings. These names are important signposts of contact with true Spirit rather than with your own mind or with entities from the astral world. Once you identify these true inner spiritual names, you will know whom you are contacting and receiving messages from.

3. Inner Vibrational Signal

The third goal is to receive and verify an inner vibrational "signal" corresponding to each inner name. Signals are subtle feelings, visions, sounds, body movements, fragrances, or tastes. By receiving a specific signal corresponding to each inner name, you can later identify each name by that signal. Thus, each signal is like an identity badge to help you test that a particular divine being is present.

Have you ever felt touched by Spirit? Perhaps you visited an art museum and a particular painting stirred your soul. Maybe at a concert you were particularly moved by a piece of music. Or you were helping a person in need or volunteering at a hospice. Or a beautiful sunset, inspiring movie, or church service moved you. At the peak point of such a stirring experience, you felt goose bumps, tingling, or an energy rush. Your hair stood on end. Such a feeling is one of your divine vibrational signals. Each signal will appear in one of the following six ways:

Vision: Clairvoyance

You may see a light of a particular color in a specific place, in your inner vision, body, or an energy center. The light might be white, gold, blue, violet, or another beautiful color. Or your signal might be a beautiful symbol, such as a rose, a tree, flower, geometric shape, Star of David, cross, sunrise, mountain, sacred place, or another pleasant vision. You might see a face or figure of a deity, saint, or beautiful, shimmering angel. Perhaps you will see Jesus, Buddha, Krishna, or another divine being.

Sound: Clairaudience

You might hear a pleasant sound in your mind. Perhaps you hear a tone, bells, chimes, harps, celestial flutes, violins, or another musical instrument, celestial symphonies, music of the spheres, angelic choirs, chanting, falling rain, rustling leaves, rushing water, wind, ocean waves, the sound of the universe, a hum or OM, or another sound.

Taste: Clairgustance

Gustatory signals are subtle flavors tasted in your mouth or throat. It tastes as if you have eaten something delicious, although you have eaten nothing. This is called *clairgustance*. You might taste a sweet, pleasant flavor. It may be familiar, such as coconut, banana, carrot, apricot, orange, peach, pear, raspberry, pineapple, tangerine, grape, cashew, almond, rosewater, milk, or another pleasant, ambrosial taste. Or it may be a completely unfamiliar and unrecognizable yet luscious flavor.

Fragrance: Clairscent

Olfactory signals are celestial fragrances that you "smell" with your inner senses. This is called *clairscent*. As you detect these wafts of sweet smells, you might look for someone wearing perfume nearby, but no one is. Instead your inner sensing is picking up a heavenly aroma. You might sense a lovely fragrance of rose, jasmine, lilac, gardenia, lavender, honeysuckle, pine, eucalyptus, sandalwood, orange, lemon, vanilla, peach, cinnamon, nutmeg, or other charming scent. It might be a recognizable or unrecognizable pleasant aroma.

Feeling: Clairsentience

A kinesthetic signal is a subtle feeling in your body. This is called *clairsentience*. You might receive an unusual, pleasant sensation in a particular part of your body or all over your body. Perhaps you sense energy moving in your body. You might feel heat, warmth, or a cool breeze. An extremity, such as an arm, leg, or toe, might tingle or pulsate. Maybe a rush of energy or tickling sensation travels up your spine. Energy or electricity might course through your body. You may feel something surrounding, cloaking, or protecting you. Or you might sense something literally touch your body. Perhaps your body seems to change size or shape. It may appear to expand or contract, become numb, or disappear. You might lose body sensation altogether. The body boundaries could dissolve. You might experience tears of joy. You may get strange sensations, such as spiraling or another geometric shape. Or your signal might be another bizarre experience that is difficult to describe.

Body Movement: Psychokinesis

When you get a physical movement signal, a body part or your whole body moves, rocks, or shakes. This is nothing to fear. It is a sign that God is present. Perhaps your head rocks or swivels back and forth. Your head or whole body might make circular movements. Your head may move or tilt in a particular direction, or bob or rock. Your entire torso might rock or move. Your eyelashes might flutter. Perhaps your head tilts backward or tips to one side. Maybe your eyes roll back in their sockets. An extremity might lift, rock, or move. Perhaps you appear to dance. You may smile or make another facial expression. Certain muscles might move or twitch. Your whole body might rock, shake, or quake. Remember the Shakers and Quakers? There is a reason they were given those names.

4. "Speaking-Through" Messages

The fourth goal of the Breakthrough session is to receive and verify a message from Spirit and speak the message that you receive audibly.

This message is a thought, a vision, or a feeling, which you speak aloud as you receive it within your mind or heart.

How You Can Have A Breakthrough

This book can offer some steps to help you have your own Breakthrough. Since the entire Divine Revelation process is based upon the principle, "Ask, and it shall be given you," your Breakthrough can occur by simply asking for the experience!

By getting quiet, comfortable, going into deep meditation, and then asking Spirit, it is possible for you to experience a breakthrough. Begin your meditation with an opening prayer. Then, as you go deeper, you will pass through various levels of consciousness, step-by-step. First, notice the environment. After that, become aware of your body, your conscious mind, and subconscious mind. When you are ready, walk through the façade barrier—the veil that has separated you from the divine presence. Then experience Spirit within as your own higher self.

This state is not a trance or leaving the body. It is a deep meditation and relaxation in which you are fully alert and awake. Walking through the door to your higher self may be very inspiring or very ordinary. You might feel as though you were in deep meditation or not deep at all. It depends upon your make-up and past experiences.

Once you are in meditation, you can call upon aspects of God and inner teachers, such as Holy Spirit, Jesus, Jehovah, Krishna, Buddha, Babaji, St. Germain, etc., to help you get inner signals and receive messages from Spirit. If you receive a vibrational signal, ask for the name. If you get the name, ask for the signal. Once you get the name and signal, ask for the message. *"Ask, and it shall be given you."*

The important thing is to let go and allow the process to happen. If you fight the process or try too hard, then it might take longer to have your breakthrough. You can deal with any resistances to breaking through by using healing prayers in my books *Divine Revelation, How to Hear the Voice of God,* and *Instant Healing.* These prayers help you let go so you can break through more easily. You can also take deep breaths or sink into your heart any time you feel stuck during the process.

You might be thinking, *I know that I won't be able to relax. It will be difficult for me.* Or, *I know that I will try too hard. I never have spiritual experiences. I will just sit there like a log and nothing will happen.*

If you have such doubts, then answer this question: Even with these doubts in your mind, are you still able to think a thought? Anyone who can think can receive divine messages. If you can think a thought, then you can receive a thought from Spirit. It is simply that easy.

It is natural to have doubts about something you have never done before. But be assured that you can have a Breakthrough experience. It just takes a willingness to learn. It may take longer for one person to break through than another. But I have never encountered a willing person who was unable to break through.

During the breakthrough, most people have feelings of joy, bliss, happiness, relief, inner peace, deep relaxation, fulfillment, wholeness, inner strength, self-authority, and self-confidence. It is usually a moving, emotional experience as you come home to God, who welcomes you with open arms.

You may receive a message of unconditional love and acceptance that speaks personally to you. This message might be a visual experience that tells a story. Then you can describe this vision out loud. Or it may come as thoughts or words in your mind, which you can speak audibly as you receive. Or you may receive an inner feeling or emotional experience, which you can describe.

Everyone who has taken the Divine Revelation course has succeeded in receiving the four goals of the Breakthrough Session. To help with your Breakthrough, you can use the meditation on page 217 of this book. And I recommend that you read and study my books *Divine Revelation* and *How to Hear the Voice of God.* I also suggest that you subscribe to my mailing list at *www.drsusan.org*, where you will be notified about classes. Contact one of the qualified teachers at *www.divinerevelation.org/Teachers.html*. You can get a downloadable Divine Revelation Breakthrough Meditation audio MP3, offered at *www.spiritualityproducts.com/secure/Order.html*. That meditation is also available with the hard copy book *How to Hear the Voice of God*, which you can order at *www.amazon.com*.

Developing ESP

The best way to develop ESP is to practice and use it regularly. Just like any other skill, you can master ESP skills through consistent dedication. Here are some exercises to help you develop confidence in your ability to open to Spirit and receive clear messages from the inner voice. These should all be done while in a meditative state. Be sure to keep taking deep breaths to stay connected to Spirit while doing these practices. Before practicing, study the Ten Tests of Spiritual Discernment in Chapter 16, presented in more detail in my books *Divine Revelation* and *How to Hear the Voice of God*.

Speaking Through

During meditation, when you receive a divine intuitive message, speak that message audibly. How do you know what to say? If you are getting a vision, describe it. For example, say, "I see an egg cracking open with a chick emerging." If you are getting a feeling, describe it. Say, "Peace," or "Love," or "My body is disappearing," or whatever you are feeling. If you are getting words, say the first thing that pops into your mind, *without editing*. At first you might hear just one word. Say that word aloud. Then two words, then a whole sentence may come. This is an incredibly powerful way to develop your ESP abilities and higher consciousness.

Singing Through

Ask divine Spirit to sing through you. You may not think you can sing, but if you let Spirit do the singing through your throat, you might be surprised. Just take a big deep breath, open your mouth, and let the tones come out. At first, the tones might come just one note at a time. Trust, and let it happen.

Dancing Through

Let divine Spirit dance through you. Put on music that you love. Stand up and let your body be an instrument of Spirit. No one is watching, so let it all hang out. You might become a ballerina or a banshee. No matter what, allow it to happen, as long as you stay connected to Spirit.

Writing Through

Allow divine Spirit to write through your hands. You can use a pencil, a pen, or a computer. Stay in contact with Spirit and write from your soul. Beautiful poetic expressions of great genius can come from ordinary people while connected to Spirit.

Drawing, Painting, or Sculpting Through

Whether or not you have any artistic ability, take out some paper and begin to draw or paint from Spirit. Or get some clay and let Spirit play. Allow your higher self to be the artist. Get your mind out of the way, along with all preconceived notions about art. Stay connected to the divine artist in your heart.

Playing Music Through

If you know how to play an instrument, let the inner musician play through you. If not, just use a drum, a rattle, a xylophone, or other percussion instrument. Improvisational divine music can come when you allow your hands to be led by Spirit. Divinely inspired music lifts your vibration and soothes your soul.

Spiritual Psychokinesis

Psycho means mind, *kinesis* means movement. Psychokinesis is a way to move objects by spiritual means. Learn to use muscle testing, pendulum, dowsing rod, L-rods, bobber, planchette, or a table to receive divine messages. Instructions are in my book *The Power of Auras*. Once you learn the basics, you can let Spirit answer your questions with these devices. Be sure to study the Ten Tests in Chapter 16 and use them diligently.

Mirror Gazing

At night, with all the lights out, sit in a chair about three feet in front of a mirror. Close your eyes and take some deep breaths while you place attention on each part of your body, separately and progressively, from the soles of your feet to the top of your head.

Then open your eyes and stare at your forehead with steady gaze, without focusing sharply. Let your eyes relax into soft focus, as if looking at a picture with embedded 3D objects in it. Relax your eyes and look beyond your image, as if you were looking at something far away. As you gaze, your mirror image might change, disappear, or black out. Other faces may superimpose over it. You might see fog-like images moving around your body. You may see lights or an aura. Practice this exercise for five to ten minutes. It can help you develop clairvoyant sight.

Psychometry

Ask for an object that someone is wearing, such as a watch. Hold it in your non-dominant hand while in a meditative state. Ask your higher self to give you impressions, feelings, or a message about the person who wears this object. This will help you develop clairvoyance, clairaudience, and clairsentience.

Why Follow Inner Guidance?

You might think it is cool to get inner guidance and be led by Spirit every day. The only drawback to asking questions of Spirit is—you will get the answer! If you do not want to hear the answer, this can be a problem. Following inner guidance means listening to the voice of Spirit and following the wisdom it gives you.

It is easy to communicate with Spirit. We learned how to do that by asking for it. It is also easy to figure out whether the message is clear. You can learn that in Chapter 16, and in my books *Divine Revelation* and *How to Hear the Voice of God*. The most difficult part is trusting what you get and then actually following the guidance!

This is challenging because your higher self wants you to evolve as quickly as possible. For that to happen, you have to step out of your comfort zone and stretch the edge of your envelope. If you are willing, your higher self will give you assignments that stretch you to the max.

Following inner guidance is like jumping off a cliff. You have to learn how to fly really quickly—or else trust God will catch you. This can be the greatest adventure of your life, or the most difficult. But with trust in Spirit and a little chutzpah, your life can be one of great power, energy, magnificence, and glory. You just need the faith to follow your inner guidance, with Spirit as your in-house counselor.

In the next chapter, we will learn how to open your third eye through meditation, and how to receive the Breakthrough Experience.

15

| The Breakthrough Experience |

*Beholding beauty with the eye of the mind, he
will be enabled to bring forth, not images of
beauty, but realities (for he has hold not of an
image but of a reality), and bringing forth and
nourishing true virtue to become the friend of
God and be immortal, if mortal man may.*

—Plato

Practicing meditation is the most profound way to open your third eye, and thereby transform your life in powerful, positive ways. In this chapter you will learn meditations that can cleanse, heal, awaken, and open your third eye. These are guided deep meditations, practiced by following the instructions here.

Please read these meditations aloud very slowly, gently, and softly while you record them onto your computer to create mp3 files, or onto another recording device. You can burn CDs or play the mp3 files on your computer, handheld device, or other apparatus. In this way, your own voice will guide you into meditation.

You can meditate sitting in a chair, couch, bed, or any other comfortable place. The most important instructions for meditation are:

1. Be comfortable.

2. Do not strain or exert any effort.

3. Let go and do nothing except follow the instructions.

Other details about meditation can be found in my books *Exploring Meditation, How to Hear the Voice of God*, and *Divine Revelation*.

Pillar of Light Visualization

Visualization can help you create a powerful sphere of divine protection. Many people imagine a sphere, bubble, or column of light surrounding and protecting them. Here is a way to visualize divine protection, increase energy and charisma, and feel lighter and lifted:

Close your eyes and imagine a beauteous sphere of protective divine light of whatever color (white, gold, violet, pink, or another color) above your head. Then see a ray of that light streaming down through the midline of your body, all the way from the top of your head to the tips of your toes. Visualize this light ray vibrating, radiating, and expanding outward from your energy centers, until it engulfs your entire energy field.

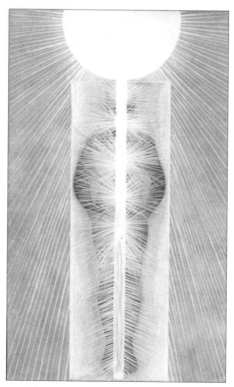

Image 15a. *Pillar of Light Visualization*

This beauteous light fills your energy field with divine love, invincibility, joy, and fulfillment. Feel this divine light vibrating and radiating within and around you. This light now expands beyond the boundaries of your energy field to create a pillar of divine light, which brings you strength, power, and energy. Say audibly, "I AM divinely protected by the light of my being."

Qigong Third Eye Meditation

Lie on your back comfortably with your head on a pillow. Put your arms and hands at your sides with your palms facing up. Place your legs in a natural position, with your feet as wide as your shoulders. Allow your feet to relax.

Look up at the ceiling. Then let your eyes look at your third eye in your forehead, at the point between your eyebrows, without straining. Next look inward, into the center of your head, in the area of the pineal gland. Then look at the point at the back of your head. Finally, look at your third eye in your forehead again and fix your eyes there.

Close your eyes, while your eyes continue to look at the area of your third eye. Close your mouth and jaw. Your upper and lower teeth should be together. Place your tongue on your upper palate with tip of the tongue touching inside the upper teeth. Breathe in and out deeply into your belly, slowly and smoothly.

Then, as you breathe in, imagine all the genuine qi from the heavens entering your third eye and moving into the center of your head. Then, imagine the qi from the center of your head radiating out through your third eye to the far distance—to the end of the universe. Breathe in and out twenty times. Then change to natural breathing while seeing all the beautiful scenery in the sky.

When you practice this meditation, your body may tend to move or shake. You may receive information from the universe. Also, you may see something beautiful in the sky. If this happens, do not be alarmed. This is completely natural. This meditation can help you open your third eye. It can calm your mind, relax your body, and release fatigue.[1]

Trataka Meditation

Trataka or Tratakum meditation, a practice from India that involves gazing at an object, is a traditional way to increase concentration and to open your third eye. When you gaze at the object with eyes open, that is called *Trataka*. When you close your eyes and see the object in your mind's eye, it is *Saguna Dhyana* (meditation with form). When you move beyond the form, the object will disappear and you will enter *Nirguna Dhyana* (abstract meditation). Through this practice, you can attain siddhis and spiritual powers.

Begin by gazing at the object for two minutes. Then increase the period very gradually. Be patient, because mastering Trataka requires steady practice. If your mind is one-pointedly focused on the object, then you are succeeding. If your mind is wandering, then continue your practice until your mind settles down.

If you find it impossible to fix your gaze steadily with eyes open, despite several attempts, just close your eyes and gaze at a spot between your two eyebrows. Do not tax your eyes by overdoing Trataka. Any time you feel tired, close your eyes and continue to imagine the object in your mind's eye.

Trataka improves eyesight, concentration, willpower, steady mind, clairvoyance, mind-reading, and spiritual healing, and helps you develop psychic powers. It can help you overcome mind-wandering, distraction, ADD, and mental problems. It can stimulate the frontal lobes of your brain and open your third eye.

Candle Gazing

One of the objects used in Trataka meditation is a candle. A beeswax or soy wax candle is nontoxic and burns longer than paraffin. Better yet, make a ghee lamp by twisting real cotton into a wick shape, dipping it in ghee (clarified butter), placing it into a small receptacle of ghee, and lighting it.

How to Practice

Wear comfortable, loose clothing. Sit comfortably in a quiet, darkened room with a comfortable temperature. Place a nontoxic, lit candle about three to four feet away, with the flame at the height of your eyes.

Take at least three deep breaths into your belly. Inhale and exhale through your nose. Then breathe normally and naturally, and let the breath go. Focus on the flame and view the corona of light around the flame for one minute. If thoughts come, do not try to resist them, push them away, or hang onto them. Just imagine them burnt in the flame.

Notice the area just under the hottest tip of the flame at the dark spot, where light and dark coexist. Focus on that spot with fixed concentration for one more minute, while you attempt to refrain from blinking.

See the flame and its light without trying to see hallucinations or movies in the flame. Imagine the flame entering your body through your eyes, illuminating your inner being.

Any time your eyes begin to water, close your eyes, see the afterimage in your third eye area, and hold it steady for as long as possible. At first it will be an afterimage, but later it will exist only in your mind's eye.

After the image fades, keep your eyes closed, rub the palms of your hands together vigorously to warm your hands, and then place your palms over your eyes, without touching your eyeballs. Breathe deeply for a few moments.

Horizon Gazing

Practice Trataka meditation by fixing your eyes at a point on the horizon (indoors or outdoors), and open your eyes as wide as possible. Take long, deep breaths while you focus on your breath and prana flowing into your eyes. Continue to gaze without blinking for two minutes. Then take a deep breath, close your eyes, and focus on the flow of pranic energy for another 30 seconds. This exercise increases pranic energy in your eyes and your third eye.

Star Gazing

Lie down outside on a mat at night, and gaze at a bright star or the full moon. Breathe deeply into your belly as you continue to gaze at that point, without blinking, for two minutes. Then take a deep breath, close your eyes, and focus on the flow of pranic energy for another 30 seconds.

Open your eyes again and continue to gaze at that star or moon. After awhile, you might see various colors, or one particular color. At times, all other surrounding stars will disappear from view. You may see a great mass of light all around you. Perhaps you will see two or three moons, or the moon might disappear altogether.

Gazing at a Divine Being

Pictures of saints and divine beings can be used as objects of Trataka meditation. By gazing at a saintly person or a deity, you can begin to imbibe his or her holy qualities. I recommend experimenting with different pictures, as they can help you absorb different traits. Pick a photo or picture with light in the eyes of the divine being. A photo with a neutral, direct stare can heal you and connect you with your higher self. By practicing this meditation, you can attain higher consciousness through the grace of that guru or deity.

How to Practice

In a dark room with a comfortable temperature, place the photo of a saint or deity three to six feet away, at the level of your eyes. Put one or two candles in front of the picture so you can see it clearly.

Sit comfortably. Open your eyes wide without straining, and gaze into the eyes of the divine being in the picture. Stare continuously with little to no blinking. Still your body and mind, and your breathing will become quieter, lighter, and more refined. As you gaze into the eyes of the picture, notice the light and pranic energy emanating from them. Imagine that you travel mentally through the picture to the source of the light.

Gaze at the picture for two minutes, while keeping your focus on the light in the eyes. Any time your eyes start to water, close your eyes and envision that face and those eyes in your third eye.

Here are other Trataka meditations that you might practice:

Black Dot: Place a black dot on a light-colored wall, or draw a black mark on a piece of white paper, and hang it on the wall.

OM: Place the Sanskrit letter *OM:* ॐ on a piece of paper and hang it up on the wall.

Sky: Close to sunrise or sunset, lie down on a mat ouside, and choose a point in the open sky. Gaze at it steadily. From this practice, you will receive new inspirations.

Mirror: Sit in front of a mirror and gaze at the pupil of one of your eyes.

Brow Center (Bru Madhya): Gaze at the space between your two eyebrows.

Nose or Toes: Gaze at the tip of your nose or your toes while walking rather than being distracted by sights and sounds around you.

Ajna Chakra: With eyes closed, gaze at the center of your head, in the area of the pineal gland.

Sun: With the help of a yogic master, gaze at the sun at sunrise and sunset. Do not attempt this on your own without expert guidance, as it can seriously damage your eyes.

Deep Meditation to Open Your Third Eye

The Divine Revelation® Meditation practice is a powerful way to open your third eye and develop clairvoyant, clairaudient, and clairsentient abilities. In Chapter 14, you learned about the Divine Revelation Breakthrough. Here you will practice a meditation to help you achieve that Breakthrough Experience.

One way to get your Breakthrough is to take a workshop or session from a qualified teacher. However, you can identify your own inner names and signals and receive inner messages with a simple meditation: Just sit down, close your eyes, take a few deep breaths, get quiet, comfortable, still, balanced, and centered, and then ASK.

ASKING is the key. In fact, the entire Divine Revelation methodology is based upon a single principle: "Ask, and it shall be given you."[2] By asking, you receive the signal. By asking, you receive the inner name, the healing, the blessing, the answer to your questions. Just ASK.

What follows are meditation instructions to help you receive inner divine names, signals, and messages. Before attempting this, however, please study the remainder of this book and learn how to use the Ten Tests of Spiritual Discernment in Chapter 16, Chapters 8 and 9 of my book *How to Hear the Voice of God,* and Chapters 12 and 13 of my book *Divine Revelation.*

1. Begin With a Prayer.

Speak aloud a prayer, such as:

> *I recognize that there is one power and presence in the universe, God the good, omnipotent. I am one with this power and presence of God. Therefore I claim my perfect divine signal and divine message to come to me now with divine order and timing. I call upon* (name of a divine being) *to give me a divine signal and message. I release any seeming blockages that have prevented me from receiving my perfect divine signal and message now. I release and let go of all ideas that I am separate from God or that God is out of reach. I accept and welcome with open arms my perfect divine contact with God now. Thank you, God, and SO IT IS.*

In the blank space above, place the name of a divine being or deity that you like and that you feel comfortable with. The "inner name" is explained on page 201 of this book.

2. Take a Few Deep Breaths.

Take breaths into your body very deeply. Fill your whole body with breath. Deep breathing is essential to help you get your signal and message. Inhale and exhale slowly until you feel relaxed, centered, and balanced.

With every deep breath, imagine, as you exhale, that you are sinking out of your head and into your heart. Take several deep breaths like this until you feel relaxed. Then resume your normal breathing.

3. Relax Your Body.

Say out loud, *"I now let go of the outer environment and go deeper to the physical level."* Become aware of your body. Notice any tension, pain, or other sensations, and quietly place your attention there until you feel the sensations dissipate. If you like, you can imagine relaxing each part of your body separately and progressively, starting at your toes and feet and going up to your scalp. Take more deep breaths. Sink out of your head and into your heart as you exhale and go deeper.

4. Relax Your Conscious Mind.

Say out loud, *"I now relax and become aware of my conscious mind."* Bring your attention to your mind. Imagine that your mind is quiet and still, like a still pond without a ripple, or like a candle flame that does not waver. Take more deep breaths and go deeper. Sink out of your head and into your heart as you let go of each deep breath.

5. Relax Your Subconscious Mind.

Say out loud, *"I now relax to the level of my subconscious mind."* Become aware of your subconscious mind. Enter a deep state of relaxation as you connect with deeper levels of mind, which are below surface thoughts and emotions. Take more deep breaths and relax more deeply. Sink out of your head and into your heart as you let go of each breath, until you feel connected with Spirit.

6. Connect With Spirit.

Surrender to the loving presence of God, in whatever form you believe God to be, in a state of oneness and wholeness, deeply relaxed, expanded, filled with perfect peace and bliss. If you are not in that state, then continue deep breathing, or use the appropriate healing prayers in Chapter 7 of *How to Hear the Voice of God,* or Chapter 10 of *Divine Revelation.*

7. Ask for Your Signal.

Say out loud: *"I call upon* (name of a divine being) *to give me your divine signal now. Feed it stronger, feed it stronger, feed it stronger."*

8. Let Go and Let God.

Take another deep breath. Do nothing and less than nothing. Do not look for anything or try to get a signal. Just have a neutral attitude in a state of beingness. That means let go and let God do it. This is the "do nothing" program. Give up completely. Do absolutely nothing.

9. Recognize and Verify Your Signal.

You will see, hear, taste, smell, or feel something, or get a body movement. That will most likely be your signal. If you are not getting a clear signal, then go back to step number 2 and repeat the procedure.

Once you recognize a clear signal, then say something like this aloud: *"*(name of a divine being)*, if the signal that I identify as being* (describe the signal) *is your signal, then please feed it stronger to me now."* You will notice your signal getting stronger when you ask the divine being to feed it stronger. If it diminishes or disappears, then go back to step number 2 and repeat the same procedure.

10. Ask for Your Message.

Say something like this aloud: *"*(name of a divine being)*, please tell me* (your question or request) *now."* Ask questions and have a conversation with your higher self. It is necessary to ASK. Otherwise, your higher self or divine being will not respond.

11. Let Go and Let God.

Take another big deep breath. Do nothing and less than nothing. Do not try to get a message. Just have a neutral attitude and give up completely. Be receptive. You might think you are just making up the answers, and in a sense you are, because you are that divine presence within you, and your higher self is answering your questions. Trust in what you receive.

12. Give Gratitude and Return.

Slowly come out of meditation. Take a deep breath and blow out, as you pretend to blow out a candle. Say something like,

> *I now thank God for this wonderful meditation and for all that I have received.* (Blow out a candle.)
>
> *I now return from the level of Spirit to the level of subconscious mind, knowing that my subconscious mind has been healed by this meditation.* (Blow out a candle.)
>
> *I now return to the level of conscious mind, knowing that my conscious mind is one with the mind of God.* (Blow out a candle.)
>
> *I now return to the level of physical body, knowing that my body is in perfect health.* (Blow out a candle.)
>
> *I now come back to the level of the environment, bringing back with me all the blessings I have received in this meditation.*

Then blow out four more imaginary candles and come all the way back to inner and outer balance. Then say out loud in a clear voice,

> *I AM alert. I AM awake. I AM inwardly and outwardly balanced. I AM divinely protected by the light of my being. Thank you, God, and SO IT IS.*

13. Difficulties?

If you have difficulty using this procedure, then you can:

1. Use the Divine Revelation Breakthrough Meditation, available as a downloadable MP3 at *https://www. spiritualityproducts.com/secure/Order.html*, to help you receive signals and messages.

2. Read the rest of this book and study the Ten Tests of Spirit Discernment in Chapter 16. Read my books *Divine Revelation* and *How to Hear the Voice of God*. Learn, study, and use the Ten Tests in those books.

3. Read *Divine Revelation* and use the meditation procedure in Chapter 8 and the healing prayers in Chapter 10.

4. Contact a qualified Divine Revelation teacher and make an appointment to verify your inner names and signals. For a list of qualified teachers and more information, go to *www.divinerevelation.org/Teachers.html*.

In the next chapter, you will learn the Ten Tests of Spiritual Discernment, which are essential for getting clear, reliable intuition and inner guidance.

16

Navigating the Inner Realms Safely

*There is a wisdom of the head, and...there is
a wisdom of the heart.*

—Charles Dickens, *Hard Times*

Is opening your third eye a safe practice? How do you know the experience or message you are getting is the real thing? Can you identify who or what is giving you subtle experiences or inner guidance?

Right now psychic development is very popular. It seems everyone declares him- or herself a psychic, medium, healer, or some other title. Many are opening to the inner planes, contacting guides, angels, and other messengers. But opening indiscriminately to the inner world is as dangerous as inviting strangers into your home.

Would you open your door to a stranger? That is exactly what many people do by playing with the occult without discernment. You would never open your door to vagrants, so why open your awareness without identifying whom or what you are contacting?

Becoming Spiritually Street-Smart

You are street-smart when it comes to your home and property. You know how to conduct yourself on the street or subway. Now it is time to get spiritually street-smart and practice safe spirituality when you visit the inner realms. Know the territory by following a road map to your inner life. Attain true spiritual discernment.

Some people say, "I get intuitive messages and hear inner voices daily. I don't know who's giving me advice, but I follow it." Is this intelligent? It does not take rocket science to determine that following the advice of unidentified voices in your mind would be confusing and dangerous.

Deep within yourself is all that you need. If you would trust the divine and allow Spirit to be your guide, you would not seek guidance from counterfeits. There is a big difference between the true voice of Spirit and whatever else is in your mind. You can learn to tell the difference.

This chapter helps you distinguish the inner voices and identify the source of intuitive messages. It provides ten ways to test whether your intuition is genuine and coming from a divine source.

Where Messages Come From

1	SPIRITUAL WORLD	Divine Voice
2	MENTAL WORLD	Internal Influences
3	ASTRAL WORLD	Lower Beings
4	ENVIRONMENT	External Influences

Image 16a. *Four Realms*

Your inner messages come from one of four basic planes of existence:

Divine Realm

The first is the true divine realm. On that level Spirit speaks to you directly. You can contact various aspects of your higher self, hear the voice of angels, archangels, prophets, saints, deities, and other divine beings. Your beloved dearly departed relatives who have moved into the divine light might communicate with you from the spiritual plane.

Mental Realm

The second realm is the mental world, where all past experiences are stored. There you might contact your subconscious mind or the collective unconscious—memories, belief systems, habits, conditioning, and societal brainwashing from parents, churches, schools, peers, society, the media, and so forth. You could tap into this erroneous mental depository and mistake it for Spirit. You could be deluded into thinking you are hearing a true divine voice or receiving divine revelations, when you are just talking to yourself!

Astral Realm

The third realm is the astral plane, where you might contact earth-bound spirits or astral entities—people who died but, for various reasons, did not go into the brilliant divine light. Discarnate entities are not on the spiritual plane, yet no longer have a body. Therefore some of them hang around the earth, trying to talk to human beings. They might be faker spirits who pretend to be "high" beings and give you "high"-sounding names. Once again, you could inadvertently contact an astral being and mistake it for a divine being.

Environmental Realm

The fourth realm is the environment. You might tap into thoughts of people around you, read their minds, or pick up general static floating in environmental thought banks. You might read the history of the planet or of humanity, which is stored in a dense mental cloud covering the earth. Then you might falsely believe Spirit is speaking to you when you are simply reading atmospheric mental flotsam and jetsam.

If your third eye is open, that does not necessarily mean you are in touch with the highest level of awareness. You can use subtle senses of seeing, hearing, and feeling to contact any invisible realm of existence on any level. Considering that you might receive messages from so many places, wouldn't it be prudent to become spiritually street-smart and learn to practice safe spirituality?

All that Glitters Is Not God

The main reason you might have trouble identifying who or what you are contacting when receiving inner messages is that you have not been trained to recognize the true divine voice.

Most religious institutions are not capable of helping you attain this experience or recognize whether it is real, even if they wanted to. Most religious leaders do not know how to do it themselves. So how could they teach anyone else?

Even in the metaphysical community, teachings of discernment are rare. Although many people learn how to open up to the inner realms, they are not taught how to discern what level they are on or what or who they are communicating with.

It is time to learn how to practice safe spirituality right now. I propose ten ways to distinguish between the true voice of Spirit and "other voices" in your mind. These ten tests help you receive divine messages clearly and precisely. Use these to test the inner messages you are receiving. Armed with these tests, you cannot go wrong. Please study these tests in much greater detail in my books *Divine Revelation* and *How to Hear the Voice of God*.

Test 1: The Experience Test

"How does this feel?"

When you are in contact with the true realm of Spirit, you will feel joyous, happy, protected, secure, satisfied, content, and loved. You will not be intimidated, fearful, anxious, conflicted or in doubt. You will experience a state of oneness, wholeness, unity, and perfection. That is what Spirit feels like. The experience of oneness and wholeness is the most important of the ten tests, since it cannot be faked by an astral entity.

Sometimes people receive divine intuition but, immediately afterward, experience negative emotions as a reaction. This common experience indicates the person contacted Spirit, but then confusion, doubt, fear, and other mental negations jumped in to deny the true divine experience.

Tests of Spiritual Discernment

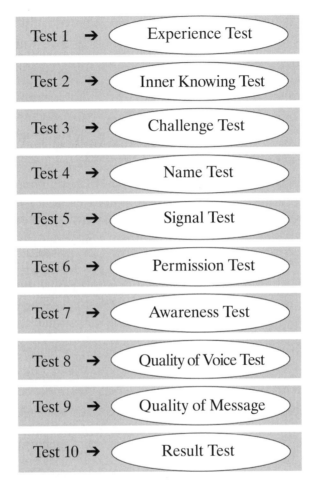

Test 1 →	Experience Test
Test 2 →	Inner Knowing Test
Test 3 →	Challenge Test
Test 4 →	Name Test
Test 5 →	Signal Test
Test 6 →	Permission Test
Test 7 →	Awareness Test
Test 8 →	Quality of Voice Test
Test 9 →	Quality of Message
Test 10 →	Result Test

Image 16b. *Ten Tests*

Test 2: The Inner Knowing Test

"Do I know this is true?"

You will know that you know, beyond a shadow of doubt. You will just *know* it. When Spirit speaks, you will experience an inner certainty and conviction that is indisputable. You will know without knowing how you know.

Have you ever had regrets such as, "I just knew I should have done that. Why didn't I listen to my intuition?" That was your inner knowing. The feeling of inner certainty is not the same as "wishful thinking," which occurs when you want something so much that you delude yourself into thinking it is true and real.

Test 3: The Challenge Test

"Do you come in the name of God?"

If a stranger knocks at your door, first find out who sent him and what his business is. Similarly, if you want to receive a message, first ask the messenger, "Do you come in the name of God?" or, "Do you come in the name of the Christ?" If you do not get a clear, positive response, then an astral entity is present. Send that entity into the divine light by using the Astral Healing Prayer below. Then ask again, "Do you come in the name of God?" until the answer is yes.

Invariably students ask whether a faker spirit from the astral world would lie in answer to this question. Thus far, I have never experienced faker spirits lying if the question is worded as recommended. Instead, they simply refuse to answer the question. In this case, immediately use the Astral Healing Prayer.

Some teachers suggest asking, "Do you come in the light?" I do not recommend using this question. Which light are you speaking about? The 40-watt light bulb or florescent light? The light of burning hell? Bud Light?

Here is the Astral Healing Prayer to say audibly, with strength and conviction, if you do not get a clear yes to your test question:

"Dear ones, you are healed and forgiven. You are lifted in love. You are united with the truth of your being. Divine love and light fill and surround you now. The vibration of the earth no longer binds you. You are free to go into the divine light now. I call forth the Holy Spirit to take you to your perfect place of expression. You are bless-ed, forgiven, and released into the love, light, and wholeness

of universal Spirit. You are bless-ed, forgiven, and released into the love, light, and wholeness of universal Spirit. You are lifted into the light of God, lifted into the light of God, lifted into the light of God. Go now in peace and in love."

Please study my books *Divine Revelation, How to Hear the Voice of God,* and *The Power of Auras* to learn a lot more about astral entities and astral healing.

Test 4: The Name Test

"What is your name?"

When a stranger comes to your door, get its calling card before letting it in. Every divine being has a name, and you can ask for it. Even God has a name. God's name is "GOD." Every aspect of your higher self and every deity, ascended master, or angelic being has a name. Do not be deceived, however. Beware of faker spirits who try to mislead you by giving you "high"-sounding false names. And do not be impressed by any entity refusing to give you a name. Instead, send that faker spirit into the divine light by using the "astral healing prayer" above.

Test 5: The Signal Test

"Give me your signal."

The signal is the sign that you are in contact with a particular aspect of Spirit. Each inner name has a separate, unique signal associated with it. For instance, Mother Mary might come to you as a vision of a pink light in your heart. To another person, Mary might give a feeling of heat in the hands. Someone else might experience Mary as a sound of celestial harps. Whenever you are in contact with Mary, you will experience her unique signal. Similarly, every divine being that you contact and identify will give you a definite sign. Whenever you are receiving clear divine intuition, the signal will be present. When the signal is over, that indicates the message is also over. Read more about the signal on pages 201 to 203.

Test 6: The Permission Test

"Do I have permission to ask this question?"

Before asking a particular question of your higher self, first inquire:

1. Is it highest wisdom for me to ask this question?

You will not be given permission in the following cases: 1) if you are seeking fortune telling, 2) if you are asking an unnecessary or frivolous question, 3) if you are asking an inappropriate question, 4) if you are not ready to hear the answer, or 5) if the wording of your question prevents your higher self from answering it. In my book *Divine Revelation,* there is an entire chapter about how to word your questions.

2. Do I have the capacity to receive a clear answer to this question?

It may be difficult to receive an insight about a quantum physics formula if you are not a physicist, or about how to do solve a complex mathematical problem if you are not a mathematician. In such cases, you might not be given permission, especially if your intuitive powers are not yet highly developed.

3. Do I have permission to ask this question?

If you are prying into someone else's business or asking something that you are not supposed to know at that time, you will not be given permission.

Test 7: The Awareness Test

"Am I alert?"

You will be conscious, awake, aware, and alert when in contact with a true divine being. You will not leave your body and let something "take over." You will not have lapses in memory. The only time you might be unconscious while receiving a divine message is when you are asleep at night during a dream.

Leaving your body and relinquishing control, as in unconscious psychic mediumship or spirit channeling, is a dangerous practice. It breaks mind-body coordination, and causes illness and early death. Unconscious mediums may try to impress people by saying, "I do not remember what happened while I was 'under.'" What is impressive about checking out of the human hotel, letting a completely unknown entity check in, and letting that entity use and abuse your body?

Test 8: The Quality of Voice Test
"Does the voice sound natural?

The intuitive voice you hear with your inner ear will sound like any other thought in your mind. If you speak your message aloud, it will sound normal and natural. You will not speak with a foreign or bizarre accent or use weird gestures or theatrics. True Spirit speaks in your own voice, your own language, and with your own accent.

There are a few possible reasons why channelers would speak in strange accents. They might be deceived by faker spirits from the lower astral plane. They could be putting on a theatrical performance. They may be unconsciously manufacturing an accent due to their own self-doubt and disbelief in their ability to receive true inner guidance. Or they might have the rare ability to let a real ghost take over their body and speak in the accent of that deceased person.

We are supposed to be impressed by channelers' strange accents. What is impressive about weirdness? Does God need to speak in a weird accent? Or does God speak lovingly, sweetly, poetically, and simply, as Jesus spoke simple words he received from Spirit?

Test 9: The Quality of Message Test
"Is the message of truth?"

The true message from Spirit will be helpful, uplifting, healing, relevant, practical, simple, loving, inspiring, and non-judgmental. The divine voice will never coerce or control you with such intimidating injunctions as "If you do not follow our religion or our deity, you will go to hell" or "Ours is the only guru and this is the only path to God." It will not threaten or judge you with statements such as, "You will be punished for your sins" or "You are subject to karmic retribution."

Divine Spirit does not decree gloom-and-doom prophecies written in stone. It will never tell you to harm yourself or another. The message will not induce fear, guilt, anger, depression, or other negative emotions. It will not present conditions or demands to fulfill, such as, "Only by reading the Bible will you get to heaven." Reward and punishment are not concepts of divine truth.

Faker spirits may try to impress you with "high"-sounding, complicated messages. Do we have such low self-esteem that we believe if we cannot understand the message, then it must be "high"? Beware of unintelligible, inane messages that contain phrases such as, "The seventh ray of the fifteenth hierarchy of the nineteenth sector of the cosmic commission in the ashtar command."

Spirit will empower you to make your own decisions and be responsible for your life. It will not enslave you with flattery. Unfortunately, humans have one major failing: susceptibility to flattery. That is how faker spirits control gullible people, and also how many gurus keep their disciples under control. Beware of messages such as, "You are the chosen ones," "You have a higher mission than others," or "You are special and misunderstood."

Test 10: The Result Test

"Do I feel energized?"

Immediately after receiving a true message from a divine voice, you will feel full, happy, elated, relieved, confident, energized, and motivated. If you feel let down, empty, hollow, drained, exhausted, or tired, then your message came from the astral or mental realm. This is one of the most important tests, since the energizing feeling cannot be faked by astral entities, which are not on the divine level.

Be aware that your subconscious mind might jump in soon after receiving a true divine message and object to the message or negate the entire experience. This simply indicates you have lost your inner divine contact and degraded to a lower realm. Do not deny or negate your divine experience.

If you are a psychic, counselor, or hands-on healer, you should feel more energized as your day unfolds. If you feel drained, it is a sure sign you are using your ego energy instead of divine energy to heal others. Let go and let Spirit do the work through you.

How to Use the Ten Tests

Be sure your inner message passes all ten tests. One test is not enough. All ten must be passed in order for you to be sure you are in contact with a divine voice and not other voices. It only takes about eight seconds to use the ten tests. Yes, you read that right. EIGHT SECONDS. The only thing that takes time is asking, "Do you come in the name of God?" "What is your name?" "Give me your signal," and "Do I have permission to ask this?" All the other tests are immediate and automatic.

In the next chapter, you will read about experiences reported by people who have opened their third eye.

Bliss

of the

Third Eye

17

| Third Eye Experiences |

It's not what you look at that matters,
it's what you see.

—Henry David Thoreau

This chapter is devoted to those who have so kindly written to me about their third eye experiences. Some of the many inspirational accounts I have received are related here.

White Light Experience

Melissa Drake Johnson, a jewelry designer from Fayetteville, Arkansas, described her experience:

"I went to bed one night. I had physically overdone it and was feeling kind of achy. I believe in energy frequency work, so I started calling in the energy of Archangel Raphael to heal the discomfort and tension in my body—to relax it. And it was working really well. Then it just occurred to me to call in the Christ healing frequency. So I started doing that.

"The next thing I knew, the entire inside of my head lit up like an airport runway. This massive blast of white light inside my head totally blinded me with light. Then my whole body shuddered for about a minute. When it was over, I thought, Wow."

A Premonition Dream

Michael Dimura from Middlesex, New Jersey, author of *Between Heaven and Hell,* reports:

"I was always interested in the paranormal and psychic phenomena, even at an early age. There were times I sensed things before they happened, but usually wrote it off as coincidence. Until one summer night in 1994.

"It started with a dream where I was driving through what looked like a tunnel at night—nothing in front of me but pitch-black darkness. Until I saw two lights coming towards me at high speed. I had nowhere to go as it got closer, and I startled awake just as both our vehicles were about to collide. Again I wrote it off, until two nights later.

"I had dropped my girlfriend off at her house and was returning home around midnight. I turned on to a small side road I used as a shortcut between the two main roads in town— a trip I'd made 100 times before. Until I noticed lights coming towards me that seemed to be driving on my side of the road! Instantly I remembered my dream. Looking around, I realized the canopy of tall trees in summer made the road appear like a tunnel—just like in the dream.

"I clenched the wheel tightly and immediately made a right turn onto one of only two side roads on that street and pulled over. Looking back, I watched as a car passed and was indeed driving on the wrong side of the road. I drove the rest of the way home, very shaken by what had just happened.

"Since that night, I've always paid close attention to any dreams or bad vibes I get from any situation."

Prescience of a National Tragedy

Daryl Hajek from Los Angeles, California, author of *Blood Blossom,* says:

"I am a deaf 50-year-old man who is clairvoyant (since child-hood). I do not conscientiously practice my skills. Rather, it occurs spontaneously on occasion. One particular experience is a vision I saw on September 9, 2001—two days before the September 11 terrorist attacks.

"I was in bed, and as I dozed off, I saw in my mind's eye a plane repeatedly slamming into a tall building. The vision repeated itself 10 times or so before I forced myself awake and sat up in bed, breathless and shaken. It took me about an hour before I went back to sleep.

"Two days later, on September 11, my mother came into my bedroom, crying. I asked her if the dog died (we had a small, 15-year-old dog that had been ill for some time). She said no and beckoned me into the living room. She pointed to the TV and I saw one building with smoke coming out of it; then the other building next to it had an explosion.

"At first, I couldn't comprehend what I was seeing. I kept thinking an air-conditioning unit shorted out and exploded. I asked my mother what had happened. She explained that planes flew into the buildings. I got chills and remembered the vision from two nights before. I felt sick and nearly vomited. That's when fear gripped me because I realized it was reality—not a Hollywood movie.

"The experience left me shaken for several months. It took me a long time to learn how to handle a vision like that."

Visions of the Dearly Departed

Bryan Mattimore, an author and marketing innovation consultant from Stamford, Connecticut, says:

"My father died of cancer when I was 21. Shortly after his death, I had several profound inner spiritual experiences with him—all lucid (extremely real, clear, more real in some sense than being awake and conscious on this physical plane). The first set of experiences, I was with him on an inner plane and I was trying to convince him that he was dead. He was a bit disoriented with his transition to this new world of being, and he could not understand why people on the physical plane could not hear or speak with him.

"Initially, when I awoke from these experiences, I felt badly—telling him he was dead, because of course, on an inner plane, he was not dead. But then I realized I was simply trying to help him make the transition to his new life. The final experience I had with him, several months after his passing, he was established on an inner world, living in a small, beautiful house on a crystal clear blue lake. We hugged before I left.

"These experiences with him, of course, made his passing so much easier to accept. Yes, I grieved, but it was wonderful to know he was okay. I had a similar experience with my beloved English Setter, Clyde, who, after he left this world, was escorted by an inner master to his next life."

Developing the Third Eye

Dr. Joy S. Pedersen, president of Express Success of Lakeland, Florida, reports:

"Archangel Michael appeared to me asking me to write his book, *Wisdom of the Guardian,* and join him in a healing practice. I had asked him how many chapters, and he said 22. I agreed. I started my practice using an ancient spiritual healing method called Ho'oponopono. This clearing process helped unblock gifts I had.

"During sessions with my clients, I began to notice I could see the hidden causes of their challenges. I learned I could connect and speak with their soul. Ancestors, relatives, angels and ascended masters began to communicate their messages to my clients through me. I discovered I could see history back to the beginning of time. My gifts unfolded, or I became aware of them, due to inspired events that helped reveal them.

"Different events occurred that prompted specific gifts becoming known. I believed in reincarnation and was invited to experience my own past lives through a past-life therapist. After the third session, I noticed the memories of past lives seemed to be 'right there' below the surface. That realization opened the door for me to recall past lives anytime without a therapist. Years later, during a client session, I realized I could see their past lives as well.

"I found the whole experience of tapping into my intuitive gifts and supernormal senses came over time. I now gratefully combine all to serve others."

Spiritual Practices to Awaken the Third Eye

Acharya Sri Khadi Madama, author, speaker, and visionary, from Toms River, New Jersey, described her experience of opening the third eye:

"Back in 1967, at age 19, I had the grand good fortune of meeting my Yoga mentor, Muriel Schneider, in lineage to the saint of India, H.H. Sri Swami Sivananda Saraswati. She would hold discourses with me that ran into the wee hours of the morning. I sat spellbound at her feet. One of the first stories I heard was about 'Opening the Third Eye' from the book *The Third Eye* by T. Lapsang Rampa. His story, illustrating the opening of the portal connected to the ajna chakra, described a tiny wedge of wood being driven into a point on the forehead to force open this hidden gateway.

"However, in reality, the only way to open this point is by aligning one's life to the higher frequency by which this chakra will correspond. After the initial intrigue of the story, and relieved that a tiny sliver was not about to be driven into my forehead, we got down to the real practice of opening this portal. That would be accomplished by building high character, moral and spiritual life, and the regular practice of Tratakum—the art of controlling the movement of the eyes to stay focused, working in unison with igniting the energy of the optic nerve and increasing the ability to hold one's inner vision in order to locate the hidden spot where the gate of light exists.

"I was taught that I had to be of particular good character so that my frequency could open the gate when the vision was in the exact place. I used a white candle for this purpose with very specific directions on how to practice Tratakum. I found the process works with steady practice, as it develops clairvoyance and distant viewing. I have never had a bad experience due to this added sense. I believe we all have it if we learn to cultivate it properly. We are all supposed to develop this ability for the good of mankind.

"Developing the third eye or ajna chakra requires not only staring into a candle flame, but also a being-consciousness-humility-purity lifestyle that resonates with the opening of the portal. Otherwise one would simply be staring into a candle, like standing in front of a door and never knocking to see if anyone is home.

"In the beginning this is mere eye training, but then I started to accurately see images of people or objects at a distance. I learned, through experimentation with a student who lived far away, that I could 'see' her surroundings, even though I never visited her across country nor saw photos of the house. The information was very specific and accurate such as: 'You have a cardboard box behind your sofa, all the flaps are inter folded,'—to be told at first, 'No, I don't.' Then, when checked, sure enough the box was there. I have successfully done this more than a dozen times.

"By accessing the central cortex by turning my inner vision upwards into the ajna spot, I am able to retrieve intuitive data when working with individuals. In fact, I received most of the data for my book, *From Lost Horizon to Finding Shangri La* through this method. This is something that took me years to develop. I believe everyone has this latent talent, which can be developed."

See how to practice Tratakum meditation on page 214 of this book.

God's Voice Prevents Danger

Lee Dawson emailed me a description of the following experience:

"I was on a rock climbing expedition. My rope leader did something that he should not have done. Without telling me, he took me on a route far more difficult than my current skill level. I found myself two thirds of the way up a sheer rock face, without a way of continuing forward, or without a way of coming back down. I thought that this was the end, and that I was going to die.

"Suddenly, I felt a reassuring presence. From somewhere, a 'voice' instructed me on what to do. I seemed to suddenly gain skills, and energy that I know I did not have before. I found myself making it to the top, and then the rope leader said to me, 'I knew that you could do it!' I scolded him for taking me up that route nevertheless!

"I found my way to a series of Light Body courses. Since taking these courses, I have had the feeling of channeling information either from my own higher divine self, or from some other higher-level source. The revelations and insights I have had could not possibly come from my own ordinary mind. I was witnessing synchronicities and connections that went far beyond my ordinary conscious ability to comprehend.

"In addition, I have developed an odd ability to sense energies in a way that I had never been able to do before. These newly developed 'senses' are entirely unlike the five known physical senses. The energy perceived is difficult to describe with words. It is vaguely similar to the sensation of being on a roller coaster, but without the true sensation of physical movement.

"There is also a strong 'flowing' sensation within and around the body. These energies twist and turn as they flow, similar to the visual properties of the sun's plasma, moving the magnetic field lines of the sun in arcs and twists."

Encountering Angelic Beings

Mollie Jensen, a writer and intuitive channel from San Rafael, California, stated:

"It started with a light, much like a star, descending down and centering in front of my third eye, right in front of the center of my eyes. This light then took on the form of what I would describe as an angelic being—somewhat of a human form, though more an outline of a human form, and filled with light.

"This being then offered me a symbol that looked like a multi-pointed star and told me that it was mine to use if I wanted to create a clearer connection with other dimensional beings. Of course I responded with a 'YES, please!' The being then reached in between my eyes and inserted this symbol. I was told that I could use this as a sort of transmitting device that would help me pull in higher guidance information.

"I remember feeling very blissed-out during the experience, even though what transpired seemed to take just a few minutes. Then the being ascended, leaving the symbol in my third eye area, and although it appeared to leave, I've never felt as if it truly left.

"I firmly believe that my interaction with this being is what set the path toward my work as a channel. I have found the experience invaluable in that it has helped me make important life choices with better clarity. Since that experience, I honed my skills and became an intuitive channel who works with this divine guidance to help my clients. I also coach them to pull in a symbol of their own into their third eye area to open intuitive channels for themselves.

"I now can call on guidance whenever I need help for others and myself. Of course, sometimes my silly humanness still gets in the way of hearing them, though when I truly stop enough to listen, it's always there. I know this is possible and normal for everyone and is just part of what we're supposed to do."

Third Eye Opening through Detox

Author Angela Mia White wrote:

"My experience of my awakening my third eye has been quite a journey. As I was trying to heal and live through a debilitating sickness that was unnamable and undiagnosed, I came upon some YouTube videos on chakras and the third eye awakening. In wanting to open my third eye, I was also led to videos that explained that our pineal gland, where our third eye is, becomes calcified with flouride. This stops the third eye from opening and thus creates a blockage to creativity and awakening the soul.

"I detoxed my body for over a year on just fruits, fresh juice, vegetables and herbs. As I did this, much more became apparent than what I'd ever consciously known before. The first person I learned from was Carol Tuttle. She explained that you could take a few deep breaths and visualize the color indigo as a ball of energy in front of your third eye—then gently bring the indigo ball into your forehead, and bounce it like a ball. You could also visualize your third eye fluttering as if you were waking up in the morning—visualize your third eye physically opening.

"This led to opening of my chakras, talking to Angels, Mother Mary, Jesus, and conversations with God. After this awakening, I was directed to write a book called *From Sick to Bliss to Conversations With God.* I was given the title, and I was told how it was going to be published and paid for by the angels. So far, they are correct. This book is for the planet. It was written about the mass awakening."

Opening to Animal Communication

Denise Mange, from New York, described her third eye experiences:

"St. Francis always spoke to me. Mainly because he spoke to animals—something I had always wished I could do. I spent my childhood studying any living creature that crossed my path. During holidays in the fields of my family's house in the mountains, many afternoons, I communed with caterpillars, beetles, butterflies, baby chickens, frogs, horses, and, when lucky, the occasional dog. All so I could intently watch and possibly even share a thought or two with one of the amazing little souls I so revered, and intuitively knew had a message for my kind and me.

"Regardless of these childhood experiences and desires, it was with some trepidation and skepticism that I signed up for an animal communication course in the summer of 2014, at age 33. As a child, I had been intuitive and somewhat of an empath, but a few eerie encounters caused me to block those gifts through my teen years and twenties.

"The course was both a homecoming and an awakening to what happens after years of blocking my third eye. What once had felt very natural, then eluded me. My intuitiveness and empathic sensibilities were rusty. What I thought would be a simple tuning into a pre-programmed radio station proved to be the most worthwhile journey back to that little girl, who, through the oneness of all and paradox of time, was still in that field, with those same animals, holding that same desire for a heart-centered connection.

"I diligently practiced connecting telepathically with animals as instructed. My first experience in animal communication was with Miss Nellie, who later told me she liked that title. Nellie was an English bulldog who came into my life via her guardian, Richard, a gentle yogi who became my biggest cheerleader in the process of reopening my connection with myself, my third eye, and ultimately to the vastness, oneness, and awesomeness of the universe.

"During a meditation, Miss Nellie showed me an image of herself on a bed, with Richard lying next to her, facing the window. Miss Nellie also showed me Richard heading downstairs in their home towards the very computer where he would be answering my email, telling me the meaning behind what my mind's eye saw.

"Miss Nellie also showed me an orange tabby cat. Richard later clarified that he considered this particular cat to be one of his angels, and a big reason why he adopted Miss Nellie. Pictures were brought to my mind's eye. And although they seemed oddly trivial, they elicited so much love, gratitude, and were dots that connected to weave a much broader story.

"As I continued to open up to the possibilities afforded by my third eye, I experienced death for the first time—seeing my beloved dog's spirit leave his body as an orb of light. As Paco took his final breath in my mother's arms across the country, his soul appeared and shined in a bright, incandescent sphere right in front of me, then drifted up to the corner of the room, and away to the big field in the sky.

"Then, while losing my grandfather a few months later, I was comforted by the presence of what I later learned was the Angel of Death, who appeared as a beautiful being in a robe, a helmet of light, holding a book he was writing in with a large, luscious plume. When I asked this stunning being its name, I heard 'Asreal.' In the age of Google, it was made clear who Asrael was through a quick online search, and the awesomeness of the gift I received through his visit—the comfort of knowing he would be guiding my grandfather to the other side, where he would join Paco, and eventually me, when the time came.

"When accessing the theta brain state, I am able to call upon an animal's higher self for connection and receive communication through visuals, smells, words, and a deep knowing of what needs to be made clear.

"Everyone has a third eye. It is just waiting for our intent to be activated, making us privy to unparalleled beauty, grace, love, compassion, joy, lightness, and oneness."

God's Unconditional Love

Orea De Sa'Hana wrote to me about her experience:

"About 20 years ago, I experienced God's unconditional love for about a 45-minute period. It was like the scales suddenly fell off of my eyes, and I could see. I sobbed most of the way through it. There aren't words to describe the completeness and extravagance (a new word that my guides recently used) of that love. The most doting parents on the planet pale by comparison.

"We humans, who love to put things in words, will keep trying to describe the indescribable. For my part, it's because, as I told God during that experience, 'I've got to tell them, help me to tell them!' That was all my soul asked for, to spread the news of God's love.

"At the same time, I think we have to be careful not to spend too much time and energy intellectualizing about it when we could be...loving."

In the next chapter, we will discover the true value of opening the third eye, and how it relates to our spiritual evolution.

18

| Third Eye Fully Awakened |

We are such stuff as dreams are made on;
and our little life is rounded with a sleep.

—William Shakespeare[1]

The goal of this book is not only to develop supersensory perception. Although awakening your intuition, receiving divine messages, perceiving subtle experiences, and experiencing dimensions other than the physical world are all laudable goals, these attainments pale in comparison with the real treasure that is locked in the center of your being.

Your third eye is not just a way to see the invisible realms. It is an eye by which you can perceive the truth. Therefore, in this chapter, we will explore the ultimate goal of human life—spiritual enlightenment in the realization of your true Self.

The word "enlightenment" is used in many contexts. It means gaining greater insight, opening to new ideas that were previously unknown, and exploring greater knowledge. But the real meaning of enlightenment is much more. It is a state of higher consciousness and expanded awareness. Those who truly attain enlightenment live in an entirely different dimension from other people. They see the world differently, and they know who they really are.

So you might ask, "Who am I, really?" Well, the answer is that you are not this body, this mind, these emotions, or any possessions that you own. You are not your history, your education, or the money in your bank account. You are something much greater than these small things. You are a multidimensional being of light—radiant, exquisite, unlimited, and magnificent.

And you might wonder, "What is this world?" The answer is, "It is your creation. You manufactured it through your own imagination." Does this sound fantastic? Yes, it is. And it is the ultimate truth. I am not the first person to conceive this idea. It is not my invention. If you read the ancient scriptures of many cultures, you will see that many wise humans of antiquity knew and taught this truth.

Vasishtha, a great seer of ancient India, stated, *"Bondage is none other than the notion of an object. The notions of I and the world are but shadows, not truth. Such notions alone create objects; these objects are neither true nor false. Therefore abandon the notions of I and this, and remain established in the truth."*[2]

Vasishtha also said, *"When in a pure mind there arise concepts and notions, the world appearance comes into being. But, when the mind gives up the subject-object relationship it has with the world, it is instantly absorbed in the infinite."*

Lord Shiva is quoted as saying, *"It is the mind alone that is the root-cause of experiencing the world as if it were real; but it cannot be truly considered such a cause since there can be no mind other than pure consciousness. Thus, if it is realized that the perceiving mind itself is unreal, then it is clear that the perceived world is unreal too."*

Vasistha described this material world as a "long dream": *"It is on account of ignorance that this long-dream world-appearance appears to be real: thus does the individual self come into being. But when the truth is realized, it is seen that all this is the Self."*

Edgar Allan Poe mused, *"All that we see or seem is but a dream within a dream."* Iris Murdoch declared, *"We live in a fantasy world, a world of illusion. The great task in life is to find reality."* And Albert Einstein opined: *"Reality is merely an illusion, although a very persistent one."*

Allegory of the Cave

In Plato's best-known work *The Republic,* Book VII, he illustrated how the soul ascends from the darkness of ignorance, where the third eye is closed, into the light of true enlightenment, where the third eye opens wide. In his book, a dialogue takes place between the philosopher Socrates (mentor of Plato) and Glaucon (philosopher and Plato's older brother).

Through an allegory, Socrates intends to show Glaucon to what degree our nature is enlightened or unenlightened. He describes prisoners held in an underground cave. The mouth of the cave opens to the light. But the prisoners' necks and legs are chained so they cannot turn their heads. They can only see straight ahead of them, toward the wall of the cave. Above and behind them is a blazing fire, and a raised area with a low wall separating them from the fire. Men walk along the wall, carrying vessels and statues of animals. So all the prisoners see are shadows cast upon the opposite wall—shadows of themselves and of men walking to and fro, carrying statues of animals. What they hear are men talking with each other, and voices of other prisoners. Thus, the shadows cast on the wall resemble a puppet show.

Socrates further describes what would happen if the prisoners were released from their chains. As they turn toward the light, they would suffer sharp pains and the glare would distress them. They would identify the shadows that they were accustomed to seeing as real and the physical world as false, even if they were told that their former perceptions in the cave were an illusion.

If they were dragged up out of the cave and could see the sun, their eyes would be dazzled, and it would take long to become accustomed to the light. The night sky and stars would be more comfortable than the blazing daytime sun. Eventually, however, they would see all that exists in the physical world, and they would realize the shadows of the cave were illusory.

No matter what the prisoners had believed while in the cave, and no matter what skills or honors they had acquired during their life in the cave, those who were freed would never want to return to the enslavement of the cave.

If those who had seen the sun then returned to the cave, they would find it difficult to see anything, and it would take long to readjust to seeing clearly in the cave. The other prisoners would ridicule their blindness and consider their own situation to be superior to those who had seen the light. They might go so far as to put to death any offender who would lead others into the light.

Socrates states that in this allegory, the prison-house is the world of sight, the fire is the sun, and the journey out of the cave is the ascent of the soul to higher consciousness, into a greater light—the true light of spiritual enlightenment. Bewilderment of the eyes (and of the mind's eye) exists in both cases: while opening to the light or while returning to darkness. Therefore, we should never deride anyone whose eyes are becoming accustomed to either light or darkness.

Socrates further explains that the power and capacity of learning is inherent in the soul, and not granted by professors of education. And just as the eye cannot turn from darkness to light without the entire body, so also the intellect can only turn from the world of becoming into that of being by virtue of the movement of the whole soul, and "learn by degrees to endure the sight of being, and of the brightest and best of being, or in other words, of the good."

It is incumbent upon rulers of State to not simply remain in the heavenly realms of light, but also to become benefactors of the State, and to descend into the cave and thereby lift those who are in darkness. Socrates warns against political ambition and lauds virtue and wisdom as the true blessings in life. He concludes: "The process, I said, is not the turning over of an oyster-shell, but the turning round of a soul passing from a day which is little better than night to the true day of being, that is, the ascent from below, which we affirm to be true philosophy."[3]

World as Illusion

Although this physical reality appears to be real, it is like the shadows on the walls of Plato's cave. We human beings are prisoners in our own cave of false perception. Until we open our third eye and see the blinding light of the true spiritual Sun, which is the glory of God, we remain bound and chained in darkness of ignorance.

Advaita ("non-dualism") *Vedanta* (literally "the end of the Veda" or "supreme knowledge") was propagated by Adi Shankara (509–477 BC). He was perhaps the greatest saint to ever walk the earth. In his writings and commentaries, he speaks of the eternal reality of the Self, which is far from the ignorant perspective of chained prisoners in Plato's cave.

The scriptures of *Vedanta* and the *Upanishads* are the origins of Advaita. In this philosophy, our perception of the world and our concept of the self are in error. The way we see either the darkness of the cave or the brilliance of the world outside the cave—that is the distinction between ignorance and enlightenment.

Here are a few sayings of Adi Shankara, from his work titled *Aparokshanubhuti* ("direct experience" or "self-realization"). These profound aphorisms speak for themselves. They are marked according to the verse-number quoted:[4]

2. *Herein is expounded (the means of attaining to) Aparokshanubhuti (Self-Realization) for the acquisition of final liberation. Only the pure in heart should constantly and with all effort meditate upon the truth herein taught.*

5. *The seer [Self] in itself is alone permanent, the seen is opposed to it, transient—such a settled conviction is truly known as discrimination.*

11. *Knowledge is not brought about by any other means than enquiry [vichara], just as an object is nowhere perceived without the help of light.*

12. *Who am I? How is this world created? Who is its creator? Of what material is this world made? This is the way of that enquiry.*

13. *I am neither the body, a combination of the five elements of matter, nor am I an aggregate of the senses; I am something different from these. This is the way of that enquiry.*

21. *Self is Eternal, since it is Existence itself; the body is transient, as it is non-existence in essence; and yet people see these two as one! What else can be called ignorance but this?*

53. *When duality appears through ignorance, one sees another; but when everything becomes identified with the Self, one does not perceive another even in the least.*

54. *In that state when one realizes all as identified with the Self, there arises neither delusion nor sorrow, in consequence of the absence of duality.*

70. *Just as a rope is imagined to be a snake and a mother-of-pearl to be a piece of silver, so is the Self determined to be the body by an ignorant person.*

84. *Just as when clouds move, the moon appears to be in motion, so does a person on account of ignorance see Self as the body.*

87. *Thus through ignorance arises in Self the delusion of the body, which, again, through Self-realization, disappears in the Supreme Self.*

94. *The Vedanta scriptures declare ignorance to be verily the material cause of the phenomenal world just as earth is of a jar. That ignorance being destroyed, where can the universe subsist?*

95. *Just as a person out of confusion perceives only the snake leaving aside the rope, so does an ignorant person see only the phenomenal world without knowing the Reality.*

96. *The real nature of the rope being known, the appearance of the snake no longer persists; so the substratum being known, the phenomenal world disappears completely.*

141. *The wise should always think with great care of the invisible, the visible, and everything else, as his own Self which is consciousness itself.*

142. *Having reduced the visible to the invisible, the wise should think of the universe as one with Reality. Thus alone will he abide in Eternal felicity with mind full of consciousness and bliss.*

Adi Shankara and many other great saints, from the ancient seers Veda Vyasa and Vasishtha and the 19th century Advaita Ramana Maharishi, to the 21st century mystic Byron Katie, have all extolled self-inquiry as a royal road to self-realization and spiritual enlightenment. "Who am I?" is the question to which all must discover the ultimate answer. The answer is that the true Self, your higher Self, is "not this, not that" (*neti neti,* according to Shankara), and not anything in the material world.

Your true Self is the imperishable, immutable, eternal, nameless, formless, beginningless, endless, limitless, unbounded, and unmanifest. It is beyond name, form, and phenomena. It is infinite and absolute. It is one and only one. According to the *Upanishads,* it is "one without a second."[5] In other words, there is no number two. There is no duality. There is only one. And that oneness, that wholeness is within me, within you, and within all things. We are all one. The ancient scriptures, the *Upanishads,* declare the *Mahavakyas* (literally, "great statements" or "supreme affirmations"). Here are a few, which summarize the supreme reality:

"I am that" *(Aham Brahmasmi).*[6]

"Thou art that." *(Tat Tvam Asi).*[7]

"All this is that." *(Sarvam khalvidam brahma).*[8]

"That alone is." *(Tad eva brahma tvam).*[9]

The Garden of Eden

The allegory of the Garden of Eden in the Judeo-Christian Bible is about humanity's fall from an enlightened state of oneness into the ignorance of duality.[10]

This story is not a history lesson, and it is not about an event that occurred thousands of years ago. It is an allegory about the human condition right here, right now, in each moment.

Adam, the first man, who represents all humankind, lives in the Garden of Eden, the paradise of immortal life, perfect union with God, and spiritual enlightenment. In this garden, God provides beautiful fruit trees and plants for Adam to eat.

There are two special trees in the middle of the garden. One is the tree of life, which grants immortality and eternal life. It symbolizes oneness, wholeness, and spiritual enlightenment. Its kundalini energy is flowing upward and opens all the chakras, including the third eye.

The other tree is the tree of knowledge of good and evil. What does "the knowledge of good and evil" symbolize? These are the two polarities of duality, such as white and black, right and wrong, reward and punishment, peace and war. Dualistic thinking is the cause of isolation and separation from God. It is ignorance. Its kundalini energy flows downward and blocks the third eye and other chakras.

God instructs Adam that he can eat the fruit of every tree in the garden except one—the tree of knowledge of good and evil. God warns that if Adam eats from that tree, he will "surely die." He will no longer be unified with God or immortal. For eating of that tree represents partaking in dual thinking.

God creates Eve, the first woman, out of Adam's rib, and they are "both naked" and are "not ashamed." They are "naked" because they are without pretense. They know and express who they really are, without shame, and without the false mask of ego. Their third eyes, fully opened, see the truth about their real identity. Adam and Eve live in wholeness, innocence, love, and contentment—without guile, greed, or need. They are immortal divine beings, one with God, at peace with themselves, and harmonious with nature.

The absolute oneness is called *Paramashiva* (*sat:* absolute). When Eve is created out of Adam, duality is born from oneness. Adam and Eve represent two aspects of the absolute: the male or *Shiva* aspect (*chit:* consciousness), and the female or *Shakti* aspect (*ananda:* bliss). These male and female polarities are known as *yin* and *yang* in Confucianism. Adam and Eve live in paradise, because yin and yang are in balance, equilibrium, and peace.

But Eve is tempted by a serpent to eat the fruit of the forbidden tree. The serpent manages to convince her that she will not die. So she eats the fruit and shares it with Adam. Then the "eyes of both of them were opened, and they knew that they were naked." Their third eye closes, and their two physical eyes, which represent duality, are opened. Now they are ashamed, so they make garments of fig leaves to cover their true selves. That garment represents the ego, the false sense of identity.

Before eating the fruit, Adam and Eve do not see duality. Their expanded consciousness sees with their third eyes. They perceive everyone and everything as one with themselves. They are fully enlightened and therefore do not differentiate between themselves and God. They live in wholeness.

Now, after eating the fruit, they fall into *avidya* (ignorance) and limitation. They experience the ego as a separate entity, and they falsely identify themselves as that ego. Disobeying God and eating the fruit opens Adam's and Eve's eyes to shame and destroys their innocence. This is called the "fall of man" or "fall from grace."

The serpent is "more subtle than any beast of the field which the Lord God had made." This snake represents kundalini, a form of prana—the life-force energy that breathes life into the cosmos. It is the subtlest element of nature. Kundalini can either rise up through sushumna nadi, which elevates consciousness and is the pathway to eternal life; or it can descend, which lowers consciousness and leads to death. When the mind identifies with the ego, kundalini flows downward. It descends to the level of muladhara chakra, the lowest chakra in the seven-chakra system. And it remains there, coiled up and asleep.

When Adam and Eve partake of the apple of the tree that represents duality, the belief in good vs. evil is born. This belief is erroneous, a delusion of false identification with duality—*pragya aparadh* in Sanskrit, "the mistake of the intellect." They no longer see the truth. Instead they mistake themselves to be limited, isolated, and separate from God. They identify themselves as the ego, rather than the true Self.

When Adam and Eve eat of the forbidden fruit of duality, the ego is born. Isolation from God is born. Suffering and shame are born. The façade is born. They search for fig leaves to cover their inadequacies. By eating from this tree, they will "surely die." The false identification with ego is dualistic thinking, which separates humans from their true nature of immortal, pristine purity. Thus death is born.

The birthright of Adam and Eve (humanity) is to live eternal life in paradise—a state of oneness with God, without shame, guilt, or other negative beliefs, habits, and conditions. This is eternal life, without false beliefs. In this state, they are fully awakened to their true nature, and they are spiritually whole.

Because Adam and Eve misuse their free will and choose duality rather than unity, God drives them out of the paradise and immortal life of Eden. God expels them lest they also "eat of the tree of life and live forever" in their state of ignorance. Cherubim and a flaming sword are placed at the gate so they can no longer enter the garden. Immortal life is thus closed to anyone who eats of the tree of good and evil (those who falsely identify with ego and thereby judge themselves and others with condemnation).

Only by remaining in the state of eternal paradise (oneness with God) are you granted the privilege of immortality. The gate to the garden is the psychic barrier or façade barrier—the false belief in separation from God, which separates your mind from Spirit. By experiencing oneness with God, you are admitted back into the garden, and eternal life is yours:

> *To Him that overcometh will I give to eat of the tree of life,*
> *which is in the midst of the paradise of God.*

> —Revelation 2:7

Spiritual Enlightenment

This book is not just about opening your third eye or developing psychic abilities. It is a guidebook and pathway to the ultimate reality, which is realized at the end of a very long road of evolution on which you have traveled throughout many lifetimes. As you fully awaken your third eye, your spiritual sight develops, and with it, you eventually attain full realization in God consciousness.

When you discover your true identity, when you realize who-you-really-are (as opposed to who-you-thought-you-were), then you are no longer bound by seemingly endless rounds of birth and death. Your karmic seeds are burnt, and you attain *moksha* (literally "freedom")—the true realization of the Self and the ultimate reality. You are no longer a part of the insanity that created this illusory world. Now you are free.

What are the implications of finding your true Self? You no longer need to reincarnate. That means you are at liberty to live in the celestial realm as a divine being of light, or you can choose to merge fully with the absolute Brahman and thereby attain the supreme pinnacle of spiritual evolution. As you unite fully with the infinite, your identification with the mind, ego, and intellect disappears, and you identify yourself only as the absolute pure consciousness, infinite and perfect.

In that state, you are the vast infinite divinity without boundaries. You are complete and whole. You are content and at peace. You are full. You are finally liberated. You are fully merged with and one with the "all that is." You are Brahman. You are the absolute. You are that oneness. And you are home at last.

| Notes |

Chapter 1: What's a Third Eye, Anyway?
1. Matthew 6:22.

Chapter 2: Lore of the Third Eye
1. Genesis 32:30.
2. James Mason-Hudson, photographer: Creative Commons Attribution-Share Alike 3.0 Unported license.
3. Wikimedia Commons.
4. Luis García (Zaqarbal), photographer: Creative Commons Attribution-Share Alike 2.0 Generic license.
5. David K. Osborn. "Did the Greeks Have Chakras?"
6. Frank Cole Babbit, ed. "Plutarch, De Iside et Osiride."
7. Mark Beck, ed. *A Companion to Plutarch,* page 91.
8. *http://www.greatdreams.com/eye/eye.htm*
9. John D. MacArthur. "Charles Thomson—Principal Designer of the Great Seal."
10. John D. MacArthur. "Source of Novus Ordo Seclorum."
11. John D. MacArthur. "Annuit Coeptis—Origin and Meaning of the Motto Above the Eye."
12. John D. MacArthur. "Source of Novus Ordo Seclorum."
13. S. Brent Morris, P.M. "Eye in the Pyramid."
14. Robert Ingham Clegg. *Encyclopedia of Freemasonry, Volume 1,* page 52.

15. *http://afiftabsh.com/2010/05/30/secret-societies-free-masons/masonic-tracing-board/*

16. *http://www.abovetopsecret.com/forum/thread928223/pg1*

17. "The Ancient Connection Between Sirius, Earth and Mankind's History." Humans Are Free.

18. Jimmy Dunn. "Horus, the God of Kings in Ancient Egypt."

19. Shira. "Symbols from the Middle East."

20. "Eye of Horus, Eye of Ra." Symboldictionary.net.

21. Alan H. Gardiner, *Egyptian Grammar.*

22. Benoît Stella alias BenduKiwi, illustrator: GNU Free Documentation license.

23. "The Eye of Horus." Ancient Egypt Online.

24. David Flynn, "October 8." Watcher.

25. H. Peter Aleff, "The system of Horus Eye fractions."

26. "What does the pharmacist's symbol 'Rx' mean?" The Straight Dope.

27. "Udjat Eye." The Global Egyptian Museum.

28. *http://en.wikipedia.org/wiki/File:Romtrireme.jpg*

29. John H. Taylor, ed., *Journey Through the Afterlife*, page 130.

30. Captmondo, photographer, from British Museum: GNU Free Documentation license.

31. Walters Art Museum: Creative Commons Attribution-Share Alike 3.0 Unported license.

32. Melissa Troyer, "The Eye of Horus and the Pineal Gland."

33. Wikimedia Commons.

34. "Totafot," Balashon Hebrew Language Detective.

35. T. Lobsang Rampa. *The Third Eye,* pages 75–77.

36. Traveler100, photographer: Creative Commons Attribution-Share Alike 3.0 Unported license.

Chapter 3: Seat of the Third Eye in the Brain

1. Gert-Jan Lokhorst. "Descartes and the Pineal Gland."

2. Ibid.

3. Ibid.

4. Ibid.

5. Ibid.

6. Ibid.

7. Ibid.

8. Helen Hattab. "Descartes's Body-Machine."

9. Gert-Jan Lokhorst. "Descartes and the Pineal Gland."

10. "Chronobiology." Polimedica.

11. Willard L. Koukkari, Sothern, Robert B. *Introducing Biological Rhythms.*

12. Jeremy Pearce. "Aaron Lerner, Skin Expert Who Led Melatonin Discovery, Dies at 86."

13. Kim Kiser. "Father Time." *Minnesota Medicine.*

14. Robert Y. Moore. "Loss of a circadian adrenal corticosterone rhythm following suprachiasmatic lesions in the rat."

15. Friedrich K. Stephan. "Circadian Rhythms in Drinking Behavior and Locomotor Activity of Rats Are Eliminated by Hypothalamic Lesions."

16. Rae Silver. "The Suprachiasmatic Nucleus is a Functionally Heterogeneous Timekeeping Organ."

17. Joseph S. Takahashi. "The Human Suprachiasmatic Nucleus."

18. Alfred J. Lewy. "The dim light melatonin onset, melatonin assays and biological rhythm research in humans."

19. David C. Klein. "Evolution of the vertebrate pineal gland: the AANAT hypothesis."

20. Allan F. Wiechmann. "Melatonin: parallels in pineal gland and retina."

21. Julie Ann Miller. "Eye to (third) eye; scientists are taking advantage of unexpected similarities between the eye's retina and the brain's pineal gland."

22. Masasuke Araki. "The evolution of the third eye."

23. Julie Ann Miller. "Eye to (third) eye; scientists are taking advantage of unexpected similarities between the eye's retina and the brain's pineal gland."

24. Masasuke Araki. "The evolution of the third eye."

25. Allan F. Wiechmann. "Melatonin: parallels in pineal glad and retina."

26. Richard Cox. "The Mind's Eye." *USC Health & Medicine.*

27. David C. Klein. "The 2004 Aschoff/Pittendrigh Lecture: Theory of the Origin of the Pineal Gland—A Tale of Conflict and Resolution."

28. "Banisteriopsis caapi (BLACK) Peru." Shamanic Extracts.

29. R. Gucchait. "Biogenesis of 5-methoxy-N,N-dimethyl-tryptamine in human pineal gland."

30. Rick J. Strassman. *DMT: The Spirit Molecule.*

31. N.V. Cozzi. "Indolethylamine N-methyltransferase expression in primate nervous tissue."

32. S.A. Barker. "LC/MS/MS analysis of the endogenous dimethyltryptamine hallucinogens."

33. D. Beach Barret, "An Introduction to Metatonin, the Pineal Gland Secretion That Helps Us Access Higher Understanding."

Chapter 4: The Third Eye Through the Eyes of Science

1. "Melatonin." Encyclopedia Britannica.

2. Dr. Neil Cherry. "EMR Reduces Melatonin in Animals and People."

3. "Melatonin." Encyclopedia Britannica.

4. "Scientists discover a new function of the dopamine in the pineal gland, involved in sleep regulation." Universitat de Barcelona.

5. Dr. Neil Cherry. "EMR Reduces Melatonin in Animals and People."

6. Ibid.

7. R.J. Reiter, and J. Robinson. *Melatonin: Your body's natural wonder drug.*

8. E.F. Torrey. "Seasonality of births in schizophrenia and bipolar disorder: a review of the literature."

9. Frank McGillion. "The Pineal Gland and the ancient art of Iatromathematica."

10. Ibid.

11. Richard Boyd. "The Scientific Basis for the Spiritual Concept of the Third Eye."

12. Scott Thill. "4 Things You Should Know About Your 'Third Eye.'"

13. "Jimo Borjigin, PhD." Medical School, Molecular and Integrative Physiology, University of Michigan.

14. Bradford S. Weeks. "Scientific Electromagnetic Field 'EMF' Studies."

15. Kavindra Kumar Kesari. "Biomarkers inducing changes due to microwave exposure effect on rat brain."

16. Bary W. Wilson. "Evidence for an Effect of ELF Electromagnetic Fields on Human Pineal Gland Function."

17. Dylan Charles, ed. "Do Electromagnetic Fields Affect the Pineal Gland?"

18. Shu-qun Shi. "Circadian Disruption Leads to Insulin Resistance and Obesity."

19. David Salisbury. "Circadian clock linked to obesity, diabetes and heart attacks."

20. "Itai Kloog: Harvard School of Public Health." PubFacts Scientific Publication Data.

21. Scott Thill. "4 Things You Should Know About Your 'Third Eye.'"

22. Itai Kloog. "Does the Modern Urbanized Sleeping Habitat Pose a Breast Cancer Risk?"

23. Jennifer A. Evans. "Individual differences in circadian waveform of Siberian hamsters under multiple lighting conditions."

24. David W. Frank, "Time-Dependent Effects of Dim Light at Night on Re-Entrainment and Masking of Hamster Activity Rhythms."

25. "Scientists discover a new function of the dopamine in the pineal gland, involved in sleep regulation." Universitat de Barcelona.

26. N. Ongkana. "High accumulation of calcium and phosphorus in the pineal bodies with aging."

27. R. Mahlberg. "Pineal calcification in Alzheimer's disease: an in vivo study using computed tomography."

28. Jennifer Luke. Fluoride Deposition in the Aged Human Pineal Gland.

29. Paul Connett, PhD. "50 Reasons to Oppose Fluoridation."

30. National Research Council. "Fluoride in Drinking Water: A Scientific Review of EPA's Standards."

31. "How to Decalcify the Pineal Gland (Third Eye/Ajna Chakra)?" Decalcify Pineal Gland.

32. Walter Last. "The Borax Conspiracy: How the Arthritis Cure has Been Stopped."

33. Joanne Powell. "Orbital prefrontal cortex volume predicts social network size: an imaging study of individual differences in humans."

34. "Science Confirms Third Eye Chakra," 2012. Merovee.

35. Serena Roney-Dougal. "Some Speculations on the effect of Geomagnetism on the Pineal Gland 1." Psi Research Centre.

36. "Gale Encyclopedia of Occultism and Parapsychology: Rosa Kuleshova." Answers.

37. Sheila Ostrander. *Psychic Discoveries Behind the Iron Curtain.*

38. Ibid.

39. Vladimir Petropavlovsky. "The Third Eye Mystery."

40. Anneli Rufus. "Third Eye Science."

41. Sara W. Lazar. "Meditation experience is associated with increased cortical thickness."

42. Chien-Hui Loou. "Correlation between Pineal Activation and Religious Meditation Observed by Functional Magnetic Resonance Imaging."

Chapter 5: Your Subtle Body

1. Svatmarama. *Hatha Yoga Pradipika,* Chaper 2:3.

2. Gopi Krishna. *Kundalini.*

3. B.K.S. Iyengar. *Light on Yoga,* 439-440.

4. Swami Harinanda. *Yoga and the Portal.*

5. Parmahansa Yogananda. *The Second Coming of the Christ,* Volume 1, page 87.

6. Ibid., page 109.

7. Matthew 6:22.

Chapter 6: Ajna: Your Third Eye Chakra

1. Subramanian, *Saundaryalahari of Shankaracharya,* 36, pg. 20.

Chapter 7: Overcoming Psychic Blocks

1. "Brow Chakra Meditation to connect with your 'third eye.'" Watkins.

2. Santosh Ayalasomayajulam. *Veerabrahmendra, the precursor of Kalki.*

Chapter 8: Developing Your Super-Senses
1. Matthew 7:7.

Chapter 9: The Seat of Siddhis
1. Maharishi Mahesh Yogi. *Bhagavad Gita*, 6:19.
2. Swami Hariharananda Aranya. *Yoga Philosophy of Patanjali*, 1:2–3.
3. Maharishi Mahesh Yogi. *Bhagavad Gita*, 4:22.
4. Maharishi Mahesh Yogi. *Bhagavad Gita*, 2:58.
5. Swami Hariharananda Aranya. *Yoga Philosophy of Patanjali*, 3:24.
6. Ibid., 3:23.
7. Ibid., 3:25.
8. Ibid., 3:26.
9. Ibid., 3:27.
10. Ibid., 3:28.
11. Ibid., 3:29.
12. Ibid., 3:32.
13. Ibid., 3:33.
14. Ibid., 3:34.
15. Ibid., 3:35.
16. Ibid., 3:36.

Chapter 10: Third Eye Alchemy
1. Eric Steven Yudelove. *100 Days to Better Health, Good Sex and Long Life*, page 9–10.
2. Fabrizio Pregadio. "Cinnabar Fields (*Dantian*)."
3. Ibid.
4. Ibid.
5. Tom Bisio. "Daoist Meditation Lesson Eight Theory: Golden Fluid and The Micro-Cosmic Orbit."
6. "The Microcosmic Orbit." YuLi QiGong: Jade Power QiGong.

Chapter 11: Nectar of Immortal Life
1. John Freed. "The Mesopotamian Winged Genies."
2. Wikimedia Commons.

3. H.H. Wilson, trans. *Rgvedasamhita, Mandala 9.* 9.001.01, 9.001.02, 9.001.03.

4. H.H. Wilson, trans. *Rgvedasamhita, Mandala 9.* 9.113.07, 9.113.09, 9.113.10.

5. *Hatha Yoga Pradipika*, 3.43–45.

6. R.B. Jefferson. "The Doctrine of the Golden Mercuric Sulphur (Cinnabar)."

7. Tao Lin. "DMT: You Cannot Imagine a Stranger Drug or a Stranger Experience."

8. Iona Miller. "Soma Pinoline." Pineal DMT.

9. Cliff Pickover. "DMT, Moses, and the Quest for Transcendence."

10. Iona Miller. "Soma Pinoline." Pineal DMT.

Chapter 12: Third Eye of the Yogis

1. Hatha Yoga Pradipika, 4:17.

Chapter 15: The Breakthrough Experience

1. JungOccult. "Styles of Chi Kung Opening Third Eye."

2. Matthew, 7:7.

Chapter 18: Third Eye Fully Awakened

1. *The Tempest.* Act 4, scene 1, 148–158.

2. Yoga Vasistha—The Art of Realization."

3. "Plato, The Allegory of the Cave." The History Guide.

4. Vimuktananda, Swami, trans. "Aparokshanubhuti."

5. Max Muller, trans. *The Upanishads.* Chandogya Upanishad 6:2:1.

6. Max Muller, trans. *The Upanishads.* Brihadaranyaka Upanishad 1.4.10.

7. Max Muller, trans. *The Upanishads.* Chandogya Upanishad 6.8.7.

8. Max Muller, trans. *The Upanishads.* Chandogya Upanishad 3.14.1

9. Max Muller, trans. *The Upanishads.* Kena Upanishad. 1:5 to 1:9.

10. Genesis: 3:2–3.

| Bibliography |

Books

Aranya, Swami Hariharananda. *Yoga Philosophy of Patanjali.* Calcutta, India: University of Calcutta, 1963.

Ayalasomayajulam, Santosh. *Veerabrahmendra, The Precursor of Kalki.* Goa, India: CinnamonTeal Print and Publishing, 2010.

Beck, Mark, ed. *A Companion to Plutarch.* Hoboken, N.J.: Wiley-Blackwell, 2014.

Clegg, Robert Ingham. *Encyclopedia of Freemasonry, Volume 1.* Chicago: The Masonic History Company, 1929.

Gardiner, Alan H. *Egyptian Grammar, Being An Introduction to the Study of Hieroglyphs.* Oxford, U.K.: Oxford University Press, 1927.

Harinanda, Swami. *Yoga and the Portal: Swami Harinanda's Guide to Real Yoga.* Jay Dee Marketing: 1996.

Iyengar, B.K.S. *Light on Yoga: Yoga Dipika.* New York: Schocken Books, 1977, 439–440.

Koukkari, Willard L., and Robert B. Sothern. *Introducing Biological Rhythms: A Primer on the Temporal Organization of Life, with Implications for Health, Society, Reproduction, and the Natural Environment.* New York: Springer Publishing Company, 2006.

Krishna, Gopi. *Kundalini, The Evolutionary Energy in Man.* Boston: Shambhala Press, 1967.

Mahesh Yogi, Maharishi. *Bhagavad Gita, a New Translation and Commentary with Sanskrit Text.* International SRM Publications, 1967.

National Research Council. *Fluoride in Drinking Water: A Scientific Review of EPA's Standards*. Washington, DC: The National Academies Press, 2006.

Ostrander, Sheila and Lynn Schroeder. *Psychic Discoveries behind the Iron Curtain*. New York: Bantam Books, 1970.

Rampa, T. Lobsang. *The Third Eye*. London: Transworld Publishers Ltd, 1956.

Reiter, R.J. and J. Robinson. *Melatonin: Your Body's Natural Wonder Drug*. New York: Bantam Books, 1995.

Shumsky, Susan. *Ascension*. Franklin Lakes, NJ..: New Page Books, 2010.

———.G. *Divine Revelation*. New York: Fireside, 1996.

———. *Exploring Meditation*. Franklin Lakes, N.J.: New Page Books, 2002.

———. *How to Hear the Voice of God*. Franklin Lakes, NJ: New Page Books, 2008.

———. *Instant Healing*. Pompton Plains, N.J.: New Page Books, 2013.

———. *Miracle Prayer*. Franklin Lakes, N.J.: New Page Books, 2006.

———. *The Power of Chakras*. Pompton Plains, N.J.: New Page Books, 2013.

———. *The Power of Auras*. Pompton Plains, N.J.: New Page Books, 2013.

Strassman, Rick J. *DMT: The Spirit Molecule. A Doctor's Revolutionary Research into the Biology of Near-Death and Mystical Experiences*. Rochester, Vt.: Park Street Press, 2000.

Subramanian, V.K. *Saundaryalahari of Shankaracarya*. Delhi, India: Motilal Banarsidass Publishers, 1998.

Svatmarama. Pancham Sinh, trans. *Hatha Yoga Pradipika*. Allahabad, India: Sudhindra Nath Vasu, the Panini office, Bhuvaneswari Asrama, 1914.

Taylor, John H. ed. *Journey Through the Afterlife: Ancient Egyptian Book of the Dead*, Cambridge, Mass.: Harvard University Press, 2013.

Yogananda, Parmahansa. *The Second Coming of the Christ: The Resurrection of the Christ Within You*, Volume 1, Los Angeles: Self-Realization Fellowship, 2004.

Yudelove, Eric Steven. *100 Days to Better Health, Good Sex and Long Life, A guide to Taoist Yoga & Chi Kung.* Woodbury, Minn.: Llewellyn Publications, 2002.

Scientific Research Citations and Articles

Barker, S. A.; Borjigin, J.; Lomnicka, I; and Strassman, R. LC/MS/MS analysis of the endogenous dimethyltryptamine hallucinogens, their precursors, and major metabolites in rat pineal gland microdialysate. *Biomed. Chromatogr.* 2013; 27: 1690–1700. doi: 10.1002/bmc.2981.

Chien-Hui Loou, Chang-Wei Hsieh, Jyh-Horng Chen, Chang-Wei Hsieh, Si-Chen Lee, Chi-Hong Wang. "Correlation between Pineal Activation and Religious Meditation Observed by Functional Magnetic Resonance Imaging." 24 June 2014. *www.theragem.nl/ KristalLichtTherapie/Resources/pineal_gland.pdf/*

Cox, Richard. The Mind's Eye. *USC Health & Medicine.* Winter 1995. In Craft, Cheryl M., ed., *EyesightResearch.org.*

Cozzi N.V., Mavlyutov T.A., Thompson M.A., Ruoho A.E., Indolethylamine N-methyltransferase expression in primate nervous tissue. *Society for Neuroscience Abstracts* 2011; 37: 840.19.

Evans, Jennifer A.; Elliott, Jeffrey A.; and Gorman, Michael R. "Individual differences in circadian waveform of Siberian hamsters under multiple lighting conditions." *J Biol Rhythms.* Oct 2012; 27(5): 410–419.

Frank, David W.; Evans, Jennifer A.; Gorman, Michael R. "Time-Dependent Effects of Dim Light at Night on Re-Entrainment and Masking of Hamster Activity Rhythms." *J Biol Rhythms.* April 2010; 25(2): 103-112.

Gucchait, R. Biogenesis of 5-methoxy-N,N-dimethyl-tryptamine in human pineal gland. *J. Neurochem.* 1976; 26: 187-190.

"Itai Kloog: Harvard School of Public Health." PubFacts Scientific Publication Data. 11 July 2014. *http://www.pubfacts.com/author/ Itai+Kloog/*

Kesari, Kavindra Kumar; Kumar, Sanjay; Behari, J. Biomarkers inducing changes due to microwave exposure effect on rat brain. General Assembly and Scientific Symposium: URSI, 2011.

Kiser K. "Father Time." *Minnesota Medicine.* 2005; 88(11): 26.

Klein, David C. "The 2004 Aschoff/Pittendrigh Lecture: Theory of the Origin of the Pineal Gland—A Tale of Conflict and Resolution." *J Biol Rhythms* 2004; 19: 264.

———., "Evolution of the vertebrate pineal gland: the AANAT hypothesis." *Chronobiol. Int.* 2006; 23(1-2): 5–20.

Kloog, Itai; Portnov, Boris A.; Rennert, Hedy S.; Haim, Abraham. Does the Modern Urbanized Sleeping Habitat Pose a Breast Cancer Risk? *Chronobiology International,* 2011; 28(1): 76–80.

Lazar, Sara W.; Kerr, Catherine E.; Wasserman, Rachel H.; Gray, Jeremy R.; Greve, Douglas N.; Treadway, Michael T.; McGarvey, Metta; Quinn, Brian T.; Dusek, Jeffery A.; Benson, Herbert; Rauch, Scott L.; Moore, Christopher I.; and Fischl, Bruce. "Meditation experience is associated with increased cortical thickness." *Neuroreport.* Nov 28, 2005; 16(17): 1893–1897.

Lewy, Alfred J. The dim light melatonin onset, melatonin assays and biological rhythm research in humans. *Biol. Signals Recept.* 1999; Jan-Apr; 8 (1-2): 79–83.

Luke, Jennifer. Fluoride Deposition in the Aged Human Pineal Gland. *Caries Res* 2991; 35: 125–128.

Mahlberg, R.; Walther, S.; Kalus, P.; Bohner, G.; Haedel, S.; Reischies, F.M.; Kühl, K.P.; Hellweg, R.; Kunz, D. "Pineal calcification in Alzheimer's disease: an in vivo study using computed tomography." *Neurobiol. Aging.* 2008 Feb; 29(2): 203–9.

McGillion, Frank. "The Pineal Gland And The Ancient Art Of Iatromathematica." *Journal of Scientific Exploration.* 2002; 16(1): 19–38.

Miller, Julie Ann. "Eye to (third) eye; scientists are taking advantage of unexpected similarities between the eye's retina and the brain's pineal gland." *Science News.* Nov. 9, 1985. In Thefreelibrary.com.

Moore, Robert Y.; Eichler, Victor B. Loss of a circadian adrenal corticosterone rhythm following suprachiasmatic lesions in the rat. Brain Research. July 1972; 42 (1): 201–206.

Ongkana, N.; Zhao, X.Z.; Tohno, S.; Azuma, C.; Moriwake, Y.; Minami, T.; Tohno, Y. "High accumulation of calcium and phosphorus in the pineal bodies with aging." *Biol. Trace Elem. Res.* 2007 Nov; 119(2): 120–7.

Pearce, Jeremy. "Aaron Lerner, Skin Expert Who Led Melatonin Discovery, Dies at 86." *The New York Times.* Feb. 17, 2007.

Powell, Joanne; Lewis, Penelope A.; Roberts, Neil; García-Fiñana, Marta; Dunbar, Robin. "Orbital prefrontal cortex volume predicts social network size: an imaging study of individual differences in humans." 1 February 2012. The Royal Society Publishing. 3 November 2014. *http://rspb.royalsocietypublishing.org/content/early/2012/01/27/rspb.2011.2574/*

Roney-Dougal, Serena; Vogl, Gunther. "Some Speculations on the effect of Geomagnetism on the Pineal Gland 1." 2012. Psi Research Centre. 26 June 2014. *www.psi-researchcentre.co.uk/article_10.htm/*

Salisbury, David. "Circadian clock linked to obesity, diabetes and heart attacks." 21 February 2013. Vanderbilt University. 12 November 2014. *http://news.vanderbilt.edu/2013/02/circadian-clock-obesity/*

"Science Confirms Third Eye Chakra," 2012. Merovee. 7 November 2014. *http://merovee.wordpress.com/2012/02/01/science-confirms-third-eye-chakra/*

"Scientists discover a new function of the dopamine in the pineal gland, involved in sleep regulation." 2012. Universitat de Barcelona. 8 November 2014. *http://www.ub.edu/web/ub/en/menu_eines/noticies/2012/06/060.html/*

Shi, Shu-qun; Ansari, Tasneem S.; McGuinness, Owen P.; Wasserman, David H.; Johnson, Carl Hirschie. "Circadian Disruption Leads to Insulin Resistance and Obesity." *Current Biology.* March 4, 2013; 23(5), 372–381.

Silver, Rae; Schwartz, William J. "The Suprachiasmatic Nucleus is a Functionally Heterogeneous Timekeeping Organ." *Methods Enzymol.* 2005; 393: 451–465.

Stephan, Friedrich K.; Zucker, Irving. "Circadian Rhythms in Drinking Behavior and Locomotor Activity of Rats Are Eliminated by Hypothalamic Lesions." *Proc Natl Acad Sci U S A.* Jun 1972; 69(6): 1583–1586.

Torrey, E.F.; Miller, J.; Rawlings, R.; Yolken, R.H. "Seasonality of births in schizophrenia and bipolar disorder: a review of the literature." *Schizophr Res.* 1997 Nov 7; 28(1): 1–38.

Weeks, Bradford S. "Scientific Electromagnetic Field 'EMF' Studies." 28 May 2008. WeeksMD. 16 July 2014. *http://weeksmd.com/2008/05/references-about-the-science-of-emf-danger/.*

Wiechmann, Allan F., "Melatonin: parallels in pineal glad and retina." *Exp. Eye Res.* Jun 1986; 42(6): 507–27.

Wilson, Bary W.; Wright, Cherylyn W.; Morris, James E.; Buschbom, Raymond L.; Brown, Donald P.; Miller, Douglas L.; Sornmers-Flannigan, Rita; Anderson, Larry E. "Evidence for an Effect of ELF Electromagnetic Fields on Human Pineal Gland Function." *Journal of Pineal Research.* 1990; 9: 259–269.

Internet Sources

Aleff, H. Peter. "The system of Horus Eye fractions." Recoveredscience. com. 24 July 2014. *www.recoveredscience.com/const102horuseye. html/.*

Araki, Masasuke. "The Evolution of the Third Eye." February 2007. Nikon. 4 June 2014. *www.nikon.com/about/feelnikon/light/chap05/sec02.htm/.*

Babbit, Frank Cole, ed. "Plutarch, De Iside et Osiride." 25 June 2014. *http://data.perseus.org/citations/urn:cts:greekLit:tlg0007.tlg089. perseus-eng1:51/.*

"Banisteriopsis caapi (BLACK) Peru." 2007. Shamanic Extracts. 13 November 2014. *www.shamanic-extracts.com/xcart/shamanic-products/banisteriopsis-caapi-black-peru.html/.*

Barrett, D. Beach. "An Introduction to Metatonin, the Pineal Gland Secretion that Helps Us Access Higher Understanding." 2002. Metatonin Research. 3 October 2014. *http://metatoninresearch. org/.*

Bisio, Tom. "Daoist Meditation Lesson Eight Theory: Golden Fluid & The Micro-Cosmic Orbit." 24 April 2013. New York Internal Arts. 15 November 2014. *www.internalartsinternational.com/free/daoist-meditation-lesson-eight-theory-golden-fluid-the-micro-cosmic-orbit/.*

Boyd, Richard. "The Scientific Basis for the Spiritual Concept of the Third Eye." 2011. Energetics Institute. 8 July 2014. *www.energeticsinstitute.com.au/page/third_eye.html/*.

"Brow Chakra Meditation to connect with your 'third eye.'" 10 July 2014. Watkins. 10 September 2014. *www.watkinspublishing.com/brow-chakra-meditation-third-eye/*.

Charles, Dylan, ed. "Do Electromagnetic Fields Affect the Pineal Gland?" 20 November 2012. Waking Times. 15 July 2014. *www.wakingtimes.com/2012/11/20/effects-of-electromagnetic-fields-on-the-pineal-gland/*.

Cherry, Dr. Neil. "EMR Reduces Melatonin in Animals and People." 26 July 2000. EMF Guru. 25 July 2014. *www.feb.se/EMFguru/Research/emf-emr/EMR-Reduces-Melatonin.htm/*.

"Chronobiology." Polimedica. 23 June 2014. *www.polimedica.org/?p=1652/*.

Connett, Paul, PhD. "50 Reasons to Oppose Fluoridation." 2012. Flouride Action Network. 5 November 2014. *www.fluoridation.com/fluorideindrinkingwater.htm/*.

Dunn, Jimmy. "Horus, the God of Kings in Ancient Egypt." 2012. Tour Egypt. 15 July 2014. *www.touregypt.net/featurestories/horus.htm/*.

"Eye of Horus." Ancient Egypt: The Mythology. 19 June 2014. *www.egyptianmyths.net/udjat.htm/*.

"Eye of Horus, Eye of Ra." 2009. Symboldictionary.net, a Visual Glossary. 20 July 2014. *http://symboldictionary.net/?p=519/*.

Flynn, David. "October 8." Watcher. 24 July 2014. *www.mt.net/~watcher/OCT8.html/*.

Freed, John. "The Mesopotamian Winged Genius." 23 February 2013. Near Eastern Archaeology. 3 June 2014. *http://nearchaeology.blogspot.com/2013/02/the-mesopotamian-winged-genius.html/*.

"Gale Encyclopedia of Occultism and Parapsychology: Rosa Kuleshova." 2001. Answers. 15 September 2014. *www.answers.com/topic/rosa-kuleshova/*.

Hattab, Helen. "Descartes's Body-Machine." 2001. Experience and Experiment in Early Modern Europe. 12 September 2014. *www.folger.edu/html/folger_institute/experience/textures_hattab.htm/*.

"How to Decalcify the Pineal Gland (Third Eye/Ajna Chakra)?" 2012. Decalcify Pineal Gland. 7 November 2014. *http:// decalcifypinealgland.com/how-to-decalcify-the-pineal-gland/*

Jefferson, R.B. "The Doctrine of the Golden Mercuric Sulphur (Cinnabar)." The Doctrine of the Elixir. 17 November 2014. *http://duversity.org/elixir/.*

"Jimo Borjigin, PhD." Medical School, Molecular and Integrative Physiology, University of Michigan. 27 July 2014. *http://medicine. umich.edu/dept/molecular-integrative-physiology/jimo-borjigin-phd/.*

JungOccult. "Styles of Chi Kung Opening Third Eye." 3 December 2013. Scribd. *www.scribd.com/doc/188841262/Styles-of-Chi-Kung-Opening-Third-Eye/.*

Last, Walter. "The Borax Conspiracy: How the Arthritis Cure has been Stopped." Health-Science-Spirit. 7 November 2014. *www.health-science-spirit.com/borax.htm/.*

Lin, Tao. "DMT: You Cannot Imagine a Stranger Drug or a Stranger Experience." 5 August 2014. Vice. 25 November 2014. *www.vice. com/read/dmt-you-cannot-imagine-a-stranger-drug-or-a-stranger-experience-365/.*

Lokhorst, Gert-Jan. "Descartes and the Pineal Gland." 18 September 2013. Stanford Encyclopedia of Philosophy. 25 June 2014. *http:// plato.stanford.edu/entries/pineal-gland/.*

MacArthur, John D. "Annuit Coeptis—Origin and Meaning of the Motto Above the Eye." 2014. Great Seal." 6 June 2014. *http:// greatseal.com/mottoes/coeptis.html/.*

———. "Charles Thomson—Principal Designer of the Great Seal." 2014. Great Seal. 6 June 2014. *http://greatseal.com/committees/ finaldesign/thomson.html/.*

———. "Explanation of the Great Seal's Symbolism." 2014. Great Seal. 6 June 2014. *http://greatseal.com/symbols/explanation.html/.*

———. "Source of Novus Ordo Seclorum." 2014. Great Seal. 6 June 2014. *http://greatseal.com/mottoes/seclorumvirgil.html/.*

"Melatonin." 30 January 2014. Encyclopedia Britannica. 3 June 2014. *www.britannica.com/EBchecked/topic/373799/melatonin/.*

Miller, Iona. "Soma Pinoline." 2006. Pineal DMT. 25 November 2014. *http://ionaparamedia.50megs.com/whats_new_1.html/.*

Morris, S. Brent, P.M. "Eye in the Pyramid." Masonic Service Association. 6 June 2014. *www.msana.com/eyeinpyramid.asp/.*

Muller, Max, trans. Sacred Text Archive. *The Upanishads, Part I.* 8 August 2014. *http://www.sacred-texts.com/hin/sbe01/index.htm/.*

———. Sacred Text Archive. *The Upanishads, Part II.* 8 August 2014. *http://www.sacred-texts.com/hin/sbe15/sbe15076.htm/.*

Osborn, David K. "Did the Greeks Have Chakras?" Greek Medicine. 25 July 2014. *http://www.greekmedicine.net/b_p/Greek_Chakras.html/.*

Petropavlovsky, Vladimir. "The Third Eye Mystery." 19 August 2003. Pravda.ru. 20 May 2014. *http://english.pravda.ru/science/tech/19-08-2003/3551-introscopy-0/.*

Pickover, Cliff. "DMT, Moses, and the Quest for Transcendence." *http://sprott.physics.wisc.edu/pickover/pc/dmt.html/.*

"Plato, The Allegory of the Cave." 2012. The History Guide. 5 May 2014. *www.historyguide.org/intellect/allegory.html/.*

Pregadio, Fabrizio. "Cinnabar Fields (*Dantian*)." 2014. The Golden Elixir. 25 November 2014. *http://www.goldenelixir.com/jindan/dantian.html/.*

Rufus, Anneli. "Third Eye Science." 27 August 2009. Psychology Today. 25 June 2014. *www.psychologytoday.com/blog/stuck/200908/third-eye-science/.*

Shira. "Symbols from the Middle East." 27 June 2014. *www.shira.net/culture/symbols.htm/.*

Takahashi, Joseph S. "The Human Suprachiasmatic Nucleus." Howard Hughes Medical Institute. 14 September 2014. *www.hhmi.org/biointeractive/human-suprachiasmatic-nucleus/.*

"The Ancient Connection Between Sirius, Earth and Mankind's History." 2014. Humans Are Free. 17 November 2014. *http://humansarefree.com/2014/03/the-ancient-connection-between-sirius.html#sthash.WwubMkaz.dpuf/.*

"The Eye of Horus." Ancient Egypt Online. 2010. 19 June 2014. *http://www.ancientegyptonline.co.uk/eye.html/.*

"The Microcosmic Orbit." YuLi QiGong: Jade Power QiGong. 14 November 2014. *www.yuliqigong.com/MicroOrbit.html/.*

Thill, Scott. "4 Things You Should Know About Your 'Third Eye.'" 22 March 2013. Alternet. *www.alternet.org/personal-health/4-things-you-should-know-about-your-third-eye?paging=off&current_page=1#bookmark/.*

"Totafot." 2007. Balashon Hebrew Language Detective. 3 October 2014. *www.balashon.com/2007/01/totafot.html/.*

Troyer, Melissa. 21 January 2013. "The Eye of Horus and the Pineal Gland." Resonates with Me. 14 July 2014. *http:// resonateswith.me/the-eye-of-horus-and-the-pineal-gland-connection/#sthash.1rc2Xip5.DGjN2kvm.dpbs/.*

"Udjat Eye." The Global Egyptian Museum. 18 June 2014. *www. globalegyptianmuseum.org/glossary.aspx?id=384/.*

Vimuktananda, Swami, trans. "Aparokshanubhuti." Sankaracharya.org. 13 September 2014. *www.sankaracharya.org/aparokshanubhuti. php/.*

"What does the pharmacist's symbol 'Rx' mean?" 17 May 1999. The Straight Dope. 24 July 2014. *www.straightdope.com/columns/ read/1641/what-does-the-pharmacists-symbol-rx-mean/.*

Wilson, H.H., trans. *Rgvedasamhita, Mandala 9.* 13 September 2014. *www.theasis.net/RgV/rv9_2.html/.*

Yoga Vasistha—The Art of Realization." *http://yogi.lv/files/yoga_vasistha. pdf.*

| Index |

| About the Author |

Dr. Susan Shumsky has dedicated her life to helping people take command of their lives in highly effective, powerful, positive ways. She is a leading spirituality expert, highly acclaimed and greatly respected professional speaker, sought-after media guest, New Thought minister, and Doctor of Divinity.

Dr. Shumsky has authored *Divine Revelation,* in continuous print with Simon & Schuster since 1996, as well as four award-winning books: *Exploring Chakras, How to Hear the Voice of God,* and *Ascension*, published by New Page Books; and *Miracle Prayer,* published by Penguin Random House. Her other titles include *Exploring Meditation, Exploring Auras, How to Hear the Voice of God, Instant Healing, The Power of Auras,* and *The Power of Chakras,* published by New Page Books. Her books have been published in several languages worldwide, several were number one Amazon.com best-sellers, and two were One Spirit Book Club selections.

Dr. Shumsky has practiced self-development disciplines since 1967. For 22 of those years she practiced deep meditation for many hours daily in the Himalayas, the Swiss Alps, and other secluded areas, under the personal guidance of enlightened master from India Maharishi Mahesh Yogi, who was founder of Transcendental Meditation, guru of the Beatles, and guru of Deepak Chopra. She served on Maharishi's personal staff for seven of those years in Spain, Mallorca, Austria, Italy, and Switzerland. She then studied New Thought and metaphysics for another 25 years and became a Doctor of Divinity.

Dr. Shumsky has taught yoga, meditation, prayer, and intuition to thousands of students worldwide since 1970 as a pioneer in the consciousness field. She is founder of Divine Revelation®, a unique, field-proven technology for contacting the divine presence, hearing and testing the inner voice, and receiving clear divine guidance.

Dr. Shumsky travels extensively, producing and facilitating workshops, conferences, ocean cruise seminars, and tours to many sacred destinations worldwide. She also offers teleseminars and private spiritual coaching, prayer therapy sessions, and spiritual Breakthrough sessions.

All of Dr. Shumsky's years of research into consciousness and inner exploration have contributed to her books and teachings, which can significantly reduce many pitfalls in a seeker's quest for inner truth and greatly shorten the time required for the inner pathway to Spirit.

On her website, *www.drsusan.org*, you can:

▷ Join the mailing list.

▷ See Dr. Shumsky's itinerary.

▷ Read the first chapter of all of Dr. Shumsky's books.

▷ Listen to dozens of free interviews and teleseminars with Dr. Shumsky.

▷ Invite Dr. Shumsky to speak to your group.

▷ Find Divine Revelation teachers in your area.

▷ See the Divine Revelation curriculum.

▷ Register for Divine Revelation retreats and teacher training courses.

▷ Order a CD, downloadable files, or laminated cards of healing prayers.

▷ Order books, audio and video products, or home study courses.

▷ Order beautiful, full-color prints of Dr. Shumsky's illustrations.

▷ Register for telephone sessions and teleseminars with Dr. Shumsky.

▷ Register for spiritual tours to sacred destinations worldwide.

When you join her mailing list at *www.drsusan.org*, you will receive a free, downloadable, guided mini-meditation plus access to her free weekly teleconference prayer circle and her free online community group forum.

As a gift for reading this book, please use the following special discount code when you register for one of our retreats or tours at *www. divinetravels.com*: THIRDEYE108.

Dr. Shumsky wants to hear from you. Please write about your personal experiences of opening your third eye and send them to divinerev@aol.com.